HERBERT W. RIDYARD

DO
YOUR
BEST

Family, Friends, Mentors
and the US Army Guide
a Boy to Manhood

 FriesenPress

Suite 300 - 990 Fort St
Victoria, BC, V8V 3K2
Canada

www.friesenpress.com

ISBN
978-1-03-910397-9 (Hardcover)
978-1-03-910396-2 (Paperback)
978-1-03-910398-6 (eBook)

Biography & Autobiography, Military

Distributed to the trade by The Ingram Book Company

DEDICATION

In memory of my mom and dad,
Emily and Herbert Ridyard, and my brothers Tom and John,
Immigrants all, from the Old Country.

TABLE OF CONTENTS

TABLE OF ILLUSTRATIONS

ACKNOWLEDGEMENTS

My journey toward the book, Do Your Best, began when I discovered my ancestors thanks to Derek Horrocks and Charlotte Cowe, family history researchers from my father's birthplace in Lancashire, England and my mother's birthplace in Dumbarton, Scotland, respectively.

Next was the interview with my mother in 1977 that sparked my interest in writing stories of the past, which led to the need for honing my writing skills as a member of the Lancaster Life Story Writers under the leadership of Marge Keene.

Since then I have spent several years writing my memoirs in earnest and subsequently submitting the manuscript to the publisher in mid-2020, a feat that could not have been accomplished without the support of my family to whom I owe many thanks.

Special thanks go to my dearest wife, Nancy Lou, who read and edited every draft and rewrite, found more appropriate punctuation, words and phrases and suggested the title, all the while providing sustenance, clean and ironed clothes and brightening my day in her loving manner.

I would be remiss if I did not specifically acknowledge all the other helpers: son Rob who came to my rescue showing how to prepare illustrations for the publisher, as well as grandson Jamie who taught me the way to wrap text around photos, son Herb Jr. and his wife Kris who encouraged and advised us on pandemic issues during weekly phone calls, daughter Amy and spouse Jeff, our nearest contacts, who dropped everything to lend a hand with heavy lifting or grocery shopping, daughter Leslie, my iTunes consultant, who arranged big band music for my enjoyment while I was writing and finally the entire family providing support via family Zoom meetings, in-person meetings in our garage and the ever-present Nixplay digital photos of grandchildren and great-grandchildren. Halleluiah! God is Good!

PART I

ANCESTRY

CHAPTER 1

FAMILY HISTORY

have always been interested in our family history, having as a child listened while my parents were telling their stories in conversations with Mom's immigrant relatives—Uncle James Barnett, his wife, Aunt Agnes, Uncle William "Willie" Barnett (my namesake) and his wife, Aunt Emmy—or with their friends the McKays, the McKinnons, and the Fergusons. If these names sound Scottish while mine, Ridyard, is most decidedly English, therein lies the story of my ancestors.

Thanks to Derek Horrocks, a family history researcher, we know that seven generations of the Ridyard family resided in southern Lancashire (Lancs.), England, in small towns like Pennington and Golborne, located about midway between Liverpool and Manchester. The nearest town in the vicinity of Pennington and Golborne big enough to be found on most maps is Wigan, one of the coal-mining towns in the area.

In the eighteenth century, several generations of Pennington Ridyards—namely Samuel, his son Samuel[2] and grandson William[3] were saddlers and later, in the nineteenth and early twentieth centuries, the Golborne Ridyards, Peter,[4] his son Thomas,[5] and grandson Thomas[6] were coal miners.

I find it wonderful that I know this much about my ancestors through Horrocks' research, but I feel sad that I missed seeing my grandfather Thomas[6] Ridyard, who was living when I was a young boy. After my dad immigrated to the United States in 1923, we could not afford to travel back to his birthplace. This sense of loss has deepened because I have never met my grandparents on either side of the family.

For a detailed list of all members of the Ridyard Family Lineage, see Appendix 1.

Note: the superscripts attached to the given names of my ancestral Ridyards are those in direct line of my heritage and give the order in that line from Peter[1] Ridyard, who represents the earliest extent of our Family history research.[1]

CHAPTER 2

GRANDPARENTS

My grandfather Thomas[6] Ridyard, a colliery grocer, baker, and labourer, born on April 29, 1859, in Golborne, Lancs., married Sarah Potter, a dressmaker born on November 2, 1858, in Gullet Aspull, Lancs., on March 16, 1880, in the Free Methodist Church of Wigan, Lancs. The marriage was witnessed by James Potter and Mary Potter, probably siblings of the bride. I found it interesting that although both bride and groom were about twenty years old, the marriage certificate shows that both of their fathers, Thomas[5] Ridyard, a coal miner, and James Potter, a colliery labourer, were deceased at the time of the wedding, and both in mine accidents. This is one of those déjà-vu-all-over-again moments because I am reminded that our great-great grandparents, Peter[4] Ridyard and Thomas Coates, also were deceased due to mine accidents at the time of the marriage of their children, Thomas[5] Ridyard and Martha Coates. [1]

Great-grandfather Thomas[5] Ridyard died on August 17, 1875, at age fifty-three when the mine roof collapsed. Maternal Great-grandfather James Potter died on April 3, 1879, at age fifty-five when he was crushed between the cage and the rod in an ascending lift (elevator) in the pit (mine) shaft. I have a newspaper article and an obituary detailing this latter tragedy that records that James Potter's son was the one who accidently started the elevator going up before his dad was completely in the elevator. Tragedy upon tragedy.[2]

The good news is that James Potter's Free Methodist Church Sunday School Class marched in the funeral procession as a show of respect for their teacher, James Potter. When I read this story and every-time I think about it, I feel an upwelling of pride. That is why I tell it here. We do not have a lot of information about our ancestors, but what little we know says that the Ridyards have been good guys for generations so let us, the off springs, follow their example.

Grandfather Thomas[6] Ridyard and Sarah's children include:

James Thomas, born September 28, 1880, in Golborne;

Harriet Alice born March 12, 1883 in Golborne and died November 12, 1899, at age sixteen of acute peritonitis followed by cardiac failure;

Herbert[7], my father, born April 7, 1889, at Heath St., Golborne;

Annie, born September 7, 1891, at Heath St., Golborne,

Eveline, born December 21, 1898, at Heath St., Golborne.[3]

Family history records show that Grandfather Thomas[6] was a sawyer in the mines at age forty. My mother told me that Grandfather injured his hand in the mines and subsequently worked in the coal company store as a grocer and baker. Thomas[6] Ridyard died October 24, 1941, at age eighty-two at 72 Heath St., Golborne, of a cerebral hemorrhage and arteriosclerosis. Thomas[6] was listed on his death certificate as a colliery watchman and a former coal salesclerk. [4]

I will never forget that sad day in 1941 at our home at 1432 Hottle Ave. in Bethlehem, when my dad received a letter from his sister Anne, saying that his father, Thomas[6], had passed. The story I remember was that he had died as a result of a cold caught from having to get up at night to go to the bomb shelter. That story does not jive with the death certificate mentioned above and is another family history mystery. How faulty is my memory after all these years? It is true I never read the letter from Aunt Anne. I only know what my parents said about it. It is of some interest to note the timing of Thomas's death, about a year after the famous "Air Battle of Britain" and six weeks prior to the Japs' attack on Pearl Harbor, Hawaii. If the air raid shelter story is true, Thomas's[6] death was just another casualty of Adolf Hitler's mad desire to conquer Europe.

My maternal grandfather, John Barnett, was born in 1857, in Burnfoot, Ireland, near Londonderry. As a young man, John was trained to be a journeyman rope spinner. He married Isabelle Neilson, a Presbyterian on December 31, 1878, in Bridgeton, Glasgow, Scotland. Their children in approximate order of birth were: Robert, Mary, Matthew, Isabella, John, Walter, Emily (my mother), William, James, Joseph, and Annie. Mom clarified that Matthew died as an infant. I had never heard of Mary[5] until doing family history research.

Grandfather Barnett developed a successful business making and selling bicycles called the Express Cycle. He expanded his business by opening another bicycle shop in Glasgow, leaving his shop in Clydebank in the hands of a partner who did something that ruined their business. John Barnett returned to Clydebank, where he worked for Singer Sewing Machine Company as a machinist.

CHAPTER 3

MOM AND DAD
IN THE OLD COUNTRY

The little I know about my parents before they came to America I gleaned from conversations over the years with my mother; however, the greater portion of that information was obtained one day in an interview when Mom was in her later years. My father rarely spoke about his life there. In this chapter, I have woven together their stories with my family history research.

My father, Herbert[7] Ridyard, was born in Golborne, Lancashire, England, on April 7, 1889.[1] There, he attended school, and though I don't believe he moved up to secondary school, he did have very nice handwriting, wrote well, and had no trouble with arithmetic. Mom informed me he often had to stay home from school with his mother who had a breathing problem.

Dad's passport shows he was a steel driller, five feet, eight inches tall, with dark brown hair and grey eyes. Mom told me he worked at Nathan's Machine Shop in Golborne; however, my research discovered that there was a Naylor Brothers Machine Shop[1] in Golborne, from 1890 to 1965, so perhaps Mom meant to say Naylor's not Nathan's. It is a mystery and a blessing that he was not a miner because Golborne and many other villages in the area had collieries. It could be that his father's injury in the mine influenced him to look elsewhere for employment.

Since he was a machinist not a miner, during WW I he was recruited to go to Scotland by Scouts from the Scottish shipyards. Dad and a friend named Bill Marsh went to work in Beardmore's Shipyard in Clydebank, where Dad became a plater's helper. Beardmore's and John Brown's shipyards in Clydebank are renown for having built huge ships, including the Queen Mary, Queen Elizabeth I and II, and battleships for the British Navy. Mom owned a yellow ribbon from the christening of the battleship, HMS Repulse.

I do not know when Dad moved to Scotland, but he was at least twenty-five when WW I started in 1914. The good news here is obvious: he was saved from going into the dreaded trenches in Belgium or France.

While in Clydebank, Dad boarded at the home of Robert Barnett, my mother's oldest brother. I assume that is where he met my mother-to-be, Emily Paterson Barnett. They were married on April 18, 1919, at Liberal Hall, Alexander Street, Clydebank, after banns, according to forms of the Union United Free Church, a Presbyterian sect. Dad was thirty and Mom twenty-six. Uncle William Barnett and Agnes Parks were witnesses. [2]

My mother, Emily Paterson Barnett Ridyard, was born July 14, 1893 at 11:30 a.m., at Hillside Terrace, in Clydebank, Scotland, one of eleven children. She loved her parents. Her father, John Barnett, called her Jean, a term of endearment. [3]

They were rather strict, as I suppose most parents were in those days. Once, Mom's mother, Isabelle Neilson Barnett, said she had heard some young person was seen smoking and she hoped none of her children were smoking. Mom's brother James said, "Not me, Mother, I quit," giving away that he had. Mom thought that was funny but never told me whether James was punished.

At sixteen, Mom passed the achievement exam and was approved to go on to high school because she was a good student. Unfortunately, the family needed her to work, like her father, so she secured a job at Singer Sewing Machine Factory as a machinist. Her work entailed polishing the eyes of the needles. I've seen her demonstrate how, holding about ten needles between her thumb and pointer finger, she simultaneously put a thread through all of the needles.

My parents had two children born in Clydebank; Thomas was born December 7, 1919, and John on June 17, 1921.[4] One of my mother's stories about their life in Scotland was that they lived in a flat, a term for apartment, on Agamemnon St., in Dalmuir, a suburb of Clydebank, where she had a difficult time because she had to carry the baby carriage up several flights of stairs after taking the babies out for fresh air.

Another of Mom's stories about the early days of their marriage concerned one of their first visits to the Ridyard in-laws in Golborne. Apparently, the children's crying greatly disturbed Uncle Jim, but Dad's mother, Sarah, told Mom not to worry about Jim. Mom said she was a "peach"!

Farewell to the Old Country—After World War I, there was a depression in Scotland; Dad was out of work for eighteen months. Nathan's or Naylor's Machine Shop in Golborne, England, had promised that after the war they would take my father back, but that promise was not kept. Consequently, Mom and Dad decided to come to America, referring to it as the land of milk and honey. It was necessary to sell all their wedding presents to buy a ticket for Dad to go to America to find a job. Wow! What a daring and dramatic decision that must have been. Leaving home and crossing the Atlantic Ocean took a great deal of faith and fortitude.

Herbert Ridyard's Passport Photo

Dad's passport, No. L082782, indicates that he applied for it at the Foreign Office in Liverpool on March 27, 1923. On June 2, 1923, he applied to the American Consulate in Glasgow, Scotland, for a visa with the intention of remaining in the US indefinitely. The visa cost $10. Dad sailed to the US on the Cunard Line RMS Franconia (1922), departing from Liverpool, England and arriving at Ellis Island on July 3, 1923. The RMS Franconia was built by John Brown & Co., in Clydebank, Scotland. Note that there were two ships called the Franconia. The first was sunk during WW I. I understand from historical records that the second, called the Franconia (1922), the one that brought Dad to the US, was sunk during WW II.[5]

RMS Franconia (1922)

My father was fortunate to secure a job with the Bethlehem Fabricators, which I understand was located along the Lehigh River in West Bethlehem, Pennsylvania, between 8th and 13th Avenues. That building is no longer there.

Soon after coming to the United States, Dad fell and hurt his arm so badly he could not write. Mom was desperately worried when she did not hear from him, but eventually money arrived from him to cover the cost of passage to the US for Mom, Tom, and John. They departed Glasgow, Scotland, on the RMS Cameronia, landing in the US on September 28, 1924, after a separation of about fourteen months. My mother carried a bottle of Scotch whiskey in her luggage but became worried about the customs' inspection so, before departing the ship, she gave it to a sailor. She also had a small washboard strapped to the outside of her suitcase, because she did not know how women washed their clothes in the US and, inside her bag, a pair of clogs, a type of wooden shoe worn in the laundry room.

Emily Paterson Barnett Ridyard with sons Thomas and John

On the trip over, my brothers Tom and John participated in races in the corridors of the ship. At an early age, I remember seeing a picture of Tom and John with Mom, when they were young. They had ruddy cheeks in the black-and-white picture. Mom said those were rosy cheeks because of the healthy air in Scotland. In more recent times, Tom gave me a copy of that picture, which he said was from their passport. It is the only one I have of my mother when she was a young woman. Thanks, Tom.

As a side note, the Cameronia was built by Wm. Beardmore & Co., of Glasgow, the place where Dad had worked. It was launched on December 23, 1919, so it is possible that he helped build it. The history of the Cameronia tells us that it was the largest troop ship that took part in the D-Day invasion on June 6, 1944. [6]

PART II

CHILDHOOD

CHAPTER 4

MY BIRTH STORY
AND FIRST MEMORIES

The Ridyard family began life in their home in the New World at 916 Cayuga Street, in the suburbs of North Bethlehem, Pennsylvania, sometime in 1924. In this area between Linden Street and Stefko Boulevard are many streets named after trees, such as Beech, Elm, Laurel, Locust, Maple, and Sycamore. Although Cayuga Street is located in this same area, it is named after a Native American Indian Tribe. Cayuga Street is unique for another reason: it tees into Stefco Boulevard, which had a trolley line that provided Dad convenient transportation across the Lehigh River to his place of work at the Bethlehem Steel Co.

The very next year there was good news and bad news. I, Herbert[8] William Ridyard, was born on July 6, 1925, at St. Luke's Hospital, Bethlehem. The world took little note of my birth. Everyone in the States was waiting for the Scopes trial to begin; Hitler was busy publishing *Mein Kampf*; the Vatican was complaining that Fascists were attacking Catholics, but Herbert and Emily Paterson Barnett Ridyard were celebrating because now they had a little Yankee in the family.

I remember little about our home on Cayuga Street. I'm told it was a nice row home; however, I do remember, albeit vaguely, having fun rocking vigorously in my rocking horse when I was a tiny tot.

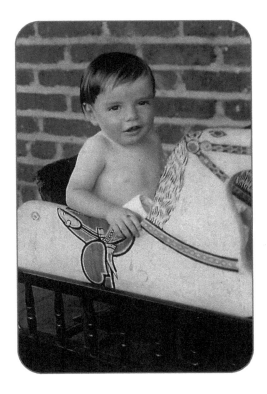

Herbert William Ridyard, age two

The year I was born Mom lost both parents; her father, John Barnett, died on January 25, and her mother, Isabelle Neilson Barnett, on December 20. That was a hard blow as there was no possibility of affording a trip to the funerals and very sad because she loved and idolized them so much. Mom was told that after dinner on the last day of her life, her mother said she was tired, lay down for a nap and passed peacefully in her sleep, that was some consolation. Whenever she spoke of her folks, she got a faraway look in her eyes remembering many wonderful times back in Scotland.

In 1927 when I was about two years old, we moved to 545 Guetter Street in downtown Bethlehem.[1] For the first few years, our next-door neighbors at 543 Guetter Street were Walter and Marie Neilson McKinnon.[2] Marie was Mom's cousin. I have often wondered whether the McKinnons influenced my parents to move there.

On the other hand, the onset of the Great Depression may have required my parents to downsize. I recollect my mother telling me that Dad had been doing piece work in a machine shop at the Bethlehem Fabricators, but when business turned for the worse, he was fortunate to obtain a job as a stationary engineer in the Bethlehem Steel Company's Pump House, which supplied water for all the Steel's steam-powered turbines.[3] Dad worked three shifts there for the remainder of his working days.

One night when I was about three years old, I woke up crying because my neck hurt. Mom called Dr. Hamilton, who saw that I was taken to St. Luke's Hospital,[4] where Doctor Chase lanced an infection in the side of my neck. I have a large scar on the left side of my neck to show for it. Years later, Mom told me that I had an infection in my mastoid glands and my condition was serious. I do not think they had antibiotics to cure infections in those days. Apparently, I dodged my first bullet at the tender age of three.

While recovering in the children's ward of St. Luke's Hospital in Bethlehem, I had my first vivid childhood memory, which I recall often in my dreams. In it, I am standing in a crib bed watching a magician perform at Christmas time. I can see him folding a large napkin into the shape of a rabbit with two large ears. After placing the napkin into a top hat, he pulls out a live rabbit. I believe that was the first time I heard the magic word *abracadabra*. Soon after that, I was in St. Luke's again to have my tonsils removed. This was done while I sat in a chair. My reward for being a good boy was a large helping of ice cream.

CHAPTER 5

MY HOMETOWN, BETHLEHEM

Since the City of Bethlehem would be my hometown for the next eighteen years, I have provided a general description of its geography with the hope that it will help in understanding my family history during this time period.

Bethlehem is in eastern Pennsylvania along the Lehigh River, midway between Allentown, five miles to the west, and Easton, five miles to the east, at the point where the Lehigh flows into the Delaware River. Bethlehem is about seventy-five miles northwest of Philadelphia.

Map of Bethlehem, PA

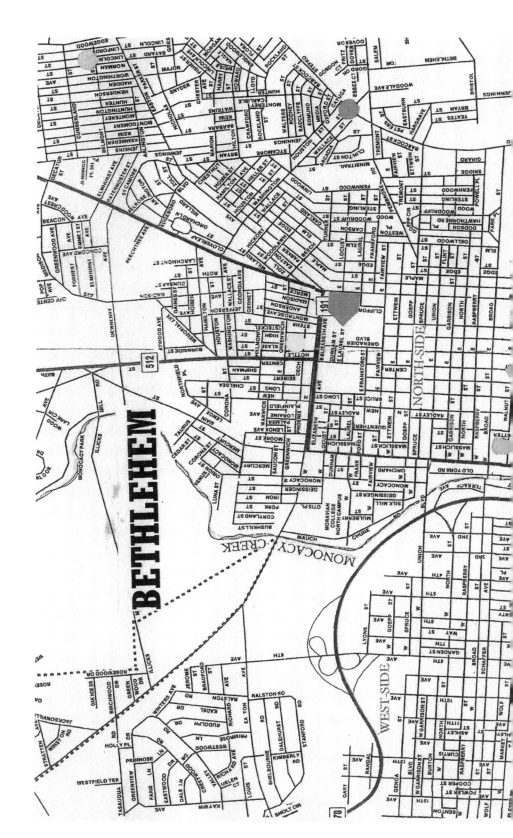

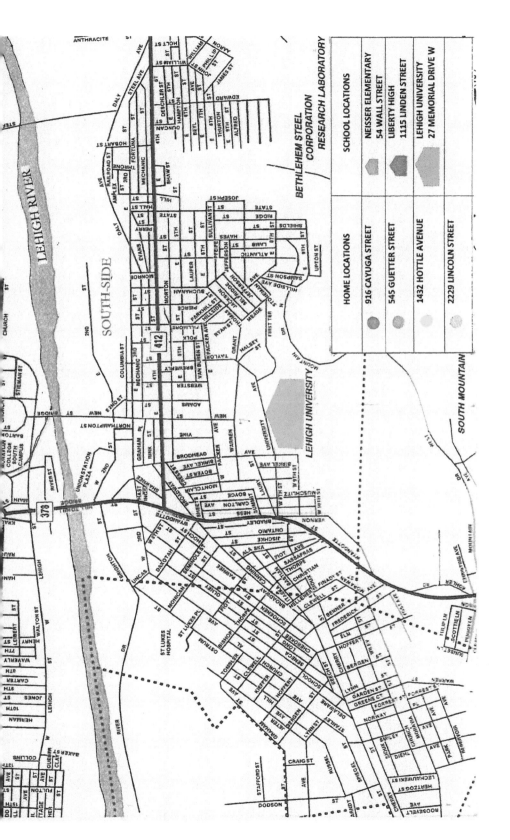

SCHOOL LOCATIONS

NEISSER ELEMENTARY 54 WALL STREET	
LIBERTY HIGH 1115 LINDEN STREET	
LEHIGH UNIVERSITY 27 MEMORIAL DRIVE W	

HOME LOCATIONS

916 CAYUGA STREET	
545 GUETTER STREET	
1432 HOTTLE AVENUE	
2229 LINCOLN STREET	

BETHLEHEM STEEL CORPORATION RESEARCH LABORATORY

LEHIGH RIVER

SOUTH-SIDE

LEHIGH UNIVERSITY

SOUTH MOUNTAIN

As shown on the accompanying map, the town is divided into two regions: North and South Bethlehem, by the west to east course of the Lehigh River. The portion of North Bethlehem to the west of the Monocacy Creek, which flows from the north into the Lehigh, is commonly referred to as West Bethlehem.

The south side of town nestles between the Lehigh River and South Mountain, which parallels the Lehigh. The main features of the "Southside" are the great structures of the Bethlehem Steel Company with railroads along the riverbank, the business district with steel workers' homes along Third and Fourth Streets, and then Lehigh University with its colleges and dormitories on the mountainside. When I was a young boy during the 1930s, we could see the flames and smoke from the steel works every night. Now it is nothing but rusty structures and empty buildings.

There are three bridges that cross the Lehigh River connecting the Northside to the Southside: the Hill-to-Hill Bridge at the south end of Main Street, the New Street Bridge, which in my childhood was called the "Penny" Bridge because that was the toll collected each way from a pedestrian (a nickel for cars), and the Minsi Trail Bridge at the south end of Stefko Boulevard. The Hill-to-Hill Bridge was built of concrete while the other two were steel trestles. The New Street Bridge is no longer a toll bridge and was rebuilt with concrete years ago.

Bethlehem's Northside, near the juncture of the Monacacy and the Lehigh, is the site of the original settlement by Moravian immigrants who traveled from their homes in Moravia in central Europe to the new world to escape religious persecution. They founded the town of Bethlehem on Christmas Eve of 1741, at which time they chose its name upon singing the Christmas carol, "Not Jerusalem, lowly Bethlehem." The Moravian Church and the neighboring buildings along Church Street are all historical elements of the original settlement.

The most populated region of the Northside, at least when I was a child, is bounded on the west by Main Street, which parallels the Monacacy Creek and runs from the Moravian Church north to Elizabeth Avenue, where Moravian College is located. It is bounded on the east by Stefko Boulevard. Broad Street is the primary artery in an east-west direction through the middle of the north side of town. This road will also take you through the

Westside all the way to Allentown. Most of the Northside shops and stores were found along Broad between Main and the next street to the east, New Street, and along Main Street between Church and Broad.

During my youth you could make the trip west on Broad to Allentown by bus or trolley. To the east, you could be transported along Broad, crossing New Street, Center Street, and High Street and then the bus or trolley line turned north along Linden and continued to Elizabeth Avenue, where Bethlehem's Liberty High School is located. The line then continued out Easton Avenue on its way to Easton.

Our home was one of six row homes on Guetter Street; they are gone now. Guetter is the alley between New and Main Streets that tees into Walnut Street, an alley parallel to Broad; hence, we were in the middle of the main thoroughfares in downtown Bethlehem.

The six row homes were located at the end of Guetter next to Walnut Street. Ours, the farthest from Walnut, was only a few minutes' walk from Broad Street. On our side of the street, between our home and Broad, was a garage or two where they butchered animals. Closer to Broad were a few doors to apartments. On the other side of Guetter was the Mohican Food Market, whose rear door was almost directly across from our front door. At night, when I was a child, this was a dark, scary part of Guetter. I usually walked in the middle of the street or ran home. Across the street from the row homes was an unpaved, delivery truck parking lot where the local children played on weekends.

At the junction of Guetter and Walnut Street was the Ross-Common Bottled Water Co. On the left side of their building there was a large door with barbed wire along the top that allowed delivery trucks entrance to their warehouse. At my young age, that door reminded me of the big door in the movie *King Kong*.

Next to the door was the Ross-Common office, whose entryway could be reached via a set of concrete steps that had a railing on two sides for safety. Those steps and the nearby large streetlight provided an inviting place for the local kids to gather in the evening to play charades and other less active games.

Our neighbors, beginning with the Walnut Street end of Guetter, were the Warners, the Sherrys, two families whose names escape me and our next-door neighbors, the Neiths. Mr. Warner was a big man who was frequently drunk. I often saw him sleeping it off on his back porch when I was on my way to Sunday School. Mrs. Warner locked him out on a several occasions when he came home inebriated. Once, he broke the window of their back door trying to get in. They had a son, Junior, whom I did not care for. His mother could often be heard yelling at him.

The Sherrys were decent people, even though they spent a lot of time drinking beer at the Fire House on Saturday nights. The Neiths left much to be desired because Mrs. Neith would play her country music or radio shows so loudly that we heard them through our rather thin walls.

CHAPTER 6

HOME SWEET HOME

Our two-story home on Guetter Street in Bethlehem was typical of most row homes. Just inside the front door was the living room, then the dining room, a short narrow passageway to the kitchen and the back porch. Upstairs were three bedrooms. Mom and Dad's room was in the front, Tom and John's in the back and mine, the smallest, was in the middle. The stairway to the second floor was in the dining room. The door to the basement stairs was in the passageway between the dining room and kitchen. The stairway to the attic was in my room. When I was little, I was convinced boogiemen lived up there.

The living room had the front door on the left side as you faced the house with a window to the right. I do not remember whether it was one or two windows, but it seemed to be wider than the other windows. There were two, small, cement steps at the front door and the door itself had a mail slot and a non-electric doorbell that, when twisted, made a ringing sound like the bell on a bicycle.

Our living room was furnished with two chairs, a small sofa, a radio, a floor lamp, and a table lamp. We had a framed picture of the steamship RMS Franconia on one side wall and the RMS Cameronia on the other. You will recall that those were the two passenger ships on which Dad and Mom, respectively, sailed to the United States.

The radio in the living room was the principal source of news and entertainment. We listened to Lowell Thomas's presentation of the evening news every night at 7:00 on station WJZ, New York. I also remember listening to exciting programs such as the Lone Ranger and Tonto, introduced by the "William Tell Overture" and highlighted by calls of "High-Yo, Silver! and Get 'em up, ke-mo sah-bee," the Gang Busters with Lieutenant Schwarzkoff of the New Jersey State Police and the Shadow Mystery Program. Who can forget Lamont Cranston's rendition of those great lines, "Who knows what evil lurks in the hearts of men? The Shadow knows. Heh! Heh! Heh! Heh!"

The living room was one of my favorite places as a child because, there, Mom read books to me while I was cuddled up to her. Also, Dad read me the comics on Sundays, drew pictures, and told me made-up stories as I sat on his lap. I loved my parents for showing their love for me in these ways. I felt safe and comfortable with them.

The dining room was seldom used for dining except on special occasions. It was a little dark, being the middle room, but it had a bright lamp hanging from the ceiling over the center of the dining room table, a bureau on the cellar door side of the room, a smaller one on the neighbor's side wall, and a chaise lounge on the opposite side. Mom called it a couch. There was a small landing at the bottom of the stairway to the second floor with a window viewing the backyard.

I remember doing homework on that table when I attended Junior High, because it was there that I was first confronted with the difficult challenge of outlining that huge seventh-grade Ancient History book. I spent many excruciating hours trying to figure out how to take notes without rewriting the whole book. That was hard, time-consuming work for me and the reason I remember it. Fortunately, it was also there I learned that writing things down was a sure-fire way for me to remember them; consequently, my effort to learn how to outline was rewarding.

That couch was another favorite spot for me. Whenever I did not feel well, for whatever reason, Mom would have me lie down there to rest and perhaps give me some medicine. If I had a sore tummy, she would rub it to make it better. She was good at that sort of thing. Sometimes, Mom took naps there, as well.

The kitchen was also a favorite gathering place for our family. That is where we had the big iron coal stove that Dad loaded up with tinder and coal from the adjacent coal bucket, lit the fire, and cleaned out the ashes, where Mom cooked, where we ate three meals a day at precise times: 7 a.m., 12 noon and 5 p.m., where in the mornings we washed up in the black slate kitchen sink and where we took our Saturday night baths, whether we needed them or not, in the big round metal tub in the middle of the floor. No, we had no bathroom—the kitchen served that purpose.

Dad's razor, shaving mirror, and strop hung on the wall near the sink. The cabinets for Mom's dishes were over the sink. The kitchen table and chairs were next to the side windows and the ice box was in the back corner. A calendar hung on the cellar door.

The nice things about living at the end of the row homes was that the kitchen windows gave a good source of light and provided a view over the communal side yard and beyond. The side yard was used as a play yard, except on days when Mom and the neighborhood ladies hung out their wash or beat their rugs. If the other row houses on Guetter had a side window in the kitchen, and I do not remember that they did, they would have looked onto their neighbor's house about six feet away.

Beyond our side yard and over its rather high wooden fence was a long yard that extended all the way to the rear of Groman's Bakery store on Broad Street. Since the Groman family lived above the store, we could see their patio furniture.

Although we had no bathroom, we did have a toilet. It was on the back porch in a small, non-insulated, unfinished room. The unique feature of this toilet was that when you sat on the seat it automatically turned water on to flush the toilet all the time you sat there. This was a huge technological improvement over the smelly backyard outhouses that had been around for years. However, this type of toilet technology did not catch on—I assume because it used too much water, for I have never seen the likes of it anywhere else. Dad kept some lye in this room that he used periodically to alleviate what little odor was present. What we did have in common with our ancestors is that in the winter it was very cold. Brrrrr!

On the outside of the living room just above the front sidewalk was a small window that gave access to the coal truck's chute used for delivering coal to the basement coal bin. We used chestnut-sized anthracite, a hard coal, for the furnace in the basement and pea coal for the kitchen stove. Anthracite coal was good for home heating and cooking because it burned slowly and efficiently, with minimal dust and smoke in the air. It was considered clean-burning coal. Of course, it would not have been clean enough for some bird brains today who want to do away with fossil fuels, but it kept us warm through the coldest of winters.

In the evening I loved to go to the cellar with Dad to see him put coal in the furnace, stoke and "bank the fire" by making a small fire in the front of the furnace, leaving a pile of un-burnt coal in the back, a method that kept the fire going all night and made it easier to start up in the morning.

The heat from the basement furnace came up through a large two-and-a-half-foot-diameter metal grate in the floor between the living and dining rooms, then was circulated by convection, keeping the whole house warm in the winter. The grate could get hot enough to burn your feet, so we were careful not to step on it without wearing shoes, but it was wonderful to stand on it to get warm after being outside on a cold day. It is interesting to note that we rented our house from the Fritch family, who were owners of the Fritch Coal Company.

As with all other row homes on Guetter Street, our back door faced the upper side of the Giant Market building. There was a walkway between our miniature backyards and the Giant. This side of the Giant building had a row of awning-type windows that were kept open during good weather for ventilation. We could look through them down to the market floor, which was far below the level of our home.

In the summer on Saturdays when the Giant raffled food baskets, we could see and hear the drawing of the tickets. One time, Mom won a basket and she had to scurry down, around and into the building to collect her prize.

Above the windows was the slate roof of the market. This was the "scenic view" at our back door. Out our front window was the Mohican Market's back door and a small parking lot. You cannot get more "downtown" than that.

Being the youngest, I was called the baby of the family. I never liked that term, but it was the reason I had my own bedroom with a small dresser, chair, and bed, where Mom would tuck me in and say prayers with me at bedtime. That bed was a real issue for me during my childhood. For the first six years or so I slept in a metal crib with sides that could be raised and lowered. I was fearful that one of my friends would discover I slept in a crib and that I would never live it down. But the bed was comfortable and warm. I do not think it could be otherwise with those scratchy wool blankets from Scotland. Thank goodness for the sheets. In spite of doing without certain luxuries in our home sweet home, I knew I was so much better off than so many others in the world and was grateful for all that we had, especially my family.

CHAPTER 7

MY FAMILY

The reason I have a right to be grateful lies with Mom and Dad. They sacrificed everything for our family. Dad worked three rotating shifts at the Bethlehem Steel Plant: day, middle, and night shifts. I recall that when Dad was on nightshift, I had to be especially quiet because Dad had to catch up on his sleep during the day.

On pay day, Dad turned over his paycheck to Mom. She ran the house and paid the bills. Monday was her wash day, Tuesday her ironing day and Wednesday through Friday were her cleaning, grocery shopping, cooking, and sewing days. Saturday morning was Mom's baking day, although sometimes Dad baked bread. Sunday was a day of rest, especially after Mom made our big Sunday dinner. Although her days were full, she loved to relax with a good hot cup of tea; that held true for Dad, as well. This is how they spent their lives, day in and day out, with only one purpose: to provide a home for themselves and their three sons. I learned about love and dedication from Mom and Dad. I owe them so much.

I also learned about honesty from them. One time, Dad came home from the Giant Food Market and counted out his change from his purchases in front of Mom. They both realized that the cashier had given Dad too much change. We are talking dimes, nickels, and pennies. He marched right back to the store to return the difference.

I remember another incident when Mom gave me a dollar directing me to take it to Mrs. Doherty, a few doors away on Walnut Street and not to mention it to Dad. The reason for giving the dollar involved the following circumstance. The Steel workers were paid on Thursday, the Paint Company workers, where Mr. Doherty worked, were paid on Friday and Mom's dollar helped tide over Mrs. Doherty's finances for one day until Friday when Mrs. Doherty would pay Mom back. That's caring friendship for you! Did I mention how tight money was during the Depression?

Occasionally, a scruffy-looking man would knock on our back door looking for a handout. Back then they were called "hoboes." Mom would make him a sandwich and give him a drink of water. Sharing, even when you have little yourself, was another important lesson for me.

Before I was old enough to go to school, Mom took me along on many daytime visits to her Scottish lady friends. They would enjoy tea and chat, and chat, and chat about "the old country." I was not allowed to drink tea because supposedly it would stunt my growth. I was given milk. These visits seemed to last forever. Children were to be seen not heard; therefore, I sat on a hard chair and squirmed as little as possible to be polite. Upon our leaving, the hostess always commended me for being patient. This was truly a difficult but effective way for a little one to learn patience.

This was also a useful means for me to understand what was happening in the adult world during those difficult times. I learned that Scotsmen drank a lot of alcohol. A few were suspected alcoholics and that was an anathema to Mom. During the Depression, the threat of losing employment always looming over the men created a huge worry for their wives. Mom would take a glass of port wine on special occasions and we always had a bottle of whiskey in our house for guests. I became aware of this when I had a bad head cold, for Mom would give me a hot toddy and smear Vicks VapoRub on my forehead and nose; that was an effective way to open my sinuses and help me get a good night's sleep.

But make no mistake, Mom could not abide anyone who got intoxicated, because there was always the possibility that they would become an alcoholic; another important lesson I learned from her.

Dad loved music. Often when he was shaving with his straight razor getting ready for work, he would sing or hum "Smoke Gets in Your Eyes." Mom told me Dad sang at their wedding. Also, when there was a Souza march on the radio, Dad would lead me in a parade around the house. This was great fun. One day I told my family that when I grew up, I wanted to lead a band, but my brothers said that was not going to happen because I needed talent to be a band leader. I did not know what the word talent meant; consequently, I was very unhappy with my brothers.

Mom liked music as well as dancing. She could dance the Highland Fling and the Sword Dance, but she did not like jazz music that was popular at that time. She said it was just noise. Later in my life I experienced the same feelings as Mom when my own children were listening to rock and roll.

I never thought about my big brothers, Tom and John separately; they seemed to do everything together. They slept in the same bed, they went to school together, they played ball together and they had the same group of friends. Because they were older than me, Tom older by six years and John by five, and because I was of a different nature than they were, happy to do things by myself, I was like an only child. These differences resulted in me being at home more than Tom and John who seemed to be outdoors all the time.

Tom and John's best friends were Herbie "Chops" Miller, Tommy George, and Dewey Roberts. The Millers lived about a block away on Walnut Street not far from New Street; Tommy George lived across New Street, where his family owned George's Restaurant, and Dewey Roberts was a member of the wealthy Roberts family, owners of the New Street Penny Bridge.

A favorite place for them was an old garage on Walnut Street, where they played Cowboys and Indians with rubber guns. When they got shot, they would stagger around before dropping dead just as the real cowboys did in the movies. We little kids played the same game, so I knew how it worked.

Tom and John went to the same schools I did, Neisser Elementary and Liberty High School. Because they were older, they paved the way for me. Teachers knew the Ridyard boys were well behaved; consequently, I was greeted with smiles by my teachers.

Tom and John (in striped sox) with Friends

Tom and John were good students, but I think they would rather have been playing ball. In high school they took the commercial course that included typing, bookkeeping, etc. which trained them to work in a business environment. Neither one ever did that. Most evenings and weekends would find them at Moravian Field, behind the Library and Moravian Cemetery, playing fast pitch softball. As they grew older, they played league games with the Celtics.

While Tom was in high school, he got a job working Saturdays in the butcher department at the Mohican Market. Tom contributed to our household finances, which was a big help to Mom and Dad.

After graduating from Liberty High School, Tom in 1937 and John in 1938, both began working at the Bethlehem Steel Company. I clearly remember that because while they were so employed, there was a strike by the steel workers' union, either the CIO or the AFL, who tried to unionize the steel workers. Tom, John, and Dad all worked during that strike. They were required to stay inside the plant for several days and not to cross the picket lines.

That was a dangerous and frightening time because of the riots in South Bethlehem. Not only were there angry marching protestors but automobiles were burned. When it was over, the union won the right to strike and negotiate for wages and benefits. I remember telling Tom and John that I was never going to join a union. I thought it was un-American and against freedom. They said I would have no choice. I felt angry and frustrated at hearing those words. For Tom and John's experiences in WW II see Appendix 2.

Three of Mom's siblings also immigrated to the US: Uncle James, Aunt Annie, and Uncle William and their families. I remember that one or two stayed at our house following their arrival in the US from Scotland.

I'm certain that their stay with us was limited as special sleeping arrangements would have been needed, since the couch was the only extra sleeping accommodation in our home. I cannot imagine how it was done; however, for close relatives, our family would have found a way. The good news is that all of them were able to find work after a short period of time.

The only person I'm certain did stay with us for a lengthy period of time was my cousin John Barnett, the son of Uncle James. I remember him because of one of his favorite sayings, "Is there any pie or cake, Auntie Emmy?" John's comment followed the main course of our meal like clockwork. It is strange how a simple remark like that, repeated over and over, will stick in your mind for so many years. It is possible that John's little sister, Nancy, stayed with us, too, but I have no recollection of her.

Uncle James was a happy person. I always enjoyed his visits because he would tell me stories, all the time smiling and laughing. Once he told me, with a wink to my father, that my Dad and he had fought the Indians. I did not know whether to believe him or not, but I wanted to.

Mom told us Uncle James could not work at the Bethlehem Steel because the dust was bad for his asthma. From time to time, we heard he had been rushed to St. Luke's Hospital in the middle of the night for a shot.

Fortunately, he secured a position as a chauffeur for an executive at the steel company, often driving him to and from New York City. From that time on, Uncle James always had the use of a car. His wife, Agnes, worked as a maid for another wealthy family in Bethlehem, the Krecksbergs.

After finding work, Uncle James and his family lived in a house near Moravian College. On one of our visits to their house, I was surprised to see that Uncle James had built a five-foot-long balsa model of the famous ocean liner, RMS Queen Mary, the original having been built in the Barnett family's hometown, Clydebank, Scotland.

That visit was also a memorable occasion for another reason. After dessert, Aunt Agnes revealed she had strained the molasses used in the cake because the flies had gotten into it. I think this was understandable during the Depression and particularly because she may not have had time or money to obtain more molasses. At any rate, I hoped the flies' germs were killed during the baking. Those were the best excuses I could think of since we did not die from fly poisoning. Aunt Agnes never lived that episode down in my mother's eyes. Whatever misgivings Mother had about Aunt Agnes, and I could tell there were some, the flies in the molasses proved her case.

Uncle James was most kind to us by driving us places whenever he could. Before he came to pick us up, Mother reminded us that Uncle James was always prompt; therefore, we had to be ready when he arrived.

Once he drove us to the train station in Bethlehem so we could catch the train to New York for a vacation with Uncle Willie. That was a memorable trip, riding the train for the first time, getting off in the great station in New York City, looking up at the skyscrapers, trying to find the subway as we were pushed along by the impersonal, rushing, jostling crowd, down the steps while carrying our heavy suitcases, exiting at Battery Park at the southern tip of Manhattan, riding the Staten Island Ferry, seeing the Statue of Liberty and finally taking another long train ride to Uncle Willie's home in Princess Bay. What an exciting trip and the first time I traveled a long distance from Bethlehem.

Another time Uncle James drove us all the way to Uncle Willie's home through New Jersey and into Staten Island without going through New York City, a much shorter trip. Uncle James loved Uncle Willie's home because the sea air there was good for his asthmatic condition.

Mom's sister Annie found a job as a domestic and her husband, Jimmy McLean, worked at St. Luke's Hospital as an orderly. Mom said he always smelled of disinfectant when he came home from work. The McLeans lived in an apartment in North Bethlehem where they had a son, Jimmy, Jr., but after a few years they returned to Scotland. I'm not sure why.

While they were in the US, I sensed a tension between Mom and Annie. Mom seemed to think her sister was putting on airs, always bragging about her husband and their prospects. Uncle Jimmy seemed very nice to me, but Aunt Annie was a bit self-centered. I never felt comfortable around her.

Aunt Bella Sharp, Emily Ridyard, Aunt Annie and Uncle James McLean (in back)

My middle namesake, Uncle William Barnett, was my favorite relative although I got to see him the least. He spoke softly, friendly and intelligently but he could also speak forcefully on a subject when he felt the need.

He worked for SS White Dental Manufacturing Company in New Jersey as a tool maker[1]. In those days this was a prestigious job. If you want to manufacture something such as dental instruments, someone must make the tools to cut the metal to the proper shape. The tools must be exact and made of special, high-quality steel. Since cutting tools are used to make multiple copies of the dental instruments, eventually, the tools wear out. The tool-maker's job is to make exact duplicates of the tools. I did not know all of this at the time, but was aware that he had an important job, seemed to be quite wealthy compared to us and that made me feel proud of him.

Uncle Willie lived in a nice home in Princess Bay, Staten Island. He boarded there in the home of Aunt Emma. Mom tried to explain this situation, but I never quite understood their relationship. It seemed they acted as if they were married but I was never sure. Perhaps he was a boarder in the beginning and later married her.

Aunt Emma was especially nice to us when we were there on vacation. She served delicious meals, even breakfast, in a rather formal way with expensive-looking dishes and tablecloths. This was rather fancy for me and I knew we had to be on our best behavior.

One evening, Uncle Willie and Emma played a duet for us, Uncle Willie on the violin and Aunt Emma accompanying him on the piano.

For Tom, John, and me, these visits were very boring much of the time. We sat on the screened-in front porch for hours. Sometimes, we went for a walk, then went for a longer walk, all the time just waiting for Uncle Willie to come home from work. After dinner he would take us for a ride around the area.

On weekends he would take us swimming at the nearby beach. Our family had a good time there enjoying the sun, the ocean view, and the swimming, but I found it difficult to wade in the water because of the many stones in the sand and I always got sunburned.

Incidentally, going and coming from the beach was when I first saw those terrible signs on the summer homes, "No Semites Allowed." I did not really understand what a Semite was, but instinctively was shocked and ashamed. It just sounded un-American.

One time, Uncle Willie drove us all the way to Asbury Park on the New Jersey coast to swim in the ocean and enjoy the boardwalk. These visits to

Uncle Willie's were true vacations for Mom and Dad; they were welcome changes from their everyday routines.

Uncle Willie came to visit us once or twice at Guetter St. He drove a Ford Tin Lizzie with a rumble seat, which was fancy in those days. Everyone should have a rich uncle. Uncle Willie was mine.

Dad and Mom with Isa McCullough, Minnie Cretsor and Uncle William Barnett

CHAPTER 8

PRE-SCHOOL DAYS

I remember that my early childhood years were mostly fun and games. This was certainly true during my pre-school days. Even during elementary school there were lots of times to play after school, weekends, holidays and summer vacations. School homework, although important, did not take up much time in the evenings until I entered high school.

During these early years I became aware of myself, my growing body, my interest in learning and my early understanding of the concept of right from wrong. I was fortunate to have the care and guidance of loving parents.

For example, I remember Mom tucking me in bed almost every night. That gave me a warm and fuzzy feeling. Then I would say my prayer: "Now I lay me down to sleep. I pray the Lord my soul to keep. If I die before I wake, I pray the Lord my soul to take. Amen." That was a profound prayer for a child, but with my mother beside me, a calming ritual. After prayers, I would soon go to sleep.

When I was three or four, I played games by myself. As I grew older, I began to play with neighborhood children, games like tag, giant steps, hide and seek, and movie star charades. I also enjoyed less active ways to have fun, such as: attending Saturday matinee movies at the Nile Theater, playing pinochle, mailing away Wheaties box tops to get secret rings and reading the Sunday funnies, to name a few. For posterity here is how some of those games were played and the life lessons learned from them.

These days if you watch the news on TV or read the newspaper you invariably learn about all the crime going on in our country. I do not know what gets into people that they want to break the law so much. On the other hand, how is it that most people would not think of committing a crime? As for me, I learned to play by the rules early in life. In fact, I was introduced to this concept while playing toy soldiers, a game I invented for my own amusement.

The soldiers and their fortifications were made with Mom's clothespins. Two pins stuck together into an X shape could be used as a cavalryman, a fence, or a barricade. An X with a pin across it represented a cannon. As part of my defense-line, I would build a log cabin to protect my army's general. In addition to the clothespin soldiers, I got a small set of US West Point Cadet toy soldiers one Christmas and two WW I Doughboys to round out my army. Having arranged my army and its defenses, I became the enemy and, using my thumb and index finger, would shoot marbles simulating cannon balls to knock down the army. Then I would reposition everything and have another battle. I played this game for hours.

Occasionally on a rainy day my brothers would play the game with me. This did not happen very often, because John and Tom were five and six years older than me and had many of their own friends with whom to play games. On these occasions it was always two against one, them versus me. They would construct their own army and fortifications and soon demolish mine because they were much more accurate with their marbles. Still, it was fun to have their company.

We had a rule that applied to any game. The last one to continue playing had to clean up. This rule, agreed upon among all three of us, was necessary to comply with our parents' rule that we were to keep our home as neat and tidy as possible. One time after all the clothespin armies were set up and the battle was about to begin, both my brothers declared, "We quit!" That meant I had to clean up by myself. They really got to me with tricks like that and I would start crying to Mom that they were not playing fair, but of course they were in the right—a rule is a rule. This was a hard way for me to learn how to play by the rules; consequently, I never forgot it. This was also one of the many ways my big brothers used to roughen and toughen me up.

The clothespin soldier game was usually played on the kitchen floor or in our tiny two-by-four backyard, but as I grew older, I was allowed outside in the neighborhood to play with other kids. If there was no one outside, you simply walked to one of your friends' house and yelled, "Yo-yo, and their name." That approach would quickly gather a group of playmates.

Most of our games were played on either Guetter or Walnut streets, where automobile traffic was almost nonexistent. No one I knew owned a car. Delivery trucks were the only problem. In the evening, there were none of those, so we had the street to ourselves.

Our favorite game, Hide and Seek, needed a large area; hence, we played it near the corner of Guetter and Walnut, where there were plenty of places to hide. These included: behind porches, fire hydrants (we were little kids), trucks in the parking lot, and in nearby barns or garages.

Most of the rules for this game were rather simple to understand. To begin playing, the person who was It stood at Home, often a telephone pole, closed his eyes, and counted to 100 while everyone else scattered to hide. Then It would walk around seeking those hiding. If It saw someone, he had to run to Home and yell, "Yonnie-Yonnie, one, two, three, caught!" And It had to do that before the Tagee got there and yelled, "Free." As you can tell, there was a lot of activity in this game, which made it fun to play.

However, there was one rule that was difficult to define and enforce: the need to set boundaries to limit the playing area. Boundaries were defined like this, "No going past Mrs. So-and-So's house and no hiding in So-and-So's garage, etc."

Some Hiders broke these boundary rules just enough so that it became impossible to find their hiding place; consequently, the game would drag on and on. Those children already Home Free would get tired of waiting and call off the game. Rule breakers like these were not appreciated and were told so in no uncertain terms. The need for well-defined boundaries is a major problem facing most everyone throughout their lives. Uncertain boundaries between countries lead to major conflicts requiring international meetings to solve.

Even when the games were going well, there would eventually come a time when someone's mother would call them, which was the signal to come home for dinner. Invariably, the kid would say, "Do I *have to?*" That never worked. When they got home, they got a good talking-to with words like,

"When I call you, you get home here as fast as your legs can carry you." When it came to rules, we all knew that parents had the last say.

The necessity to play by the rules I learned playing childhood games, reinforced by my parents and teachers, became an important guideline for my life.

In the 1930s, our favorite entertainment was the Saturday afternoon matinee movie at the Nile Theater, which was located at the northwest corner of Broad and Guetter streets, just one block from my home. In my childhood days, most movies were talking pictures shown in black and white.

Everyone I knew in my age group went to those shows and tried to get there early to get a good seat—neither too close nor too far from the front; around the tenth row was perfect. Any closer and you were straining your neck by having to look up.

Movie-Tone News was always the first feature. Here, we saw all the important news events happening in the world, including President Roosevelt's latest vacation, Adolf Hitler and his Nazi soldiers marching and terrorizing some of their own people, and the Japs mercilessly bombing Chinese or Manchurian people. These latter news stories brought out a lot of "booos" from the audience.

Next there would be a cartoon, usually Mickey Mouse, Donald Duck, or Bugs Bunny. Oh, how we would squeal with laughter. Then there would be a short subject, perhaps a documentary or a comedy starring Buster Keaton or the Keystone Cops. Again, laughter would fill the theater.

Then along would come the long-awaited serial, a movie whose weekly chapters presented a continuous story. We would be so excited, because in the final scene of the previous week's serial, the hero might have been on a train that had gone over a cliff because the bad guys blew up the track. From previous experience, we would know that the good guy was not dead because that would have ended the story; consequently, the first thing we were shown in the next chapter would be a recounting of the situation at the end of last week's movie—a replay, so to speak, but this time the good guy would jump off the train at the last second, just before it went off the cliff. Everyone would say, "I told you so! I knew he didn't die!"

Finally, there would be a full-length feature movie. Quite often it was a cowboy movie featuring Tom Mix, Hoot Gibson, or Ken Maynard, with bit parts by their sidekick, Gabby Hayes. The good guys wore white hats and the bad guys wore black. Each kid had his favorites and would argue about their attributes. Roy Rogers and Gene Autry were not my favorites because they stopped the action to play and sing songs. I wanted to see those bad guys get shot and fall off the roof yelling, "Aaaahh!" all the way down.

Occasionally we saw a movie featuring the Johnsons on an African Safari with hordes of Black warriors chanting, dancing, and brandishing their spears. They were scary enough to cause bad dreams. On other occasions, we saw several Tarzan movies. I remember seeing *Tarzan the Ape Man* with Johnnie Weissmuller, a muscular Olympic swimmer and diver playing Tarzan. We were enthralled by these movie stars. This was the Golden Age of movies produced by Darryl Zanuck, Cecil B. DeMille, Warner Brothers, etc.

The matinees were four hours long. Sometimes I came home with a headache from all the noise, but I did not tell Mom because she might not let me go again. However, there never was before, nor has there ever been since, more entertainment for your money—ten cents, a thin dime.

As a result of our exposure to the Matinee Movies, my friends and I invented a game based on characters in the movies. All five or six of us would sit on the bottom step of the stairway leading to the Ross-Common Bottled Water Company's office door at the corner of Walnut and Guetter streets. Whoever was It would pantomime or act out the performance of one of the actors in a movie we had seen.

The first one to call out the name of the actor indicated by Its charade would be rewarded by moving up one step. The first one to reach the top of the steps was the winner and became It for the next game. One of the more enjoyable parts of this game was that almost everyone got a chance to perform.

Cowboys were our favorite actors; hence, they were most often imitated in Movie Stars. Simulated shootouts required the hero to fire mythical pistols at the bad guys, who then would stagger around before dropping dead. We never tired of playing that game.

During the summer holidays, we had a lot of free time, so often someone would think of a new game to play. If we enjoyed it a lot, it would catch on and we would play it for days on end. I remember one summer we played

Pinochle on our back porch or at the Miller house every day until we got tired of it and changed to Hearts.

Another fun thing to do was to send away for items advertised on cereal boxes. I always—and I mean always—ate Wheaties for breakfast. They advertised sports heroes like Jack Armstrong, the All-American: Boy, an Olympic track star. The lyrics for the theme song Wheaties sponsored on the radio program were, "Oh, won't you try Wheaties, the best breakfast food in the land. Won't you buy Wheaties for that's the best food that am. They're crispy, they're crunchy the whole day through. Jack Armstrong never tires of them and neither will you—so won't you try Wheaties, the best breakfast food in the land?" Sending in a few box tops and a dime would reward you with a small model airplane or possibly a sports card.

Wheaties also advertised for Col. Roscoe Turner, who was the pilot of a racing airplane that held the speed record for flights across the US. The 1930s were the "Golden Age of Flying." That is when I fell in love with airplanes. Every time I heard an airplane engine in the sky, I would stop everything to look up.

I joined the Roscoe Turner Flying Club by mailing in some box tops and ten cents and receiving a secret ring with Roscoe Turner's insignia on it. That was exciting for a five- or six-year-old.

From one such promotion, my brother Tom got a baseball game played with a special set of cards. I still have them. Tom made up baseball leagues and score cards and we three brothers played against each other. Tom's favorite team was the St. Louis Cardinals, John's was the New York Yankees, and mine was the New York Giants. In those days there were only two leagues, the National and the American, with eight teams in each. We knew all the players by heart. Teams did not trade as often as they do today, so team rosters were pretty much the same year after year. I am certain that my early reading accomplishments were honed by reading the sports page of *The Bethlehem Globe-Times* to check the team standings and players' statistics.

A few years later I obtained a great football game from a cereal box promotion. It came complete with a poster board football field, a ten-yard sideline marker, a set of rules, and five dice. It was designed for grind-it-out football with percentages against the passing game. I could play two opposing teams by myself with the results based strictly on the roll of the dice. I played it for hours, much like the kids do today with computer games, but without any need for batteries or dexterity. I remember a great game I played between archrivals Michigan and Ohio State that ended with a close score of fourteen to thirteen; however, I do not remember who won.

I also learned to read using the comic strips in *The Bethlehem Globe-Times'* daily newspaper and the Sunday *Philadelphia Record*. The latter had a full set of comic strips. Dad always read the funnies to me, until I learned to read them myself. I thought the stories in the funnies were absolutely wonderful, and they provided me with a great incentive to read.

Who can forget Prince Valiant, Buck Rogers, Orphan Annie, Li'l Abner, Blondie, Mutt and Jeff, Popeye, and Terry and the Pirates with their nemesis, The Dragon Lady?

Dad liked Bringing up Father, which was about the trials and triumphs of Maggie and Jiggs. He also liked Our Boarding House, about a blustery old man, Major Hoople, who often said, "Egad."

As with the serials in the movies, many comic strips were continuous from day to day or week to week. That made them something to look forward to.

Along with these good times, like everyone else, my childhood had its trials. Although I had the usual bouts with childhood illnesses—measles, chicken pox, mumps and whooping cough—I led a rather normal healthy life, but for some unknown reason, I was always underweight, very thin, almost skin and bones. Once or twice when my mother was drying my hair after my bath she would say, "All your strength has gone into your hair."

Most of the time this condition was not a problem for me. I thought little about it until I put on a swimming suit. Then I was embarrassed. This feeling of inadequacy was exacerbated in high school, where the boys swam in the nude; however, in this instance I was not alone. One of my friends at school, Dalton "Wayne" Shelley, was skinnier than I was.

Even worse than being skinny, I remember the time I contracted influenza, which made me feel so miserable that I thought I was going to die. I prayed for God's help to save me. After I recovered and returned to my normal self, the feeling was so wonderful that I remember it to this day.

When I was six years old, I fell ill with a serious illness, scarlet fever. Our home was quarantined for thirty days. I am certain that circumstance did not make me popular with my brothers. Dad was the only one allowed out of the house, so he could go to work.

Later, my mother reminded me that Dr. Hamilton called my illness "scarlatina," implying it was not as bad as scarlet fever; nonetheless, the sign on our front door read "scarlet fever."

Mom and Dad moved my crib-like bed into their front bedroom next to Guetter Street, where there was more sunlight. I had a fever and a red rash all over my body. I have little memory of this time. I suppose that was a result of the fever. Eventually, all my skin peeled off. I was a sick little kid.

The first time I was allowed downstairs was March 1, 1932. I remember that date, because, as our family gathered around the radio at seven o'clock that evening to listen to Lowell Thomas, we learned that the Lindbergh baby had been kidnapped. The manhunt, capture, trial, and execution of Bruno Richard Hauptmann was the lead news story for years. I even remember that Herbert Norman Schwarzkopf, the superintendent of the New Jersey State Police, was the lead investigator in the case. You will remember he was also the narrator of the popular radio drama, Gang Busters. What is more, his name lived on in his son, General Herbert Norman Schwarzkopf Jr., commander of Operation Desert Storm in the Gulf War.[1]

Scarlet fever was a serious disease. I know of more than one person who had serious heart problems resulting from that disease. During my early childhood, this was the second bullet I dodged. Thank you, Father in Heaven!

Early childhood was more than fun and games for me. As I was just beginning to grow up, I learned many things: that I had loving parents, how to play by the rules, how to amuse myself, how to get along with my brothers and friends, how to plan ahead to avoid problems, to take an interest in reading, and that, although I was a skinny kid, I was strong enough to survive a dangerous disease.

PART III

SCHOOL DAYS

CHAPTER 9

NEISSER ELEMENTARY SCHOOL

n 1931 when I was six years old, it was time to grow up and go to school. At that time, there were no public kindergartens, so children in my neighborhood began their formal education in First Grade at Neisser Elementary School on Wall Street, about seven blocks from my home. Neisser was the first public school[1] in Bethlehem, a brick building with three stories and a basement or boiler room. When I went there, the third floor was not used because it was unsafe.

On that first day, you can picture me as a slender little boy with dark brown eyes and hair, long eyelashes and a very shy manner. Like most kids, I was a little afraid to go to school that first day, but Mother encouraged me by giving me a goodbye kiss and saying, "Be a good boy and do your best. No one can ask you to do more than that." I was blessed with a mom who gave me that same encouragement throughout my days at school.

So off I went up Walnut Street, but on the way, I heard Herbie Warg crying his head off and his mother yelling at him to go to school. I quietly passed by on the other side of the street while trying not to smile on the outside as I savored the moment.

Mom (My Inspiration) and I (age 10)

Herbie Warg was my nemesis. We had a "Seinfeld and Newman relation-ship" and I could not help but recall the time I had the mumps and was quarantined at home. Mom had moved me into the front bedroom for the fresh air afforded by the windows there. Early on a Saturday morning, I heard Herbie Warg outside reading the quarantine sign. He said, "Mumps—good for him!" Hearing him crying now was sweet revenge indeed and I did not have to say or do anything to enjoy it.

As I continued up Walnut, I was joined by some of my friends. When we reached New Street, we turned right (south) and walked down New and crossed over Market St., where all the rich people lived and then down past the Moravian Cemetery to Wall St. Every time we crossed over a street, we remembered to look both ways for cars and trucks. Compared to today, traffic was light, but we had been taught to be careful and never to jay-walk. At Wall

St., we turned left (east) and walked the last two blocks to school, crossing over Raspberry Alley. The whole trip was rather short, even for a six-year-old.

I don't remember ever being late to school. That was a no-no. It would show up on your report card and you would have some real explaining to do with your parents, who saw you off to school in plenty of time. Since we were kids with time on our hands, we sometimes played marbles in the gutter all the way to school.

As we approached Neisser, we passed the playground's high chain-link fence on our right and then the front door we were not allowed to enter, finally turning right down School Street—really an alley—to the entrance near the rear of the school. Our teachers greeted us there that first day and led us to our classrooms.

At first glance, our first-grade room seemed large to me, but that was because the students were split into two classes, 1A and 1B, depending on their age and advancement. In those days, if you failed to pass, they kept you behind one half-year. Our desks and seats were one piece, the desk with an inkwell and a groove for a pen or pencil near the front and just behind a top that could be opened to store your books, papers, artwork, etc. Desks were lined up in rows and columns facing a blackboard. At the top of the blackboard the teacher had written all the numbers from one to ten and the cursive letters in both upper and lower case. They were so perfect I had a hard time believing anyone could write so beautifully.

Each room had a large cloak room where we hung our coats in the cold or inclement weather and where students were paddled if they were naughty. Getting paddled was doubly bad because the teacher sent a note home to your parents and you were likely to get paddled again; consequently, that punishment only occurred once or twice in my class while I was at Neisser.

I was as prepared for school as I needed to be. I could write my name. I knew my home address. I could read simple children's books, the baseball scores, and some of the funny papers, and I could count up to ten with my fingers.

One of the many wonderful things in my life happened to me that first day. I got Miss Murray for my First-Grade teacher. I remember her as if it were yesterday. She had gray hair curled in a bun at the back of her head, her back was ramrod straight, she wore black, high-top shoes laced above her ankles and had a beautiful smile. She was the best teacher I ever had. She taught me arithmetic, to write, spell, read, and much more. I learned to respect my teachers and other adults, to be honest, to always tell the truth, to never cheat or say vulgar words, to love my country, and to care for those less fortunate than me.

Every morning we recited the Pledge of Allegiance and listened as Miss Murray read from the Bible and offered a prayer.

One Christmas, because she knew our family was relatively poor, she arranged for us to have the school's Christmas tree. By the way, I liked every one of my teachers, but Miss Murray was my favorite. I will remember her to my dying day. Many years later when I graduated from Lehigh University, she remembered and sent me a letter of congratulations. I still have it.

One of the most important things Miss Murray taught me was to pay attention when she was teaching by having us sit silently with our hands folded. I soon discovered that if I paid attention and listened to my teachers, I could remember everything they said. This was a revelation to me. Homework and tests were easy. You cannot come home with hundreds on your papers almost every time without gaining great confidence in yourself. School was fun for me.

I also developed a strong motivational drive within me that made me want to do my best every day. Part of this drive was to make sure I never missed an assignment. I might not hit a home run, but I could almost always take a base!

The source of this motivation, I did not know of such a thing in those days, was certainly derived from my mother's daily urging me to do my best, but my dad was part of it, too. I remember one time I brought home a paper with a mark of ninety-nine. Dad asked me, in a kind way, what happened to the other point. It seems that I had forgotten to write my teacher's name at the top of the paper. I never made that mistake again.

However, I believe it was Miss Murray, who encouraged and taught us the ways to learn daily, who should be given most of the credit. An example of this is her suggestion to check our subtraction problems by adding the results. That made a big impression on me. From that idea, I learned to check everything. I also learned in math that there were two ways to get to every answer and I have always wanted to find them both.

I became a painstaking student, careful in everything I did. I was the epitome of slow but sure. This approach would confound me in high school and college, but it was my strategy in elementary school.

Something happened to our Second-Grade teacher so Miss Readline, Neisser's Third-Grade teacher, took over and taught Second and Third Grade. She was younger than Miss Murray and looked a little more modern wearing some make-up. I do not remember much about those years, but I do remember she was also the school's music teacher.

We started learning music in First Grade. Miss Readline divided the group into blue birds, yellow birds, and red birds. I never was sure what those groupings meant, but my guess was that blue birds were somehow better singers. It may have been a ranking of voice ranges, but back then I did not know there was such a thing. I only knew that, for some reason I was a yellow bird, not in the top ranking, and I did not like that at all; therefore, I had misgivings about Miss Readline. But when I got to Second Grade and had her for my everyday teacher, I found that I liked her a lot.

Still, there was one time she bothered me. I took one of her math tests and, after checking my answers, I found a mistake. Unfortunately, we were doing this test in ink and not allowed to erase, so to correct my error I changed a zero to an eight by writing another zero below the first one, so it touched the one above and made it look like an eight. That did not suit Miss Readline because that was not the way to write an eight properly; consequently, I did not get my usual hundred that day. I have been bummed about that ever since.

My memories of Fourth Grade and my teacher there are totally gone, but I remember Fifth Grade, where we had Miss Hunt, because she was a winner and when Mrs. Hemsath, the Sixth-Grade teacher, moved to high school, we got Miss Hunt again, only this time her name was Mrs. White because she had married during the summer. Miss Hunt and/or Mrs. White was a very competent teacher. We learned long division, history, and other interesting subjects in preparation for high school.

As one of her star pupils I sat in the back row, but I embarrassed myself by getting caught talking to Betty Bunte, who sat beside me. Boom! Just like that we were moved to the front row. I learned to respect Mrs. White because, as nice as she was, she took no nonsense from anybody.

A lot of interesting things happened to me in Neisser School. For example, I was asked to report to Mr. Strong, the school janitor, furnace attendant, and jack of all trades. Mr. Strong would send me to a cigar store about two blocks away on the corner of New and Church Street to buy him cigars. When I returned, I was told to "keep the change." This made me feel special—and, of course, I was.

Also, I was one of those selected to have a special snack time just prior to recess. About four or five of us were sent to the basement, where we were given a small bottle of milk and some graham crackers. This must have been the beginning of school lunch programs. I think the requirement was that you were under-weight, otherwise known as skinny. I fit that bill.

My favorite time at Neisser was recess. Our playground seemed large to me. There was a high chain-link fence on the Wall St. side, to keep us from chasing balls into the street, and on the side opposite the school where there were homes. The school formed the third side and it is interesting to note that there was only a low wooden fence next to the back alley. The ground was covered with small white stones, which made running OK but was ripe for skinned knees.

Near that rear fence was a merry-go-round about eight feet in diameter. It was three feet high, had a step around the edge at the bottom and hand railings at several points. Several children pushing together could get it going fast, but it was heavy and rusty, so it slowed quickly. Most kids took a turn on it and then went off to play somewhere else. It seemed to me to be dangerous. There was also a set of swings near the back fence that were popular during recess.

Most of the time, my friends and I played touch football with a proverbial stocking football. At other times we flew paper airplanes. I loved doing that. I could make a real floater. Recess was probably only about half an hour, but it seemed like more.

At the end of our school day there was no rush to get home. As I walked past the cemetery in the spring, a detour inside led to a good place to find violets to take home as a present for Mom. In the fall I could make a large pile of leaves there and have fun jumping into them.

On Friday afternoon it was Story Time at the Bethlehem Library on Market St., just two doors from New. I loved listening to the Story Lady and the quietness of the library. I read a lot of good books from there. I found *The Bob's Hill* series and read them all. As I grew older, I read all of Joseph Altsheler's books about Frontiersmen who lived and fought during the French and Indian War. The first large book I read with over several hundred pages was *John of the Woods*. John befriended a hermit that most people shunned. Not everybody had a library on the way home from school. I made the most of it.

The most exciting event on the playground occurred on May Day. Everyone dressed up in their finest and the children danced to music that we had practised for weeks ahead. My favorite was clap-stamp-bow. We formed a circle with four boys and four girls, did our clap-stamp-bow twice, then swung our partners, do-si-do-ed and did a grand-ala-main around the ring. I had no idea we were doing a square dance. It was fun especially because our parents and teachers were there to cheer us on.

We even had celebrities and a speaker. A girl from Sixth Grade was chosen Queen of the May Day and for a finale the older girls danced the Maypole Dance, weaving those long, colorful ribbons around the tall maypole. Then we all had vanilla, chocolate, and strawberry ice-cream slabs on a paper plate with flat wooden spoons and a piece of cake donated by the parents. School did not get any better than that in the middle of the Great Depression.

Another exciting event was the time when the Sixth Graders from all the elementary schools had a half day off and walked as a class in our best clothes to Liberty High School to see the High School Operetta. I remember the musical was one by Gilbert and Sullivan, *The Pirates of Penzance*. A high school student by the name of Willard Bilheimer was the star. This was a real treat for all of us.

As an adult I have driven down Wall St. many times. Neisser School was torn down long ago. It was the oldest school in Bethlehem and now it is only a memory. Some small apartments have taken its place and I am confounded by a feeling of melancholy and mystery as I drive by. How did that big school and that huge playground ever fit into that tiny space? It does not seem possible. It is another sad example that you cannot go back . . . except in memories.

CHAPTER 10

SCHOOL'S OUT

We attended school from September to June, but only until about 3 p.m., when classes ended for the day. In the late afternoons and evenings, we had lots of free time, except for homework. We had even more free time on weekends, national holidays, and during summer holidays in July and August. During free times like these that I called "school's out," our family enjoyed many special occasions and we children engaged in various enjoyable activities and pastimes.

Birthdays were always a wonderful highlight of the year. Mom would bake a cake, usually vanilla with vanilla icing, and decorate it with the required number of candles. The birthday person had to make a wish and if they could blow out the candles with one blow, their wish would come true.

Most of Mom's cakes during the Depression were one-egg cakes. They were yellow with a light texture. Once in a great while, she made a two-egg cake of which she was quite proud. I loved them all, but the best was a pineapple upside-down cake. That was superb. I loved to find that in my lunchbox at school.

My favorite birthday present was a scooter, simply because I enjoyed it more than any other. I would ride it down Guetter Street to Broad, hop up on the sidewalk and just fly down the steep Broad Street hill, braking with my foot at the bottom and turning left down the slighter grade of Main Street. Then I would scoot uphill on Walnut Street to get back home. When I was a little boy, that was thrilling—and great exercise.

Another present that brings back fond memories was roller skates, even though I was not that good on them because there were few good places nearby to use them. The sidewalks near our house had multiple grooves that made you vibrate while skating, and expansion joints that were made for tripping; still, they were fun. I never owned a bike.

The New Year was ushered in with a simple Scottish ceremony on New Year's Eve called "Hogmanay." Dad would go out the front door before the clock struck midnight and come in immediately after, bringing in the New Year. The coming-in part was called "First Foot." If done by a man with dark hair, it was thought to bring good luck to the household throughout the year. My folks would then sing "Auld Lang Syne" and give a toast to the New Year. Since I was usually in bed long before midnight, I knew none of this until I was older.

Preparing for Easter consisted of the whole family coloring hard-boiled eggs, which Mom made. John was very good at making unique, pretty designs. Our folks placed these eggs in baskets with perhaps one large chocolate egg and a few small candy bunnies and hid them for us to find on Easter morning. After breakfast, we attended service at Wesley Methodist Church.

The Fourth of July was celebrated by watching the parade on Broad and Main Streets and attending the fireworks display at the high school football stadium. Children in our neighborhood had their own fireworks going all week. Most had a cap gun, so we played cops and robbers or cowboys and Indians until we ran out of ammo.

Many of the older boys had small firecrackers that they lit with a stick of punk and ran away before the fuse set them off. You had to be daring to do that because those fuses were ever so short. Others had cherry bombs, which made a loud noise when you threw them at a cement sidewalk. Most children had sparklers, which we lit at night and ran around twirling and drawing pictures in the air.

I had sparklers but no firecrackers; however, I did have something I thought was better: a small model of a WW I army tank that could make a big bang. It had an internal reservoir that you filled with water. To fire the tank, you scooped up about a thimble-full of Bangsite powder (powdered calcium carbide) from a small magazine on the back of the tank, dropped the Bangsite charge into the water, screwed the firing mechanism over the water reservoir, waited for some gas to form inside, and then pushed the firing pin, which made a spark inside the tank, firing the cannon with a very loud bang. I had a lot of fun with that tank until I accidentally burned my hand.

While filling the tank with water, I put too much in it and the water overflowed and ran down over the back of the tank into the Bangsite magazine, which I had forgotten to cover with its lid. The mixture flared up in the magazine and burned the center of the palm of my hand, which was holding the tank there. I received a serious chemical burn that formed a large blister and hurt like the dickens. Mom took me to Dr. Hamilton. He recommended Unguentine ointment. I was one of the many casualties from fireworks that occurred on the Fourth of July, and I wore a bandage for some time.

Of all the special days described here, none can compare to Christmas, because that Holy Day comes with its own season, Advent, starting right after Thanksgiving. During this time, Sunday School and church services reminded us of the meaning of the coming of the Christ Child. The large Star of Bethlehem was lit on top of South Mountain and the street-lamps in town and across the Hill to Hill Bridge were decorated as well as the stores and homes throughout the city. Many homes placed a few electric candles in their windows while the original Moravian homes placed candles in each window. The streets and homes were decorated so beautifully that people came from long distances to see Bethlehem, "The Christmas City."

The Moravian Trombone Quartets serenaded passers-by near the Moravian Church at the foot of Church and Main Streets and special services were held inside the church including tours of its large Putz depicting the biblical manger scene.

On Christmas Eve, our family went to Wesley Methodist Church. That was one of the special times Dad was able to go with us; often, he was not able to, because of his shift work at the Bethlehem Steel.

Of course, the stores in Bethlehem were decorated festively to encourage people to shop, but for me, shopping for Christmas presents was a challenge because I had no money.

Mom helped by taking me to Woolworths 5 and 10 Cent Store. I walked up and down the aisles trying to find something for each member of the family. Mom made enough suggestions for me so eventually I selected my presents. I bought her a nice handkerchief. During my childhood she acquired an ample collection of handkerchiefs from me.

As I grew older, I managed to save some money to buy things on my own. Uncle Willie was always good for a quarter when I saw him. One Christmas, I bought John a small red bow tie. He did not like it. I was crushed and have felt badly about it ever since.

Usually, Dad came home with a small tree and Mom and Dad decorated it while we were in bed on Christmas Eve. Tom, John, and I would get up early on Christmas morning and see that beautiful tree all decorated with bulbs, tinsel, and the star of Bethlehem on top. What a wonderful feeling. We were not allowed to open our presents until Mom and Dad got up, but we could see what was in our stockings.

The only present I remember receiving as a child was a big yellow dump truck, which I kept under my bed for years after I stopped playing with it. Once, we got a small electric train. It was put under the tree every Christmas along with some figures and bits of scenery added over time to build our "Putz." Everyone in Bethlehem used the German term "Putz" instead of *crèche*.

Mom always made a delicious Christmas dinner with raisin or mince pie. Mince pie was a ritual brought over from the Old Country. I liked the raisin pie better. Buying a fruit cake seemed to be another ritual that Mom thought was special. That cake seemed to last forever.

The only problem I had with Christmas happened when we sat at the kitchen table eating our dinner and I looked at the chimney over the coal stove and pondered, "How did Santa Claus ever get down that chimney?" Somehow, he did.

During my early school days, my mother made certain her boys wore decent clothes. Most of my clothes were hand-me-downs from my brothers. My shirts came with large tucks neatly sewn into the sleeves. Trousers were turned up with cuffs at the bottom made to fit the new owner, me. My sweaters were always oversize until I grew into them. I suspect they were warmer that way.

No matter how new or old they were or whether they were darned or patched, my clothes were clean—Mom made sure of that, just as she kept our home clean. That was one of her special skills of which she was proud, and I was proud of her for it.

Shoes were about the only thing bought to size and you were taught to take care of them. Always untie your shoes when you take them off and use a shoehorn to put them on, all this to keep from wearing out the rear of the shoe. Keep them clean, keep them polished, and never get them wet. This gives you an idea of how we lived during the Depression.

One Christmas, Mom bought me a pair of high-top boots with leather laces. Those boots looked super with knickers as did knee-high socks and were great for snowy walks to school. In the summer, we wore sneakers. They felt as light as a feather.

When I was about ten years old, Mom bought me a matching set of jacket and knickers. They were made of corduroy material, which kept me nice and warm, and were a nice gray color with black-and-white specks. I did not get new clothes very often, so to be able to wear this outfit to school was special for me.

During winter when it snowed, everyone went sledding. My brothers had large, two-person Flexible Flyers and I had a smaller one. All you needed was a good hill and a way to stop at the bottom. North Street between New and Main was one of those places. The police blocked off the top and bottom of the hill with large sawhorse barriers and spread ashes at the bottom to slow us down. All we had to do was learn how to do a belly flopper to get started at high speed. Dad filed the rust off the bottom of the runners to improve our speed. We sped down that hill and walked back up again, over and over.

There was only one problem. On very cold days, the hill became icy and, after an exciting run down it, your runners might ice up. If you did not check them and remove the ice, you could lose steering control and end up going sideways or—worse—backward. I did that more than once. It was scary and reminded me that it was time to go home. It was good we did because when we got home, we found we had frozen fingers and toes, even when wearing mittens and boots. We had not noticed the effects of the cold while we were having fun.

My scariest sledding adventure occurred on a hill behind the Moravian Seminary. There was a wonderful, steep, sloping hill that teed into an alley at the bottom. This meant you had to make about a forty-five-degree left turn into the lower alley, a turn we normally had no problem navigating.

Unfortunately, on one particular day, there was an auto parked on the right side of the lower alley. This meant we had to make a sharper left turn than usual as we entered the lower alley—again, not a problem as we successfully demonstrated over and over.

Taking one of my turns down the hill, for some unknown reason, my turn was too wide and, almost out of control, I slid right under the rear of the car. I do not know why I did not crack my head on something under the car. It was fortunate that my jacket caught on something, probably the end of the exhaust pipe, which stopped me before I was killed. Was that dodging bullet number three?

When I returned home, I was afraid that Mom would ask about the tear in my corduroy jacket; therefore, I put it way back in my closet and stopped wearing it for a long time. One day I decided to wear it and found it had been neatly sewn together. Bless you, Mom.

During the 1930s, one could indulge in the wonderful hobby of building model airplanes at minimal expense. Both the Comet and Megow model airplane companies had a line of flying model kits for ten cents apiece. These models had about a twelve-inch wingspan. A considerably larger kit with an eighteen-inch wingspan cost a quarter.

They were constructed of strips of balsa and covered with tissue paper. Fuselage, wing airfoil, and tail formers, which gave the model its shape, were provided on sheets of balsa pre-cut to shape at the factory. The kits also included three-view plans, construction directions, a rubber-loop-motor, a pre-carved propeller, a wire hook to be connected to the propeller, a hard wood plug to mount the propeller, a small piece of sandpaper, and some decorative decals—either numbers or military insignias. All this for a dime! Airplane glue had to be bought separately, much the same as today's toys with "battery not included."

Brother Tom built the first model in our family from a twenty-five-cent kit, a WW I British Sopwith Camel biplane. Brother John built a WW I German Fokker D-VII biplane and then a beautiful modern Ryan ST low-winger with a streamlined, inline engine design and two open-air cockpits. In all my attempts, I never made one that nifty.

I learned how to make model airplanes by sitting and watching Tom. One thing we had in our family was patience because that is what it took to make these models.

By the time I was eight or nine, I was making my own and flying them in neighboring fields. I always loved airplanes. I had models hanging from the ceiling in my room. Those were happy times. My head was in the clouds. Everyone needs to have a dream. It was my dream to find a career in aviation.

The first model that I made was a Boeing Pursuit. Next, I made a high-wing Polish Fighter. As my technique improved, I made a model of which I was proud, a US Army Air Corps Curtiss Helldiver biplane. I flew it from our backyard into the side-yard. One time it flew across the yard and over the neighbor's six-foot-high fence. I thought that was a great accomplishment. I had to climb that fence to retrieve it, a daring feat because, in those days, no one would dare to enter another's yard without permission.

That Helldiver never flew that far again after many attempts, so I launched it from Tom and John's bedroom window and had some great flights from there, but I never could get it to glide over the fence again. Eventually, after many crashes and subsequent repairs, I lit a match to it and watched it go fluttering down in flames just as seen in the movies, a fitting end to a great model airplane.

Tom started another pastime in our family. He bought "G-8 and His Battle Aces" pulp fiction magazines. They had wonderful stories of WW I airplane heroes. Typically, the Allies would hear that the Germans were building a secret weapon that would break the WWI trench warfare stalemate. G-8, an English spy, would parachute behind enemy lines, discover who was the mad scientist developing the weapon, sometimes getting captured but always escaping and destroying the fiendish enemy weapon by blowing up the German factory.

All these magazines had one exciting feature story and several short stories. I read Tom's magazines and occasionally bought a magazine featuring a hero named "The Lone Eagle." We enjoyed other pulp magazines, including "The Shadow," "Doc Savage," "The Spider," and one of my favorites, "Secret Service Operator #5."

CHAPTER 11

THE GANG

We called the group of friends in our neighborhood "the Gang." There was no special connotation to the term "gang." It just meant we were friends. Almost all of us had nicknames, another means of expressing our friendship. Gilbert Miller, one of Chops Miller's younger brothers, was called Bullet. His older brother was called Ralphie. The Millers lived on Walnut, not far from New Street. Roland Mease, who lived across the street from the Millers, was called Measey. His mother had a lot of chores for him, so there were times he was not available to play with us.

Then there was Gildo Ruggerio, called Gildo, a built-in nickname. For most of my early childhood, he was my best friend. I remember finding a penny and inviting Gildo to go to the candy store on Broad Street to buy five—count 'em, five—green leaves, my favorite candy, which I split with Gildo.

He lived in an apartment above a store on Broad Street about halfway between Guetter and New Street. His back door opened onto a roof where there was a metal fire escape across the roof and down to the lot where we played games. Gildo's dad was a WW I veteran who walked with crutches. Gildo said he was gassed in the war. I wondered but I never discovered whether he fought for the US or for Italy, which was an American ally in "the war to end all wars."

Robert "Bobby the Greek" Diacogiannis also lived in an apartment over his father's store on Broad Street. His father ran the popular Nick's Hot Dog

Shop, not far from New Street. I remember eating some great-tasting hot dogs and chocolate-covered Popsicles at five cents each from Nick's. Bobby's back door also had access to the lot behind the stores on Broad Street.

Bobby Schoenen, son of the proprietor of Schoenen's Meat Market on the opposite side of Broad Street, was also a member of the Gang and its largest and strongest asset when we played football. His family was the only one that could be called wealthy.

Then there was Billy Smith, whose father owned Smith's Cleaners on Broad just beyond New, but who lived in an apartment near Gildo. Billy's mother, according to my mom, seemed to put on airs and some of it rubbed off on Billy; consequently, we kids considered Billy to be a bit of a sissy, but we never let our opinions on this matter be known. Years later, my opinion changed markedly when Mr. Smith drove Billy and me to Camp Minsi, the Bethlehem Boy Scout Council's camp in the Pocono Mountains, and then stuffed my tick with straw to make a mattress for my bed.

I was the smallest and skinniest member of the Gang and was called Shadow for obvious reasons.

Jimmie Burns, who lived on Walnut, played with the gang sometimes; however, since his family was Catholic, they sent him to Parochial School. We saw little of Jimmie until school was out for the summer.

You can see that our Gang was a good example of the "immigration melting pot" we learned about in school. We had Protestants, a Catholics, and a Jew composed of Pennsylvania Dutch, Italian, Greek, Irish, and English backgrounds. The good news is that these religious and ethnic differences never entered our minds. As I said, we were just friends.

I have fond memories of being a member of the Gang. Sometimes, we played in the Millers' backyard where we could climb their cherry tree and just sit around waiting for Mrs. Miller to give us one of her baking treats. Other times, we climbed, looking for apples, on a tree near Measey's house.

Once in a while, someone from Ross-Common would ask us to unload one of their big delivery trucks full of crates of sodas. They would pay each of us with a soda. We knew we were being taken advantage of, but we did not care. It was something to do and later brag about.

Often, we just hung around Ross-Common and passed the time skinning the cat on the railings around their front steps or just shooting the bull.

Occasionally, shooting the bull led to some unkind words, followed by a few "I dare yous," then "double-dare yous," and sometimes fisticuffs. It was amazing, at this point, how quickly the bigger kids would step in to stop the fight and make the two antagonists shake hands. I was never prouder to be part of the Gang.

After enough of us had gathered around Ross-Common, we would mosey over to our playground, the lot behind the Broad Street stores, and play softball. We chose softball over hardball because our field was so small, and no one owned a baseball glove.

Remember, in those days, none of us had any money except for a penny or two we happened to find in the gutter or down a sewer grating; a stick with chewing gum on the end was sometimes successful in retrieving the penny. Our parents might come up with a dime to go to the movies, but for a glove you would need much more money. Things like baseball gloves usually showed up at Christmas time and I remember when one of the kids got a glove at Christmas, it was used by whoever was playing catcher. Another time someone got a small football with the white rings on it for playing at night. We thought we were in heaven. The softball we played with was a forlorn thing to see. It was beaten almost to a pulp and had been repaired so many times with electrical tape that it was almost completely covered. When Bobby Schoenen hit it, you could see the tape streaming behind as the ball flew over our heads.

Our games began with the ritual of choosing sides. Usually, one of the bigger kids would start off by tossing a bat with the handle end up and someone else would catch it. Then the tosser would wrap his hand around the bat just above the tossee's hand. The two leaders would work their hands one above the other up the bat until there was no more room for someone to get a hold on the top. The last one to hold onto the bat got to choose first. There was an art to catching the bat and then ending up with first choice but since I never got to pick sides, I never learned it.

Because I was the smallest member of the Gang, I was always chosen last, but notice I always got to play. Even if there was an uneven number of us, it did not matter to my friends. We could still play with uneven sides, especially if I was the extra player. I learned inclusiveness from the gang. The important thing was whose side got Bobby Schoenen if he was there to play that day.

The baseball field was classic 1930s for kids living in the city: a dirt lot no one seemed to care much about. Home plate was a large rock about twenty feet from the Millers' backyard fence, which conveniently made a backstop for the catcher. First base was the corner of a building, which jutted out from the back of a store on Broad St. Second base was another smaller rock in the middle of the field. Third base was Old Lady So and So's backyard gate, which was amongst one of several fences along the backyards of the homes that faced Walnut Street.

I do not remember Old Lady So and So's name, but we all thought she looked like a witch and we were deadly afraid of our ball going into her backyard. Only the bravest of the brave would go in to retrieve it. If she saw us there, she would come out threatening to call the cops. She would pay in spades for those complaints on Halloween. Just think about it—what gang of kids had a real witch to pull tricks on at Halloween?

I remember the Halloween someone moved her outhouse about fifty feet away. I never knew who moved it, but I imagine it had to be some of the older guys. In those days, that Halloween prank was one of the highlights of our lives and was much talked about for a long time afterward.

The biggest problem with our field was the presence, in the middle of right field, of a tall garbage can pavilion about ten feet square and high with a roof on it. At times we had fun playing and jumping off this pavilion, but when baseball season came around, it was a pain in the neck. Of course, if you could hit the ball over the pavilion, it was usually a home run. Most of us could not do that, but if Bobby Schoenen was up to bat, someone had to play back behind it.

We seldom had enough kids to form two teams, so most times we rotated positions in the field in a sequence so that after the batter got out, you moved to a new position. This rule held unless you caught a fly ball—then you immediately had a turn at bat. When there were even fewer guys to play, everyone had to bat lefty to make sure the ball went in the direction of our lone outfielder.

Because of my small hands, I had trouble catching the rather large softball, so instead of playing the outfield, I was made steady pitcher. It was important to have a good catcher (not me) at first base to throw the batter out. The good news is that my friends included me in their games no matter my capabilities. This was another way I learned inclusiveness in the Gang.

Occasionally, the Gang played touch football. Our ball was a stocking stuffed with old rags tied in a knot at one end until that magic day the Millers got that small leather football from Santa Claus.

A couple of times someone arranged a game with another group of kids from up near Center Street. It was fun because our Gang was all on the same team. We identified our teams with similar colored handkerchiefs tied around one arm.

We played the game in a small grassy yard next to the Evangelical Church near Center and Market St. It was one of the few times we played tackle football, which was possible because of the grass. Of course, our main rusher was Bobby Schoenen. It took the whole other team to get him down. Still, both teams were having a hard time scoring. Then came my moment of glory on the gridiron.

Our team decided to send Bobby into the center of the line and, after the other team was climbing all over him to try to get him down, he lateraled it to me on the end. Generally, no one paid any attention to me. That trick play worked perfectly, resulting in a big gain before I was dragged down from behind just short of the goal line. I do not remember the score or who won, but we had a great time.

I look back, remembering all those good times with the Gang. I thought they would never end, but it seems all things do. When I was about fourteen, our family moved to Hottle Avenue, a few blocks from Liberty High School. Guetter Street was a mile away. There were new kids in my neighborhood and I soon lost touch with the Gang.

I never saw Gildo again, nor the Millers. Bobby Diacogiannis and Roland Mease's photos are in my high school yearbook, but I do not remember seeing them at high school. The fact that Measey took the general course could explain that somewhat, but Bobby took the scientific course like I did and was on the student council in his senior year, as I was.

It is a mystery, a sad mystery. I can see this separation happening after graduation when we were all swept up into WW II, but not for all those years in school. I guess I will have to be satisfied and happy for all the good times I had in the Gang.

CHAPTER 12

JUNIOR HIGH SCHOOL

When I was twelve years old, I entered Seventh Grade at Liberty High School. I was taking courses at the junior high level in the high school building because there was no junior high nearby; consequently, we called the place high school, which it really was, even our report cards said so. Strange as it may seem, I spent all six years there until graduation.

This was nothing new because my two brothers, as well as students for many years past, had done the same. What was new started while I was there. When I was promoted to Eighth Grade, they removed Seventh Grade from Liberty High and likewise when I became a freshman in Ninth Grade, they removed Eighth Grade. The reason for the change was due to the construction of a new junior high on Linden Street, Benjamin Franklin Junior High. Since I did not know this was in the offing, I felt as if, in some ways, I was the "Last of the Mohicans."

Liberty High was a good mile from Guetter Street, which was not a problem except during very inclement weather. There were many ways to get there. My usual route was to walk up Broad to Center, then out to Fairview, which would bring me to the southwest corner of the school. Occasionally, I would walk out High instead of Center. If I thought I was running late, I would take an even more zig-zagging route, but then I was never late to school—never ever. In addition, that first year, I had perfect attendance.

In Seventh Grade, I had Mr. Everett for a homeroom teacher in room No. 2 in the lowest floor of the four-story building. It can best be described as a basement with its windows above ground.

I liked Mr. Everett. On my first day, he mentioned with a smile that he had had my brother John in his class. Teachers know when you come from a decent family.

As I moved into this new stage in my life, although I did very well, I was surprised to learn that our studies were more difficult than in elementary school, so that meant I had to work harder than before. It also became evident that I must not miss an assignment and get behind in my studies. I did not realize it at the time, but I was beginning to learn the secret to success, hard work.

On my first report card I continued my scholarly ways from elementary school. The first semester I received eight Es, one G and an Excuse in Swimming. You will note that Bethlehem schools did not use the A, B, C, D grading system. A grade of E stood for Excellent, requiring a numerical grade between 90 and 100, G for Good meant a grade between 80 and 89, F for Fair meant between 70 and 79 and P for Poor, a grade less than 70. My E's that year were in English, Arithmetic, US History, Geography, Spelling, Art, Chorus and Gym (physical training). The one G was in Industrial Arts. I never fully understood the Excuse in Swimming. I never missed class, but I was not good at swimming. I suspect it was a gift from my teacher, Mr. Starkey.

The second semester I got almost the same grades, except the G was in Arithmetic instead of Industrial Arts and in Swimming I got a P for poor. I went one whole year and never was able to do the dead man's float. Every time I put my head in the water it went up my nose. At some point I tried taking my breath through my mouth instead of my nose and I learned to swim. Why didn't someone tell me that a year earlier?

It is interesting that the word PROMOTED was stamped over the red P by Mr. Everett, almost hiding it. You could tell by his tone of voice that he was upset by the P that ruined my almost perfect report card.

In eighth grade I had Mr. Yeager, the Industrial Arts teacher, for my home room teacher and reported every morning to Room 20. My report card was more of the same. The first semester I received nine Es and one F, in

Swimming, and in the second semester I received eight Es, one G in Industrial Arts and another F in Swimming. Now I was at least passing Swimming.

Although I was receiving excellent grades in all of my subjects, my favorite subject was History, taught by my favorite high school teacher, Mr. McIntyre. He had a pleasant voice, was interesting, and allowed no nonsense in class. I appreciated that atmosphere because I enjoyed History and wanted to learn all I could.

All my History teachers lectured as they wrote on the blackboard and I took notes as they lectured; consequently, to keep up I began to use a very small script, almost a scribble. At home, I spent hours outlining the book and cleaning up my notes. Outlining efficiently was one of the most difficult things I learned to do in school, but when exam time came at the end of the year, all I had to do was review my notes and I did well consistently. Learning the outlining technique helped me in both high school and college.

I made one of the hardest decisions in my life while in junior high school. I had to decide whether to take the commercial, scientific, or academic course. Basically, I had to decide whether I was going to prepare to go to college or not, while knowing there was no way that my parents could afford to send me there.

I was familiar with the word "afford." When I was little and we took Saturday walks with Mom and Dad up or down Broad and Main streets, we would window shop. I enjoyed that because there were always new things to see and the store managers put the most attractive items in the store windows. When I saw a new toy, I would say something about how nice it was. Mom and Dad would say, "We can't afford it." That would end the conversation. You do not hear that phrase much these days. Back in the Depression I heard it a lot.

Tom and John had chosen the commercial course. That is the course you took if you were planning to get a job after high school. I knew I had the grades to go to college but on the other hand my mother had to give up further education when she was sixteen to go to work to help support her family. I don't know how far my dad advanced in school. If I went to college, that would be a first in our family. What right did I have to even think about it? Trying to make that decision was excruciating for me.

Mom and Dad invited our neighbor Mr. Sherry to our house to discuss the matter. He spoke about subjects you would need to take. I remember he said something about Boolean Math. I did not know what that was. In any case he seemed to be encouraging me to go to college and it appeared my parents were agreeing with him without really saying so. That broke the ice. I chose the scientific course. I chose not to take the academic course because I was told I would have to take Latin. Latin sounded difficult and a little esoteric for a steel worker's son, so the dice were cast.

There were a lot of new and interesting things about Liberty High School. We had lockers for our books, towel, and gym clothes on the days we had Gym or Swimming. There were long hallways to travel to find your next class, so you needed your schedule handy in one of your notebooks to remind yourself where to go. Notebooks were a new, necessary item and then there were study halls. That made it possible to get your homework done or started before school was over. I was amazed how some students goofed off in study hall.

In addition, there was a nice cafeteria where you could sit with your friends, eat lunch, and go over the latest happenings in school and on the radio. I enjoyed my lunch. Mom took care of that. I usually had a ham and cheese sandwich, a piece of fruit, some raw carrots, and a package of Krimpets, unless of course Mom had baked some cake or pie.

Then there were sports and other activities after school. I tried out for track but did not last long. I kept getting a stitch in my side while practicing running. Anyway, Mr. Starkey said my knees were too far apart to be a runner. The only club I joined was the Hi-Y. Mr. Dando, the Economics teacher, was its mentor. I was elected secretary and had to prepare and read the minutes.

Our Hi-Y group planned a trip to Lancaster and one time while reading my minutes I mispronounced that name, putting the emphasis on the second syllable. Everyone had a big laugh. I was embarrassed and never forgot that episode. My dad was from that county in England and I still did not know how to pronounce Lancaster.

We took a bus to Lancaster, stayed overnight in someone's home, and attended a dance where you had to ask a girl for a dance and get her to let you sign her dance card. I was too shy to ask and could not dance anyway, so it was a long evening for me, but it was still nice to be in that beautiful place and to see all those lovely girls. Truly, going to Lancaster was a big deal. I had never been farther west than Allentown until I went to Lancaster and that was the farthest west I traveled until I joined the army.

There was one touch of comedy that weekend that occurred when we got off the bus. Somehow when we were unloading, the bus backed over my friend Henry Douglas's suitcase. He never lived that down.

CHAPTER 13

BOY SCOUTS OF AMERICA

When I was thirteen, I joined Boy Scout Troop 13. We met in the fellowship hall in the basement of the Evangelical Church at the corner of North and Center streets. Our scoutmaster was an army lieutenant who seldom came to meetings. Bob Shafer, our senior patrol leader, ran the meetings and kept a tight rein on the troop. Bill Bauder was his assistant. I liked them both for conducting good troop meetings, emphasizing advancement and having fun all at the same time.

If someone did not obey the Scout Laws or acted unruly, disturbing the meeting, they had to run the gauntlet. That meant running between two rows of Scouts while being whacked on the behind with hands, first aid splints or neckerchiefs.

During our game time we loved playing Steal-the-Bacon, a game where one member of each of two teams or Patrols would try to grab a Scout Neckerchief that was lying on the floor in the center between the two teams and then race back to their team before being tagged. Each Scout took turns playing with Bob Shafer keeping score. Relay races were fun as well as the Simon Says game.

Occasionally, we played Capture the Flag, usually an outdoor game, but inside our meeting room it was played with the lights out. Each team trying to sneak up on the other team's flag at the same time could lead to mayhem, but we loved it.

After I was appointed patrol leader of the Flaming Arrow Patrol, Bob Shafer began contests between patrols where we earned points for patrol attendance, advancement, camping, etc. Since you could earn the most points for camping, my patrol went camping out at Ellicks Mill, in good weather almost every Friday night. Our patrol won the contest easily.

We loved sleeping out in the woods. There would be four of us crammed into a tiny pup tent. We cooked eggs and bacon in a frying pan and baked potatoes in the coals of our wood fire. Our cooking was sometimes yucky, but we ate it anyway because we were hungry.

While camping, we earned badges for Camping, Fire Building, Cooking, and Reading a Compass and also learned about conservation of natural resources and other community skills. As patrol leader, it was my responsibility to help other scouts pass their scout tests and watch out that no one got hurt, make sure no one damaged a tree and that our campfire was completely out, and that we picked up our trash and left the area cleaner than when we arrived. This was my introduction to serving others. I did not know it at the time, but I was beginning to learn the secret to happiness: serving others.

During the summer, I had the opportunity to go to Camp Minsi, the Bethlehem Boy Scout Council's camp in the Pocono Mountains. I do not know how Mom managed buying me a summer uniform and paying for two weeks of camp, but she did. You will recall that it was there that I formed a good opinion of Mr. Smith, the tailor, for his generosity in taking me and helping with my bedding.

Camp Minsi was a great place to earn merit badges in the shortest time. I was already a Star Scout, having earned the necessary five merit badges; however, at camp before I knew it, I had earned the ten required badges for Life Scout.

I earned a lot more badges than that while at Camp Minsi, including First-Class Swimming, which required swimming about 150 feet. A large group of us jumped into the water together and I think peer pressure helped me finish that short stretch. I was not going to let the others beat me.

Unfortunately, I realized I would probably never get the coveted Eagle rank because you had to pass the Life Saving Merit Badge. To earn that badge you needed, among other requirements, to swim a quarter of a mile—that was clear across Camp Minsi's lake.

Minsi's lake was beautiful and I often went sailing with Dean Garland, a member of my patrol and a good swimmer. One of the two boys sailing a boat had to have passed the Life Saving Merit Badge. Dean had done that. One afternoon, while sailing, we had quite a scare. Suddenly, a storm came up. Fortunately, having had some Scout training in handling small sailboats, we knew what to do. We took down our sail and rowed ashore as quickly as we could, soaked to the skin but happy to be back on shore.

One afternoon, the Scouts from Bethlehem were challenged by the Scouts from Bath to a softball game. In the last inning, Bath was leading us by several runs going into our last at-bats. We had two men on base when I was asked to pinch-hit. I thought they were crazy for asking me to bat. I managed to wait out a walk, but my walk allowed Hunk Leibert, our best hitter, to come to bat and hit a home run that won the game by one run. Our team went wild. That is one of my favorite memories, but it comes with mixed emotions. I felt inadequate at the time; pure luck made this experience end in great joy.

Bob Shafer, Sr. Patrol Leader, Troop 13, BSA

My memories of Scouting would not be complete if I forgot to tell what happened on a troop hike through the woods near Ellicks Mill led by Bob

Shafer. He suddenly became ill. We had to get an ambulance for him. A short time later we learned that he had come down with polio, a relatively prevalent disease in the 1930s. Bob would recover but walk with a limp for the rest of his life. He did not let that physical impairment hold him back from pursuing a career in Scouting at the highest level. After high school graduation, Bob became a Boy Scout district executive in New York.

As I look back, Scouting prepared me for many experiences later in life, including leadership, responsibility, serving others, and taking time to enjoy the outdoors—but most importantly, to serve in the US Army in WW II, both during training and in combat. Sleeping on the ground in close quarters with my squad or patrol is a perfect example.

CHAPTER 14

HOTTLE AVENUE

'm not certain when we moved to Hottle Avenue. I know I was at least thirteen because that is when I joined Scouts and the next summer I went to camp while still living at Guetter Street. So, I was probably about fourteen; that would make it 1939. In any case, I think the move came as a surprise to me.

We moved to 1432 Hottle Avenue, which is one block east of Center Street and one-and-a-half north of Elizabeth Avenue. That put us about five blocks from Liberty High School, which was very convenient for me. In addition, our home at Hottle Avenue had many other improvements over the one at Guetter Street.

It was still a row house, but it had a front porch with a small garden in front of it, a small closed-in back porch, a large backyard with gardens along the fences on both sides, a garage where Dad stored his lawnmower and garden tools, access to the basement from the backyard, and a bathroom. The Ridyards were moving on up in the world! I still had the middle room upstairs to myself. It was smaller than Guetter Street, but I thought it was perfect, having a nice bed, a closet, a desk with three drawers, a study lamp, and a small radio. Who could ask for anything more?

Dad had further to go to work, but the trolley and bus lines were nearby on Linden Street and Elizabeth Avenue. Also, there were small grocery stores nearby for Mom, so it made shopping for essentials easy, but to go downtown to the bank and the major stores she had to ride the bus. Mom and Dad made some sacrifices in this move, but clearly the benefits outweighed the negatives.

For me it was a no-brainer. We no longer lived in an alley and the addition of a bathroom and shower made it more than worthwhile.

As I described previously, when I moved to Hottle Avenue, I soon lost contact with the Gang. I do not remember seeing any of them at high school. On Tuesday nights, I still enjoyed attending Boy Scout Troop 13. Dean Garland was the only one there I would consider a close friend; however, since he was younger than me we did not see each other at school and eventually he moved farther away to the west side of town.

I did not know any of the neighborhood kids around Hottle Avenue. Some of them could be seen playing basketball in our back alley, but I never cottoned to them. There was one time that I did go with them to the gym at Trinity Episcopal Church on Market Street, quite a long way from my new home. We played some games there and then I was challenged to a boxing match. I think it was a set-up. Everyone else knew this other kid could box. But they dared me to do it so I could not back down. I knew nothing about boxing, so I went on defense the whole time. The bout was only three rounds and there was a referee. I got hit hard only once so I considered that a victory. I survived. The hardest part was holding my gloves up and moving for what seemed like a long time. That was the last time I went anywhere with those kids.

This resulted in my becoming a loner in my own neighborhood—but not lonesome, because I had lots of things I loved to do and tons of homework to keep me busy.

Fortunately, I found a lot of new friends at high school. I ate lunch with Andrew Pheiff, Henry Douglas, and others with whom I became acquainted.

Henry S. Douglas and I became close friends. I do not remember how or why it happened, we just always seemed to enjoy each other's company. I never felt that way about anyone else except Gildo when I was a little kid.

Best Friends- Weston Werst, Herb Ridyard and Henry Douglas

As most people are aware, by 1939, the Depression was easing up. I'm sure that is why we were able to move to Hottle Avenue and, like everyone else, the Ridyards got a telephone. This was a big deal for a teenager. Having a phone meant that Henry could call me, and we could plan to go to a movie or to do something else on weekends.

Sometimes, we met at The Cup, a few blocks from high school, to buy ice cream. It was usually Henry's idea. He was a very engaging person. He was always asking me questions about myself and seemed really interested in my answers. That became a small problem when we bought ice cream cones. Henry could eat ice cream cones faster than anyone I knew. When he was finished, he would ask me question after question and as I answered him it took me much longer to finish my ice cream. It seemed funny-peculiar at the time, but those questions were one of Henry's trademarks and one of the main reasons for our friendship.

We had a lot of things in common. That fact became obvious as we conversed every day at school. We both had straight hair. His was much longer than mine and he combed it into a big curve on his head. Henry used heavy grease of some kind to keep his hair in place; at least it looked that way. Even so, on windy days when we went outside, both our hairdos would blow all over. No one wore hats. We laughed a lot about that problem.

Then there was the problem of teenage pimples. Henry had more than his share of those. I believe he had an acne problem. We would commiserate on getting up in the morning to go to school only to find we had a new hickey to deal with. Those were the days when we thought that was the end of the world. I thoroughly enjoyed having someone like Henry with whom I could share my thoughts and problems.

Henry lived out on Easton Avenue and came from a family that was wealthier than ours. They had a car and when Henry became sixteen, he was permitted to borrow it. However, his parents were strict with him and he had to work at home washing the car and doing other chores to get to use it. During our high school years, Henry and I were often together in that car.

I cannot remember when I met Weston H. Werst and that is strange because he is hard to forget. He was quite a cut-up. He was always laughing and teasing people. He loved to make up nicknames for other students and I think he must have alienated a lot of them with all his teasing, yet he never did any of that with me. He lived on the west side of town in an old home somewhere around Eighth Avenue near Broad. I did not know it at the time, but his parents were osteopathic doctors.

One of my early memories of our friendship was of him inviting me to his home to play soldiers. I had not played soldiers in a long time and thought it was a child's game, but I went along with Weston's invitation. I was surprised to find that he had real lead soldiers, lots of them, not made from clothespins like mine, and he had cannons that fired small pellets. I found myself in a game that was more like a war. Weston knew how to fire his cannons accurately and he was merciless. He destroyed my army. That game was not fun. It was my first realization that Weston was very competitive.

Sometime later, the Wersts moved to a home on Broad Street a block or two east of New Street. The family lived on the second floor and the doctors' offices were on the first floor. Mrs. Werst carried on the osteopathic practice and Mr. Werst began the practice of optometry. It was here that I first became part of their family.

They invited me on a trip to a Phillies game with the Brooklyn Dodgers at Baker Bowl in Philadelphia. It was my first trip to Philadelphia and to a major league ball game. Most of the people at the game were rooting for the Phillies, but I was a Brooklyn Dodgers fan, having spent many evenings during the summer listening to Dodgers games with Red Barber, the greatest baseball announcer ever. I thought the Dodgers players were terrific. Carl Furrillo could throw out players from the outfield; Peewee Reese was a superb shortstop; Pete Reiser was a wonderful outfielder and clutch hitter; couple these attributes with Gil Hodges at first, Jackie Robinson at second, Ralph Branca on the mound, and Roy Campanella behind the plate and you had a top-notch baseball team. It so happened that the Phillies had lost thirty games straight to the Dodgers, but that day, with me present, the Phillies beat the Dodgers. I was completely disappointed.

After the game we went to dinner at the home of Mrs. Werst's large Italian family, where I felt a little out of place. Mrs. Werst made sure that did not happen by introducing me and making sure I was treated like family. I thought that was kind of her.

In addition to finding new friends when I moved to the suburbs, I discovered some new ways to entertain myself.

Although I continued to work hard at school and do my homework every night except Friday and Saturday when I took a break, on Sunday I was back at it again. However, even when I studied, I usually had my radio on. There were some programs that I never missed. Bob Hope, the greatest comedian ever, was on Wednesday night and everybody in school listened. The next day we retold his jokes and laughed all over again.

Jack Benny, another great comedian, was on Sunday nights with Gracie Allen and Rochester. Fibber McGee and Molly and Amos and Andy were also great comedy shows. Amos and Andy, one of Dad's favorites, was on just after the news at 7 p.m. Mystery programs were a lot of fun, too, especially The Inner Sanctum with its Creaking Door.

Because I grew up during the era when swing music was born, I learned to love music by the big bands. The first time I heard Glenn Miller's band was at Dean Garland's house on North Street, which was only a few blocks from my home at the time on Guetter Street. Dean's family had a record changer, the first I had ever seen. It was there I heard "In the Mood" for the first time. Glenn Miller's music was beautiful, with a great sound and every note in his arrangements had its special place. I often reminded myself not to just listen to the melody, but to listen to all those subtle background notes.

Dean and I loved to go to the piano and music store on Main Street and listen to records in their soundproof booth. Once in a great while, Dean would buy a record, but usually we just went for the enjoyment. The store manager did not seem to mind, probably because we were smart enough not to overstay our welcome.

After school at about 4:45 p.m., Harry James's band played on the radio for about fifteen minutes. I never missed it. I still love Harry James and his trumpet.

From time to time, I built model airplanes in my room at Hottle Avenue. My favorite was called a Monocoupe. It was made from scratch, using plans found in a Flying Aces magazine. "Made from scratch" meant I did not buy a kit. I bought all the balsa, glue, etc., and cut out all the parts. To do this I covered the plans with wax paper and traced the part—say, a wing rib—onto the wax paper with a sharp pencil and then transferred the shape of the parts to the balsa by making pin holes through the wax paper into the balsa along the outline of the part. Then I cut out the parts with a safety razor blade. It was time consuming but gave me a feeling of accomplishment.

I loved that Monocoupe for its unique, original sport design. It was a high-wing monoplane with a cabin, twin vertical tails, and a single-wheel landing gear enclosed in a steam-lined wheel pant. It flew nicely but flights were too short because I did not know enough about making good rubber-band motors and I did not make my models light enough. Still, I was very proud of that beautiful Monocoupe.

CHAPTER 15

WESLEY UNITED METHODIST CHURCH

om told me that I was baptized as a Presbyterian, but my first memory of church was when I entered the kindergarten class at Wesley Methodist Episcopal Church on the corner of Wall and Center Street. It is not there anymore; the congregation moved many years ago to a beautiful new church building in the suburbs of north Bethlehem. The word "episcopal" was dropped from their name while I was still a child. Today, it is called Wesley United Methodist Church, the term "united" being added after a merger with the Church of the Brethren.

My childhood faith had its birth through the guidance of my mother and father and was strengthened by the wonderful Sunday School teachers at Wesley Church. Though I remember those who helped my faith grow, it is still a mystery to me how it became so imbedded within me. I remember walking home from elementary school thinking about my conscience and whence it came. I knew right from wrong so clearly in those days, but it puzzled me how that little voice had come into being.

There was a disruption in my faith story when my parents took their membership to the Evangelical Reformed Church. I was suddenly attending a Sunday School with a new group of children, none of whom I knew. After some weeks, I complained to Mom and she suggested I go back to Wesley Church. She assured me that my cousin Ralph McKinnon would be there to greet me.

The next Sunday morning I walked by myself back to Wesley Church and there was Ralph, who greeted me warmly. This is one of my fondest memories. I was nine years old and proud of what I had done. Soon after, my brothers moved back, as well, followed by my parents. Someone said a little child shall lead them.

However, I never understood how Ralph happened to be there to greet me. The McKinnons did not live near us but in a neighboring township. We had no phone and no one else I knew had one at that time. Did it happen by accident that Ralph showed up outside the church at just the right moment? It is a mystery. I'm left to believe the Holy Spirit was working overtime that day.

When I was a teenager, I was asked by my Sunday School teachers if I wanted to accept Christ as my Lord and Savior. That decision was difficult for me because I knew the Lord was sinless. How could I live up to His example? However, I knew it was the right thing to do so I accepted Jesus, another important step in my life. I still have the card I signed.

Besides Ralph McKinnon, I had two other friends at church: Jack Crooks and Dick Walters, both of whom were also classmates at school. During high school I had Jack to thank for introducing me to a couple of good books, Captain Blood and Scaramouche, which later became movies starring Errol Flynn. I envied both Crooks and Walters for being able to sing music in parts in our high school chorus. As much as I loved to sing, I could not figure out how to sing the tenor notes.

Our Sunday School class members always attended church with our teacher. Our preacher was old but excellent and we had a great choir. It is no wonder because Mrs. Fitch and Miss Benfield, our high school Chorus teachers, were the directors of the Wesley Choir. Willard Billheimer, an excellent tenor in our community, often sang solos.

Dr. Frank Fornoff

However, the highlight of my time at Wesley Church was my senior high Sunday School class simply because our teacher was Dr. Frank Fornoff. As our class members gathered on a Sunday morning we would begin to chat about the events of the week. Frank would be part of these conversations, asking questions about each of us. Then without our realizing it, we would be involved in the learning process.

Frank was a Chemistry teacher at Lehigh University and, coincidentally, my brothers, Tom and John, also had a Lehigh professor as a teacher at Wesley Church, Dr. Eney.

After the war when I attended Lehigh, Frank led the Chemistry demonstration lectures for the entire freshman class, which everyone enjoyed. I never had him for a teacher, but I understood his class was a tough one, lots of surprise quizzes.

Once I stopped in to say hello to him after school. He was speaking to one of the Lehigh football players, who seemed to be asking Frank to go easy on him. Frank let him know, as kindly as possible, not to expect any different treatment than any other student. I was proud of him. Who knows what pressure coaches could bring on faculty members?

In my last year at Lehigh, Frank went out of his way to take me to the DuPont Co., in Delaware to tour the plant. He introduced me to his friend, who was a manager in the DuPont chemistry lab. I learned from Frank that his friend had been the valedictorian in their class at Kansas University and Frank, the salutatorian. This trip was an interesting and unspoken gift to me in order to help me find a job. That was Frank Fornoff's way of showing friendship. It is another example of why I consider him my greatest role model.

CHAPTER 16

LIBERTY HIGH SCHOOL

I officially entered Liberty High School when I entered Ninth Grade. My report card for Ninth Grade is missing so I can't vouch for my grades, but I believe they were much the same as in Seventh and Eighth Grade. Regardless of my performance as a freshman, I had entered into high school-level studies that were more difficult.

In tenth grade Mrs. Wilson, who taught German, was my home room teacher and I reported to Room 120 on the first floor, not the basement. She always had the song "Ach! du lieber Augustin" written on the blackboard.

My grades in English were an E the first semester and a G the second semester. In Biology, one of the toughest courses in high school, I earned an E. Our teacher, Mrs. Kutz, gave us lots of homework, requiring a detailed notebook that she reviewed periodically. We had to include sketches of every plant and animal known to man. In addition, we dissected worms and frogs and made detailed drawings of them as well as the human body. We also made a frogikin and a manikin showing all the organs in their bodies in layers. I worked on that huge notebook and our other projects almost every evening and remember going to our back door at night to look at the sky to rest my eyes. Near the end of the semester, we had an exciting time the morning we entered class and found that the praying mantis had given birth to a gazillion babies in the laboratory.

Plane Geometry class was pure heaven compared to Biology for it was there I discovered I had a real talent. Mr. Whytock had a rather dry manner but was a great teacher. He would describe general theorems on the black-board, and then ask students to demonstrate how to solve geometry problems using the theorems. For some students it was embarrassing when they made a loud screeching noise on the blackboard while using the big protractor.

Mr. Wytock also asked us to give verbal proofs for problems listed in the text. He would start with the first person in the first row near the door and, one by one, move down the row as each student stood to try and present a proof to the problem. I would count the number of students ahead of me to see which problem I was likely to get and pass the time doing that problem in my head while waiting my turn. Whenever someone made a mistake, Mr. Whytock would give that same problem to the next person in line. That meant I would be given a different problem so I would do that one in my head, as well. Before you knew it, I had done a lot of problems in my head and I became good at it. I could literally do them all. That was a tremendous confidence-builder for me. Everyone needs to find something they are good at. I had found mine.

In Eleventh Grade I had Mary Crow, a bucktoothed English teacher, for my homeroom teacher in Room 218. That was a tough year primarily because of French class but, I did very well in Algebra with all Es and 100 in the final exam. I had a wonderful Algebra teacher, Mrs. Murray, sister of my First-Grade teacher. I attended her sessions after school where one could do homework and receive help if needed. I also had straight Es in History. I think you know I love History.

Physics was a difficult subject, but I did well there, also. My teacher, Mr. "Pop" Emery, was a tough old bird and scary at times, but I earned an E the first semester and a G the second. Unfortunately, I received an F in the final exam. I do not remember why.

Pop Emery handed out our corrected test papers one at a time. If a student did not do well, he would point out a mistake and then stick his pencil through the kid's paper, accidently on purpose, as a symbol of his discontent. I also recall that he threw an eraser at a student sitting in the back row who was not paying attention.

We had only one girl in our Physics class, Betty Bunte, whom I knew from Neisser Elementary. I thought she was brave to take Physics. During WW II, she worked as an engineer at the Boeing Aircraft in Seattle.

I did not do well in English. The first semester I got all Gs, but the second I got mostly Fs. I don't remember my teacher's name and I can only imagine that we were learning to write themes for which I seemed to have no talent.

I took la français in Tenth Grade because my mother said she'd studied French. That was a mistake. I'm sure I would have done better in German or Spanish, but what do I know? I was never very good at memorizing anything. In Tenth-Grade French I did OK; Eleventh Grade was a different story.

Mrs. Mumbauer was a nice enough teacher but almost all her quizzes were surprises. I learned to hate surprise quizzes. To minimize the degree of surprise I took to walking by her classroom every morning on my way to my homeroom. If the map was down over the blackboard, the surprise quiz was a fill-in-the-blank quiz on French grammar.

When you came to class and she wanted you to translate verbally from the text, she would say, "Traduise, s'il vous plaît!" Then she would start with the first pupil in the first row on the left and move back and forth along the rows of pupils. I sat in the middle of the class, so I had some time to think. If there was a vocabulary quiz, Mrs. Mumbauer would simply say, "Prendre le papier!", which meant; take out some paper, then she read words for you to spell. To prevent you from looking in your book, she immediately said, "Fermez le livre!" which meant close your book.

These quizzes led to some comical moments, depending on your point of view.

Once, when the students were asked to translate and it became Henry Douglas's turn, he took a few moments before getting up to read. I suspected he had not studied. Then he jumped up, saying, "All right" in an exasperated tone implying, *if I have to*. Mrs. Mumbauer made him sit down. Well, I thought that was funny and so did Henry, but we could not show it on our faces.

Another time, Mrs. Mumbauer asked Sylvia Ostapchuk to translate; she started crying and said she had something in her eye. Mrs. Mumbauer sent her to the school nurse. Sylvia was a star pupil and was always ruining the marking curve. Henry and I hated her for that. When she started crying, we immediately started laughing inside—not on the outside in Mrs. Mumbauer's class, no way. We realized that Sylvia had not been prepared for class and had come up with the lamest excuse and it had worked. We could never have gotten away with it. Henry and I laughed over that episode for years.

Eleventh Grade French was not going well for me. The first term I got an F. I worked very hard and got a G the second term, but I got an F in the final exam and ended up with an F for the first semester. I was an unhappy camper. During the second semester, I got straight Fs and it was during that time that I made a big mistake.

Henry Douglas asked me to go to the movies with him on a Wednesday night. I never went to the movies during the week, but he coaxed me into it and we both paid for it the next day. That morning, Mrs. Mumbauer announced, "Prendre le papier!" Oh, baby, a surprise vocabulary quiz, and neither Henry nor I had studied. I immediately reached under my seat and brought up my French book, magically opened it to the correct page, and mentally photographed the page of vocabulary words, all while Mrs. Mumbauer was calling out, "Fermez le livre!" I got a 42 on that test and Henry got a 26. What a bummer! Now I had hit bottom. That was the only test I had ever failed in school, not counting swimming.

A 42 is a killer for chances of getting a decent grade. If you are trying for at least a G, you need a lot of good marks to offset a 42. For example, nine 80s and a 42 average out to a 76. That is still an F. You need to average nine grades of 84 to just make it to a B. That was never going to happen. What I was really worried about was failing all together. As it happened, I received Fs each term and in the final exam, resulting in an F for the semester. All that work for basically nothing.

Twelfth Grade was a breeze compared to Eleventh. The first semester I got 5 Es and 4 Gs; in the second semester, I got 6 Es, a G in Swimming, "Yippee," and an F in Health. After all those Es and Gs in previous years that F was a mystery.

To summarize my accomplishments in high school I can say that I worked hard and did well in most of my courses, especially Algebra and Geometry as well as Biology, Physics, and Chemistry. I did not do well in Eleventh-Grade English, which emphasized writing skills and I accomplished little in la français for all the effort I put into it. I appeared to have little inherent talent for either of these latter two subjects.

Still, I ranked number fifty-second in my class, which put me in the top 10 percent. I had done my best, just as my mom encouraged me to do.

Because I had to work hard for my grades, I had little time for extra-curricular activities. I enjoyed being secretary of the Hi-Y Club, I joined the French Club because I thought it was necessary. I was elected to the student council but did not have time to contribute to its work. On the other hand, I made several excellent friendships at high school and enjoyed associating with all my classmates.

I had a couple of jobs during my high school years. The first was selling programs at football games. I think they sold for a quarter and we were paid a few pennies for each one sold. By the 1940s, the Depression was coming to an end and students could afford a quarter. My friend Dick Walters recruited the salesmen, so it was a question of who you knew that helped me get the job. It was fun. I think we got into the games free and the pennies mounted up to perhaps a dollar a game, but sometimes you missed the kick-off.

I also applied for a summer job with the Bethlehem Department of Education and was put to work with the Liberty High groundskeepers. My primary task was to dig up pig ears and plantain weeds from the football field. Talk about your boring jobs—there I was, me and a football field full of weeds.

However, occasionally, I had fun when the sprinklers were on in two alternating rows along the length of the field. Temptation got the better of me, so when no one was looking, which was all the time, I ran the length of the field dodging the sprinklers. I became good at it.

Some days I was asked along with others to rake the grass after it was cut in the large, beautiful lawn next to the high school building. This was necessary when rainy days interfered with the regular cuttings. That work was a welcome break from weeding.

At the end of summer, I was glad I had taken the groundskeeper's job. The work was not difficult and the pay was decent. I earned almost a quarter an hour, $10 a week for eight weeks—real money in those days.

During my lifetime, as with most boys, girls were an important attraction for me; consequently, I'm going to treat this matter as a separate topic from my studies in school. I fell in love for the first time when I was about seven years old. Her name was Shirley Temple, the curly haired child movie star with big dimples, whom everyone else fell in love with, as well. She made some forty-two movies between 1932 and 1949 with titles like *Little Miss Marker* and *The Littlest Rebel* and sang some very cute songs, including "Animal Crackers in My Soup" and "The Good Ship Lollipop," which I sometimes still hum to myself.

A year later I fell in love with the brunette movie star Ruby Keeler, the female vocalist and dancer in the musical, *The Gold Diggers of 1933*. Musicals were big draws in those days and I loved them. When I read that Ruby Keeler married that old, bald-headed but very popular comedian and singer Al Jolson, I was crushed. That ended my "affair" with Ruby Keeler. Then her co-star Dick Powell married the other girl in the Gold Digger movie, Joan Blondell. I thought these Hollywood stars must be losing their minds. Dick should have married Ruby. I would not have minded that arrangement. I liked Dick Powell, so I forgave him. He later made a slew of movies as a private eye, Philip Marlowe, and became a great actor and director on stage, radio shows, and movies.

When I was sixteen, I fell in love with Helen O'Connell, the singer with the Jimmy Dorsey big band. I used to carry her pin-up picture around in my notebook. Two of her top hit songs that I could listen to over and over were "Green Eyes" and "Tangerine." When the Dorsey band made the movie *The Fleets In*, Henry Douglas and I sat through it twice. Sitting through a movie twice was not something I did very often but it was a common thing to do back then. We both liked her and that was OK. Somewhere I have one of her 78 records with her autograph.

As you can tell, my love life was a fantasy and the girls in it were dream girls. Real-life girls were a different story. When you are too shy to ask a girl for a date, you have a problem in school because there are girls everywhere and when you are picky like me that only makes finding a girl to date even more difficult.

When I was fourteen, I met this girl that seemed very nice, so I sent her a note asking her to go to the movies with me. She sent a note back saying she was busy. I thought of using the John Alden, Miles Standish approach where you ask someone else to intercede for you, but I never put that idea into action.

So here I was, a junior in high school with the junior prom approaching. I did not know how to dance, and I had no idea who to ask to the dance or how to ask them. John, Mom, and Dad all tried to teach me the rudiments of dancing, but until you ask someone to dance you are not going to learn for real. I had gone to a few high school dances at the Masonic Temple but never got up the nerve to ask a girl to dance.

Our class was the first to receive the principal's approval to have dances at lunch time in our high school gym. That decision did nothing to help my situation, so my friend Henry Douglas came to the rescue. He found me a blind date. Henry said she was a high school postgraduate and did not know anyone in our class.

I dressed up in my semi-formal jacket and white trousers, in vogue at the time. I suspect brother John wore them before me. I bought a corsage. Henry borrowed his father's car, picked up his girlfriend, picked me up, and I met "what's her name" for the first time at her door. I do not remember her name. I was in her company for about six hours and I have never seen her since. However, she was pretty. I can thank Henry for that. And off we went to the prom.

About halfway through the prom we left and traveled to a large dance hall near Allentown where Jimmy Dorsey's band was playing and Helen O'Connell singing. We did not do much dancing. We just listened and were enthralled. It was the only time I ever saw a big band in person. For me, for us, it was wonderful. Henry planned the whole thing. I do not think I ever had a friend quite like him. Without Henry I might never have been to the junior prom or learned to dance. A few years later, Henry would land and fight on Iwo Jima with the Fifth Marine Division and be one of the lucky ones to survive.

Toward the end of my senior year, I was invited to a party. I had never been invited to a party before and I do not know who invited me or why I was invited to this one. There were about fourteen high school students there, evenly divided between boys and girls. I recognized that most of them were in my class, but I knew none of them. We had sodas and snacks and played games. First there was "Pin the Tail on the Donkey." Like the others I was blindfolded, spun around, and invited to pin the tail on the donkey drawn on paper over a doorway. I was worried that they might open the door and let me walk into the closet but that did not happen. Don't ask me where I pinned the tail, I can't remember.

Then we sat in a circle and played what I have decided to call a "mind-game." There were no instructions provided for playing the game. The girls began to whisper messages from one girl to another. It seemed that after receiving the message the girl would hesitate before passing it to her neighbor as if she were modifying it --- at least that is what I thought was going on. However, that was only a guess, so when I received the message, I was dumb-founded and embarrassed as to what to do; consequently, I repeated what I had heard to the person next to me.

Undoubtedly, the girls had played the game before and understood what to do. To me it seemed like an inside joke was being played on the rest of us. Whether the other boys knew what was going on, I do not know, but I did not and was beginning to want out of there.

After a break for more goodies, we were told to assemble again in a circle on our knees and it was announced that we were going to play "Spin the Bottle." I had never played this game before, but was aware that when the bottle was spun by a girl, if it pointed toward you, you had to kiss the girl. I was upset to be trapped into this game. I wanted to run but there was no place to hide.

Would you believe that the first time the milk bottle was spun, it pointed directly at me—I was It. There was no denying it, so I crawled across the room and kissed the girl to the cheers of the audience. I learned that her name was Betty Will. That was a first for me. I believe those girls planned this whole party just to get kissed.

There was one good thing about that party. I was not afraid of girls anymore and I soon got up the nerve to ask Betty to the senior prom. No more blind dates. I was growing up, even if I was way behind the others.

When the hard work was over, we had a commencement ceremony and then I began to think about the future. I decided to try my best to find a way to go to college, use my academic talents to study engineering and take some classes to improve my writing skills needed to write scientific or engineer-ing reports.

In the meantime, there was a war on. Little did I know, but I was about to spend two-and-a-half years in the military, where the only writing I would do would involve brief letters home while I proceeded to forget most of what I learned about writing in high school. Commencement would have to wait.

PART IV

WW II
SERVICE IN THE UNITED STATES

CHAPTER 17

A BRIEF HISTORY LESSON
ON WW II

This brief history lesson, providing some of the highlights of WW II, is especially written for my grandchildren, so they and other generations born later can appreciate what our country was faced with and how I felt about it at the time. Before the war began, I was in school but even as a child I could see it coming. I had a feeling of helplessness as the war drew nearer and nearer to us.[1]

WW II Begins in Europe

I was fourteen when Germany attacked Poland, on September 1, 1939. Since the British and the French, the Allies, had a treaty with Poland to protect each other as a hedge against German aggression, the Allies came to the aid of Poland and that was the beginning of WW II and its spread around the world.

Keep in mind that Great Britain owned one quarter of the land in the world and France owned a large piece of Africa as well as Indo-China, today's Vietnam.

Since my parents were immigrants from England and Scotland, they of course sided with their homeland and any blow against Great Britain was one they felt emotionally. For the Ridyard family, WW II started effectively with the entrance of Britain into the war, even though the United States was not at war. As a result, our family followed the war's progress closely on the radio, *The Bethlehem Globe-Times,* and Fox Movietone News.

Our family was an anomaly because, at that time, most Americans were opposed to getting involved. You would hear people saying, "We pulled their chestnuts out of the fire in WW I and we are not going to do that again." It appeared that most Americans did not realize the danger Nazi Germany under Adolf Hitler was to the rest of the world, including us.

Germany conquered Poland in a matter of weeks and persuaded Russia to attack Poland from the east and then split the spoils between them. This stunned the world because everyone knew the Germans hated Communism and therefore Russia. Soon after taking Poland, Germany literally walked into Czechoslovakia and added it to its Greater Germany sphere of influence. They had already absorbed Austria, so Germany was growing rapidly.

In the meantime, the British deployed their army and air force into France and, outside of a few skirmishes, nothing much happened there until the spring of 1940; this was called the Phony War.

At sea, British convoys fought German submarines bringing supplies to Britain from the US and British colonies. The Germans sent two battleships to raid those convoys. The German cruiser Admiral Graf Spee fought a battle off Montevideo with three British cruisers. The Spee heavily damaged the cruiser Exeter, but was chased into the harbor, trapped there, and eventually scuttled. Little victories like this heartened the Allies.

During November of 1939, Russia attacked Finland and the Finns fought hard for four months, killing many Russians before they were beaten. Everyone thought they were brave.

In February of 1940, Germany conquered Denmark and Norway. The British landed troops in Norway but eventually had to withdraw, leaving Germany in total control. This type of retreat was to happen to the British many times and the world coined a term for it: "too little and too late." It was a very depressing time and it was to get worse.

On May 10, 1940, the Germans attacked the Allies through Belgium and Holland with seventy-two divisions. They also had seventeen divisions along the French border and forty-seven in reserve. The Phony War was over. The

Dutch had ten divisions and Belgium had twenty-two; although they fought bravely, they were soon overwhelmed by the Germans.

The British and French had fifty-one divisions spread out between Belgium and France. The Germans attack, called a Blitzkrieg, went due west through the Ardennes and the Allied Armies to the sea, making a large bulge in the Allies' line arriving at the coast of France in ten days. Most of the British and many French soldiers north of the German bulge were cut off. Fortunately, about 300,000 of the British and French soldiers were evacuated by sea at the French coastal town of Dunkirk. This was called the "Miracle of Dunkirk."

In case you are not aware, the Germans attacked through Belgium in WW I and twice during WW II—in the 1940 attack I just described and again in 1944 against the US in the "Battle of the Bulge."

After the German thrust to the sea, the main French army was pushed south. Paris was captured and France surrendered on June 23, 1940. It took only six weeks to defeat France and Britain. Unbelievable! It seemed no one could stop the Germans.

The Battle for Britain

At this time a great leader arose in Britain. Winston Churchill became prime minister and promised "nothing but blood, sweat, and tears." His leadership, oratory, and presence gave everyone hope. Wherever he went he gave the V for Victory sign with his fingers.

The Germans planned to invade Britain but had to deal with the British Navy, which controlled the sea and the Royal Air Force (RAF). The Nazis tried to soften up Britain with their huge air force under the command of General Hermann Göring. All during the summer and fall of 1940, the Battle of Britain,[2] an air-war, raged over England. The Germans had the advantage in numbers of fighters and bombers, but the British RAF had two excellent fighters, the Spitfire and the Hurricane, that were a match for the German Messerschmitt fighter.

In addition, the British had two major advantages. To attack the British, the German fighters had to fly across the channel and back, significantly reducing their fuel and flight time to engage the British fighters. Britain's other advantage was their Coastal Defense System, which included radar towers along their coast and civilian aircraft spotters that could warn when, where, and how many German fighters and bombers were coming across the channel. This defense system gave the British a twenty-minute warning so they could plan to send the appropriate number of British fighters to the areas where the attacks would be coming from, thus making up some of the difference in the strength between the two forces.

Still, the Germans came close to wearing down the RAF by attacking their airfields near the coast where their fighters were located. Then a fortunate happenstance occurred. A German bomber force lost its way and dropped their bombs by accident on London. The British retaliated by bombing Berlin. This attack incensed Hitler and he redirected his air attacks to bomb London and other British cities. After that, the British did not have to worry as much about running out of fighters or airfields. Their big problem was the fatigue of their pilots, who had to fly several sorties a day, every day.

The news broadcasts that the Ridyards listened to reported the number of planes shot down every day and it was clear that the British were winning, if only they did not run out of men and planes. This made our family proud. Churchill said, "Never in the field of human conflict was so much owed by so many to so few." By October 1940, Hitler gave up his invasion plans. The British had won their first victory—but of course it was a defensive victory. The Germans were still rulers of Europe.

When the Germans started to bomb London and other cities every day, the British had many civilian casualties. The population had to spend its nights in bomb shelters and send their children to stay with families in the countryside and even in Canada. Their cities, especially London, were devastated. The British called this bombing campaign The Blitz.

It was during this period that my parents received notice from my father's sister Anne that my grandfather Thomas Ridyard had died. I can only imagine how Dad felt, but I was too young to fully understand. They told me that Grandfather Ridyard had caught a cold because of going out at night to the air raid shelter. Many years after the war, I tracked down his death certificate, which says he died of a heart attack. I will never really know what happened. Thomas Ridyard was just another casualty of Hitler's lust for power.

Meanwhile, Italy, in a cowardly way, attacked France just before France surrendered. This was called "the stab in the back." Italy's Fascist dictator, Benito Mussolini, then invaded Albania and Greece, but the Greeks put up a strong defense, embarrassing the Italians. Early in 1941, the British landed troops in Greece to help defend it. The Germans countered by invading the Balkans. They overpowered the Bulgarians and Yugoslavians and, by April 1941, had driven the British out of Greece. Then the Germans used airborne soldiers to capture the island of Crete to gain air control over shipping in the eastern Mediterranean. The Germans continued to appear invincible, but they had just made a serious miscalculation.

The War in Russia

Hitler made plans to attack Russia in May of 1941, but the offensive in the Balkans delayed the attack until June 22. He tried to defeat the Russians before winter, but he had lost six precious weeks; that delay would come back to haunt him. The attack began with 207 divisions, twenty-five of them armored, and fifty more with Finnish, Romanian, Hungarian, and Italian soldiers.

With the help of a map of Eastern Europe and Russia, I followed the German advance by sticking little pins along the battlefront. At first, the Germans swiftly crushed and captured hundreds of thousands of Russian soldiers, moving thousands of miles toward Moscow. They got within thirty-five miles of Moscow, but for some mysterious reason they bogged down. Unbeknownst to me, the Russians' retreat caused huge supply problems for the Germans, who were far from home. When winter came early, it was very cold in Russia in October, and the Germans had not brought their overcoats. Also, none of us knew at the time that the Russians had moved a large army of Siberian soldiers west to defend Moscow. It seemed a miracle had happened that I did not understand. No one could stop the Germans, right? Wrong!

America Aids the Allies

Meanwhile back in the US, after many desperate requests from Churchill, President Roosevelt decided to help the British against the German submarines by lending them sixty old WW I-vintage, US Navy destroyers in exchange for a lease on British bases in Bermuda and the Caribbean, for which we would now provide defenses. This was called the "Lend Lease Program."

We also started convoying merchant ships partway across the Atlantic, taking over Iceland as a base for US planes and ships to guard our convoys. Eventually in 1941, we agreed to help the Russians with supplies. The US also started to draft an army. Congress passed the Draft Act by one vote. Most people here were still opposed to getting into the war, fearing that Roosevelt was doing just that, though he had promised not to send US soldiers overseas.

Russia Turns the Tide

In the meantime, the Germans advanced into northern Russia, first conquering the Baltic states of Latvia, Lithuania, and Estonia, and then laying siege to Leningrad. Having difficulty capturing it, they surrounded it and tried for 900 days to starve them into submission.

The Germans also advanced far into southern Russia, capturing most of Ukraine, the Russian naval base in the Crimea, and the Baku oil fields east of the Black Sea. Here again they ran into a stubborn Russian defense at a city called Stalingrad on the Volga River. The battle there began in August 1942 and lasted until the winter of 1942. After continuous fighting, the Russians still held onto a strip of the city on the west bank of the Volga; the Germans were worn out from having to fight continuous waves of Russian reinforcements coming across the river.

At this point, the Russians gathered a huge army, broke through the Italian lines west of Stalingrad, and surrounded the Germans in Stalingrad. Troops sent to relieve the surrounded Germans were driven back and, eventually, in January 1943, the surrounded German army of 90,000 surrendered.

This left the Germans in Baku and along the Black Sea in danger of capture, so they retreated. Although the war in Russia continued for another year, during which the great tank battle at Kursk was fought, the German advance had ended. The Russian factories in the Ural Mountains were turning out tanks that were a match for the Germans and the US supplies began to pour into Russia, keeping their armies well supplied. The German dream of defeating Russia was over.

The War with Japan

Since the 1930s, the Japanese had been expanding their empire into Korea, Manchuria, and China through brutal bombings and massacres of their populations. During 1941, the Japanese started to make their move into Southeast Asia. They occupied French Indo-China, today Vietnam; at this point, the defeated French could no longer protect it. This move threatened British Singapore and Dutch Indonesia. Roosevelt responded by freezing Japanese assets in the US and initiating an oil and scrap iron embargo. The Japs had no oil in their own country, so they demanded a free hand in Asia. We were on the brink of war, although most of us did not see it coming. Unfortunately, our military, of which we were so proud, did not see it coming either.

December 7, 1941

It was just another Sunday afternoon in the US. I was in my room at our home on Hottle Avenue doing homework and getting ready for the next day as a junior at Liberty High. While studying, I was listening on the radio to a football game between the Washington Redskins and the New York Giants. The Redskins had as their quarterback one of my favorite players, Sammy Baugh, one of the NFL's greatest passers of all time, but for some strange reason, the Redskins were getting beaten by a huge score, 50 to 0. It is no fun to have your team losing by that much, so I was feeling down, when suddenly, right in the middle of the game, came this news broadcast, "The Japanese have bombed Pearl Harbor[3], our naval base in Hawaii, early

Sunday morning, sinking several of our battleships and destroying scores of our planes at Hickham Field. There were 10,000 US casualties."

What a shock! I was stunned, frightened, and angry all at the same time,—similar to how I felt after 9-11. I ran downstairs and told my parents. We listened to more news. Not everything about the damage was really known at the time. I am sure they kept a great deal secret from us. But today we know that nine ships, including four battleships, were sunk and twenty-one were severely damaged. In all, 181 US planes were destroyed. Both army and navy bases and airfields were bombed, 2,350 were reported dead and 1,178 were wounded. Many of the dead were entombed when the Battleship Arizona blew up, capsized, and sank. It can still be seen submerged in the waters of Pearl Harbor, where a Memorial Monument has been built to honor those who were lost that fateful day.

The next day, we had an assembly in the auditorium at Liberty High School to hear President Roosevelt's talk to the country, wherein he told us what had happened and that we were at war with Japan, using these now immortal words, "Yesterday, December 7, 1941, a date which will live in infamy, the United States of America was suddenly and deliberately attacked by the naval and air forces of the Empire of Japan. Yesterday, the Japanese government also launched an attack against Malaya. Last night, Japanese forces attacked Guam. Last night, Japanese forces attacked the Philippine Islands. Last night, Japanese forces attacked Wake Island. Last night, Japanese forces attacked Midway Island. With confidence in our armed forces and with the unbounded determination of our people, we will gain the ultimate triumph, so help us, God." As an aside, allow me to comment that the main thoughts from Roosevelt's speech are carved in stone at the WW II Monument in Washington, DC, but the buggers left off the words, "so help us, God." Someone is always rewriting history.

There was not much a sixteen-year-old high school kid could do but go to school. What little I could do, I did. I saved quarters to buy Defense Savings Bonds. I still have two bonds that my mom bought for me. The deal was that if you bought a $25 bond for $18.75 and kept it to maturity, ten years, they would give you back $25. At school, we bought Defense Savings Stamps for ten or twenty-five cents. If you saved enough you could buy a bond. I was never able to save enough stamps.

The war effort needed all the scrap metal we could find to make weapons. Some buddies and I collected scrap metal and took it to the junk yard in a wagon. We were paid a few pennies for the scrap.

Finally, I remember being called by the Boy Scouts to report to Scout headquarters on Market Street. We were sent to a place on the Southside to help people sign up for Ration Cards. These cards limited how much food and other items like gasoline, shoes, sugar and the like you could buy, so people would not hoard and cause a shortage. I still have Mom and Dad's cards. The Scouts also helped keep order and served refreshments. I do not remember Mom ever having any shortage of food, but then I was not home during the entire war.

Everyone was supposed to keep their window shades down at night so bombers would not see the lights. People did that but there was no bomb threat around our town. At the beginning of the war, the Japs shelled and bombed the west coast once or twice; those people had real air raid warnings. Ours were only for practice.

For the first five or six months of the war with Japan,[4] the news was exceedingly bad. We listened to the radio broadcasts every night around 7 p.m. Early in December, the Japs captured the islands of Guam and Wake after only a few days of fighting. They invaded the Philippine Islands, destroying most of our big bombers on the ground. There were reports that our ammunition did not work. The Japs attacked Malaya and Borneo. Jap planes sank two large British battleships, the Repulse and the Prince of Wales, on December 10. They captured Singapore on February 15. The Japs landed in the Dutch East Indies of Sumatra and Java, where there were large supplies of oil. At the end of February, a combined naval force, consisting of Dutch, British, and American ships, fought the Japanese navy in the "Battle of the Java Sea" and were defeated. No one seemed to be able to stop them.

The only holdouts were the American and Philippine soldiers, who retreated into the Bataan peninsula of Luzon Island, where they held off the Japs for several months. On March 11, we learned that General Douglas MacArthur was asked by President Roosevelt to leave and go to Australia to take over the defense of the Southwest Pacific. General Wainwright took over on Bataan and, on April 8, was forced to retreat to Corregidor Island in Manila Bay. He surrendered on May 6. The only positive result is that we slowed down the Japs for five months.

The soldiers who surrendered were forced to walk sixty-five miles to a prison camp. Thousands died on the way due to mistreatment. This was called "The Bataan Death March." In the ensuing months and years, we would learn more about how brutal the Japs were to prisoners of war.

On April 18, the US struck at Tokyo with 16 B-25 bombers led by General Jimmy Doolittle by flying from the aircraft carrier Hornet in a daring raid where most of the planes crashed or landed in China after running out of fuel. Two crews were captured and three of the men were shot by the Japs as a reprisal for the raid. In spite of these losses, the Doolittle Raid was a great morale booster for Americans everywhere.

In early May, an important naval battle occurred in the Coral Sea near Australia where two US aircraft carriers, the Lexington and the Yorktown, opposed a Jap invasion fleet headed for New Guinea, a large island just north of Australia. This battle was a draw. The Lexington was sunk and the Yorktown damaged, but the Japs lost a carrier and a destroyer. More importantly, the Japs called off their invasion. This was a close call because the next target for the Japs would have been our bases in Australia.

Midway

The Japs then decided to take the war in an easterly direction by invading Midway Island, 1,000 miles west of Hawaii. Secretly, they sent a huge naval fleet with four carriers and transports filled with Jap soldiers across the Pacific and at the same time sent another to invade Alaska. Fortunately, the US Navy broke the Japanese naval code and learned the main attack would be at Midway,[5] subsequently confirmed when our search seaplanes spotted the Jap fleet.

While the Jap planes were bombing Midway, US torpedo bombers from our three carriers—The Enterprise, The Hornet, and the repaired Yorktown—attacked the Jap carriers. All of our torpedo planes were shot down, but while the Jap planes were attacking our torpedo planes at low altitude and the Jap carriers were loading up their bombers for another raid on Midway, our dive bombers arrived and sank all four of the Jap carriers and a cruiser. We lost one carrier, the Yorktown, to a Jap submarine.

Without carrier air support, the Japs gave up the invasion and sailed for home as we harassed them on their way. This was the only defeat the Jap navy received up to that time. There were more to come. The Battle of Midway, June 4 to 8, 1942, was the turning point of the war against Japan. From then on, the Japs were on the defensive.

Guadalcanal

The long road to Tokyo began when the US realized the Japs were building an airfield on Guadalcanal, the southernmost island of the Solomon Island chain, and relatively close to Australia. From there, the Japs could bomb the shipping lanes used by the US to build up supplies in Australia for our counter-offensive. The US, with an armada of ships landed the First Marine Division, capturing the airfield. This began a six-month battle involving both navies and armies. It was brutal but we won.

From there, our navy and marines under Admiral Nimitz started an island-hopping campaign over the next three years that moved ever closer to Japan. The fighting was bitter because the Jap soldiers would rather die than surrender. We had to kill almost all of them as they defended the various islands with names like Bougainville, New Georgia, Tarawa, Makin, Kwajalein, Eniwetok, Saipan, Guam, Ulithi, Yap, Palau, Iwo Jima, and Okinawa.

The Jap navy showed up to fight while we were landing on Saipan. In the resulting battle, called the "Battle of the Philippine Sea," which was mostly an air battle, we destroyed 350 Jap planes with a loss of thirty of ours. This was called the "Great Marianas Turkey Shoot." The Japs also lost three more carriers, two by a US submarine[6].

While this was going on, General Douglas MacArthur's forces began a three-year series of battles to retake New Guinea, New Britain, Morotai, and the Philippines. Note that MacArthur had his own navy for support. There were at least eight amphibious landings by the US on New Guinea and several in the Philippines. During the battle for Lae in New Guinea, on March 1, 1943, the Japs sent a naval force to reinforce their army. In the "Battle of the Bismarck Sea," the US Air Force sank ten Jap warships and twelve troop transports, drowning most of their soldiers. Earlier, the Australians had driven the Japs back over New Guinea's Owen Stanley Mountains in another brutal battle.

In 1944, the Japs sent their whole battleship and cruiser fleet to stop MacArthur's landing at Leyte Gulf in the Philippines. Part of the fleet was turned back by airplane attacks and another Jap fleet was destroyed by US ships, including the battleship USS Pennsylvania, which had been repaired after being sunk at Pearl Harbor on December 7, 1941. Note that the US had twenty-five light aircraft carriers present at the Battle of Leyte Gulf.[7] The people at home were turning out ships, submarines, airplanes, munitions, etc., in enormous quantities. Subsequently, MacArthur's forces recaptured the Philippines.

The war in the Pacific ended when President Harry S. Truman, Roosevelt's vice president, who replaced Roosevelt after he died of a heart attack on April 12, 1945, ordered the dropping of the atomic bombs on Japan. Our use of the atomic bomb eliminated the need for the US to invade Japan and saved a million or so US soldiers' lives.

I hope this brief history lesson will give the reader a sense of the horrific war we were engaged in for four years. It is not meant to be complete. For example, I have not described D-Day and the subsequent US invasion of France, Belgium, Luxembourg, The Netherlands, and Germany, with which I am hoping you are familiar. I simply recorded as much as I could from my readings of history books[8]. Nor did I describe the experiences of my brothers and me during the war. We were simply minor actors in the larger scheme of things. We did our part, as did so many others in America's response to our enemies. In all, some 430,000 American service men died during the conflict. It was a very frightening and dangerous time, but we pulled together, faced our fears and did our best, no matter what the task might be.

CHAPTER 18

RECRUITERS COME TO LIBERTY HIGH

was fourteen years old in 1939 when Hitler invaded Poland. I was fifteen in 1940 when France surrendered, and the Germans invaded Africa, Crete, and Russia. I was sixteen in 1941 when the Japs attacked Pearl Harbor. During all this time I had to be content to pursue my studies at Bethlehem, Pennsylvania's Liberty High School.

When I was seventeen in 1942, the war began to turn around. The British finally defeated the German General Rommel at El Alamein near Egypt, the Russians defeated the Germans at Stalingrad, the Americans landed in Guadalcanal in the Solomon Islands and the US and British invaded Africa. Winston Churchill called it "not the beginning of the end but the end of the beginning."

The invasion of Africa was of course our first offensive against the Germans. It was thought we were not ready to attack the Germans in Europe. General Patton captured Morocco and the US-British army captured Algeria. In both places the French, on orders from occupied Vichy France, for fear of German retaliation, gave some resistance, but soon gave up and became part of the Free French army.

My brother Tom was among those who invaded Algeria. He was a Sergeant in an anti-aircraft battalion and saw combat against German airplanes. Years later Tom told me that the British gave them a radar-guided, airplane-tracking device because they had none. This was another of many indications that the US was not prepared to go to war.

I, of course, was now a junior in high school. My English teacher, Miss Delong gave us an assignment to write a letter. I wrote one to Tom. Later she wrote a note on my paper asking me how my brother was doing. I thought that was nice.

Sometime in the spring of 1943, US military recruiters came to Liberty High. You can imagine it was quite a surprise when one morning we seniors were told to attend an assembly in the auditorium where recruiters from the army, navy, and marines were going to make a presentation. I recall that one of the women teachers was quite opposed to the idea and would not go to the meeting. There was tension in the air. I wonder if this ever happened again in a US high school.

The recruiters introduced us to a program the army called the Army Specialized Training Program (ASTP) or, for short, the A-12 program. The navy and marines had similar programs. To become part of these programs one needed to be willing to enlist in the reserves, pass a written aptitude test, and take a four-month basic infantry training course. After we passed another written test, they would send us to college. For me this was a dream come true. If you remember, I had taken the scientific course in high school with no idea how I could ever afford college. Here it was being presented as a gift for my service.

After the presentation, a few of our teachers felt they needed to comment. I do not remember anyone speaking firmly for or against the program. However, from their comments, I suspected that many of the teachers did not want us to enlist.

Mr. Emery, our Physics teacher and baseball coach, tried to put some realism into the discussion. He proceeded to go to the front of the auditorium, not on the stage where the recruiters were, but right in front of me for I sat in the second row. There, he demonstrated how you would have to stab the enemy with a bayonet and then lift your foot up to shove him off your bayonet. It was a very dramatic and shocking moment. There was hushed murmuring in the room.

In spite of Pop Emery's efforts, I went home and asked Mom and Dad if I could enlist—another dramatic moment. With pride and well wishes for my future, they gave their permission. This decision would affect the course of my life for the next two-and-a-half years.

I often wondered what my parents were thinking when they gave their permission. In those days, people like my parents seemed to keep their thoughts to themselves. I can only guess what might have gone through their minds. Enlisting gave me a chance to go to college and avoid the draft for which I would be eligible a month later. They already had one son in harm's way—my brother Tom in Africa. Was that enough? There was a terrible evil in the world; everyone had to do their part. Although they never communicated their rationale to me, I'm thankful for their support.

CHAPTER 19

ENLISTMENT IN THE ARMY SPECIALIZED TRAINING PROGRAM (ASTP)

Having obtained my parents' approval to enlist in the ASTP, I traveled by trolley to nearby Allentown, where the local recruiting offices were located. Through all my young life, I had been interested in airplanes, so I went to the Army Air Corps recruiting station, where I was given an eye test. Because I needed to wear glasses, they said I was not eligible. I left their office disappointed. Later, I would see lots of members of the Army Air Corps wearing glasses. I can understand that pilots and gunners would need perfect vision, but many others like flight engineers would not.

It occurred to me that it might have something to do with the AST program, so I looked at my ASTP booklet, "Fifty Questions and Answers on the AST Program." I had paid little attention to this booklet because all I cared about was that I was being sent to college. I found my answer under Question 1: What is the Army Specialized Training Program? Answer: It is a plan to train soldiers for specific army needs, utilizing the faculties and the facilities of colleges and universities. It is anticipated that most of the soldiers will be recommended for Officer Candidate School. Oops, I didn't know we were to become officers.

This helped me understand my rejection by the Army Air Corps. Most officers in the Air Corps were pilots and they needed to have perfect vision. An officer in the army "something else" would not need perfect vision, just good vision.

I did not apply to the navy because I had never learned to be a good swimmer, so I applied to join the army at the Armed Forces Induction Station, Sheridan School House, Grant and Liberty Street, Allentown, Pennsylvania.

This time, I was given a relatively complete physical, including an eye exam for color blindness and a depth perception test. I did well in those tests except when I was asked to stand on one foot with my eyes closed for a long period; my eyes were blinking and blinking as I tried to maintain balance.

After the tests, I met with a doctor who simply asked me, "Do you really want to enlist?" By the tone of his voice, I knew he was trying to talk me out of enlisting. Having seen me almost naked it was obvious that I was a skinny, 121-pound lightweight. Nonetheless I said, "Yes." I did not know it then but that was one of my best decisions ever. The date was June 3, 1943.

I took an oath to defend the United States of America and was sworn in as a private in the Army Enlisted Reserve Corps for the duration of the war plus six months. My army serial number was 13193892. The first digit (1) indicates that I enlisted. Members of the National Guard, like my brother Tom, had a 2 as their first digit. Draftees had a 3. I have always been proud that I enlisted to serve my country.

I. D. Card for Pvt. Herbert W. Ridyard, US Army Enlisted Reserve Corps

CHAPTER 20

CALLED TO ACTIVE DUTY

On my eighteenth birthday, July 6, 1943, the US Army sent me a letter asking the following questions:

Headquarters Third Service Command

United States Army

Baltimore, Md.

6 July 1943

Subject: Status, Enlisted Reservist.

To: Pvt. Herbert W. Ridyard

1432 Hottle Avenue

Bethlehem, Pa.

1. The records of this headquarters indicate that you were enlisted in the Enlisted Reserve Corps Unassigned on 3 June 1943, and that you became 18 years old on 6 July 1943.

2. The records further indicate that you have completed four years of high school. Information is desired as to whether you are now in attendance at a college or university.

3. In the event that you are, deferment from call to active duty may be granted you, upon request, until the completion of the current semester in which you are now enrolled, provided that completion of the semester occurs within six months from date of your 18th birthday.

4. Should you not be attending an institution of higher learning, you will be considered eligible for immediate call to active duty.

By command of Major General RECKFORD

Later that month, a number of recruits, including me, received another letter ordering us to report for active duty as follows:

SPECIAL ORDERS	HEADQUARTERS THIRD
	SERVICE COMMAND
No. 166	UNITED STATES ARMY
	BALTIMORE, MARYLAND
	13 July 1943

37. Pvt. Herman J. Koestner 12170246 1516 Second Ave Altoona PA ordered to AD 28 July 1943. WP that date fr address after name to 1301st SU New Cumberland Pa:

38. Following Enl Res in gr of Pvt ordered to AD 28 July 1943, WP that date fr address after name to 1301st SU New Cumberland Pa:

William Baumann 13158445 516 W Third St. Columbia Pa
James K Johnson 13199952 4027 Dayton Rd Drexel Hill Pa
Harry J Liddle 13194915 516 Grove St Clarks Summit Pa
Herbert W Ridyard 13193892 1432 Hottle Ave Bethlehem Pa

In lieu of T and subs while traveling FD will pay travel alws a/r 5c per mile. As an alternative to auth travel alws TNT and FD will reimb him for the actual cost of meals at not to exceed $3.00 per day under auth Par 2a Table II AR 35-4520. TDN 1-5030 P 431-02 A 0425-24. AUTH: WD Memo W50-1-43 dated 27 Jan 43.

By command of Major General RECKORD

OFFICIAL:	EDWIN BUTCHER
F.V.M. DYER	Brig. Gen. GSC
Lt Col. AGD	Chief of Staff
Adjutant General	

The army unit titled 1301st SU, New Cumberland, Pennsylvania, that we were to report to, was also known as a reception or induction center. It was just west of the Susquehanna River, south of Harrisburg, Pennsylvania, and north of the present PA Turnpike.

Uncle James drove my parents and me to the Reading Railroad Station in Bethlehem, where we said our goodbyes as I left to serve in the US Army.

Listed on that call to active duty letter were the names of eleven other eighteen-year-olds, all in the Enlisted Reserve Corps and soon to be members of the Army Specialized Training Program and army buddies. One of those, Bill Baumann from Columbia, Pennsylvania, would become a lifelong friend.

At New Cumberland we were assigned bunk beds in one of the barracks and introduced to army chow, which, although much maligned by others, I always enjoyed. We were then issued duffel bags and uniforms. Since my feet were rather narrow, the army issued me size 13 triple-A combat boots. Because they were an odd size, I had to carry three pairs instead of two in my duffel bag throughout my army career. I had never worn shoes larger than size 9 and ½, but, amazingly, those boots were perfect for me, one of the mysteries in my life.

In the following days we were given a physical exam, a tetanus shot and taken to see several movies entitled *Why We Fight* that, in effect, were a visual history lesson about the aggressive nature of both Japan and Nazi Germany. Much of this we already knew from movie newsreels back home but they were necessary for the few who may not have been paying attention.

We were also taught the rudiments of close order drill, including how to respond to the commands: Fall-In, Attention, Parade Rest, At Ease, Right and Left Face, About Face, and Dress Right (lining up in a straight row). These commands were well known to me, having learned them in Boy Scouts. Interestingly, we never saw a backpack or a weapon.

One of the most important lessons we learned at New Cumberland was to "never volunteer for anything." We were not told this by anyone in an official capacity; however, we did witness a perfect example of this fact.

One morning, we were told to fall-in outside the barracks. After we lined up, the sergeant in charge asked if any of us had an engineering background. Several recruits who volunteered were told to step forward and then were marched away. The rest of us were marched to a movie theater, where we were shown a movie and encouraged to laugh and cheer so they could make a motion picture of us enjoying the show. I never understood why that was done; however, for us in the audience, it was simply a lark. When we got back to the barracks, we learned that the "volunteer engineers" had to dig a hole for a swimming pool—so much for volunteering!

After several weeks at New Cumberland, we packed our duffel bags and set off for places unknown. New Cumberland was the farthest West I had ever been, a record that was about to be broken by a huge margin.

A large group of us were taken to Harrisburg, where we entrained on a Pullman car. We wore our brand-new US Army dress uniforms and thought we looked nifty. Having lunch and dinner in the dining car and sleeping in a Pullman bed for the very first time was truly high adventure! We never tired of seeing the cities and the countryside along the way, although some portions of the cities near the railroad tracks were ugly.

Disembarking in St. Louis, we were met by an army officer who helped us change trains. This one headed south and since it was early August, the temperature rose higher by the hour. We traveled through Missouri and Arkansas, eventually stopping briefly in a place uniquely called Texarkana on the Texas-Arkansas border.

Finally, we arrived at North Camp Hood, which is in the middle of Texas about 120 miles south of Ft. Worth and ninety miles north of Austin, the capitol. It is important to recognize that North and South Camp Hood were temporary parts of the larger complex, Fort Hood, a permanent US Army base named after Confederate General John Bell Hood. During WW II, Fort Hood was primarily a Tank Destroyer Training Center. Tank Destroyers, or TDs, were partially tracked, armored vehicles carrying anti-tank guns. However, to meet the growing needs of WW II, Fort Hood was expanded to include two additional army bases, North and South Camp Hood, to conduct basic infantry training. These camps have long since disappeared.

Upon our arrival, we were taken to two barracks near a mess hall. Most of the new arrivals were in one barracks and a few others, including me, were in the neighboring barracks. I believe the powers that be forgot about those of us in the second barracks for a few days. That was a good thing because I came down with a miserable stomach ailment.

This sudden illness resulted from my first visit to the mess hall. There, we were instructed to be sure to take salt tablets or we would have heat stroke. I began to eat my first meal in Texas and decided to have a cup of coffee, something I had never tasted before. I soon learned it was the only hot drink in the army. While enjoying my meal, I noticed there was a bowl of salt tablets on the table and proceeded to wash down a few with my coffee—big mistake! The coffee melted the tablets in my mouth and made me instantly sick to my stomach; I remained that way all day and all night.

Fortunately, no one came to roust us out the next morning. I worried about having to start training while not feeling well. That evening, I noticed a tent with a red medical cross nearby and reported my plight to the doctor therein. He was very nice. He asked me where I was from. I said Pennsylvania. He let me know that he was from the north, as well, and understood the big change I was going through. He gave me a chit to take to the mess sergeant who in turn gave me some soup. That hit the spot and I was soon feeling much better—and just in time because we started basic training in earnest the next day.

Basic training was to be an important milestone in my life, a new beginning of a much-improved, healthy lifestyle. I would feel great and never need to see a doctor again for the next year and a half, until I was overseas in combat for many months.

CHAPTER 21

BASIC TRAINING AT NORTH CAMP HOOD, TEXAS

T he new recruits from New Cumberland, Pennsylvania, and other parts of the country were transferred to their new address: Company D, 142nd ASTB, 6th Regiment, North Camp Hood, Texas. ASTB stands for Army Specialized Training Battalion.

Our company's designated quarters was 200 square feet. In the center of one side there was an entryway from one of Camp Hood's main streets into the Company's ninety-foot-wide Parade Ground, which ran from the entryway down the center of the Company Area, almost to the opposite end. The surface of the Parade Ground was composed of caliche, which is formed when particles of soil are bound together by calcium carbonates commonly found in the arid lands of the southwestern US.

On one side of the Parade Ground there were four one-story wooden barracks arranged parallel to each other with the barracks' front doors facing the Parade Ground. On the other side was a series of buildings that included the Officer of the Day's quarters, the supply building, and the latrine, in that order with the OD's quarters nearest the entryway.

Across the end of the Company Area, opposite the entryway, was the large mess hall, kitchen, and kitchen staff's billets, all under one roof.

The newly arrived trainees were divided into four platoons, one for each of the four barracks. Each platoon had four squads with twelve men per squad; hence, there were forty-eight men per barracks. The first platoon occupied the barracks nearest the mess hall while the 4th platoon's barracks was near the entryway. The second and third platoons' barracks were in between in numerical order.

Inside the barracks were twenty-four double-decker bunks constructed with two-by-four wooden frames, twelve on each side, arranged parallel to each other with an aisle down the center. Each bunk had a mattress, mattress cover, two sheets, a blanket and a pillow made up by the trainees with the pillow against the outside wall.

Between each bunk along the outside wall were foot lockers for storing extra clothes and personal articles. Class A uniforms were hung on the outer wall of the barracks while helmets, combat packs, and rifles were hung on the ends of bunks at the center aisle. Boots were stored under the bunks. Ammunition was not permitted in the barracks.

The corporal assigned to each training cadre of the company had a small room near the front door. His main function seemed to be to yell at us to wake up in the morning or to go to sleep at night, even though the bugler gave the same messages. A small pot-belly stove was located near the front door but was not needed during the summer while we were there.

I slept in the top bunk near the front door of the barracks. Charles Remington, another trainee from Pennsylvania, a guy that looked even skinnier than me, slept on the lower bunk.

When we lined up on the Parade Grounds alphabetically in the morning for roll call, I happened to be the tenth man in the third squad of the third platoon. Remington was next to me, as number nine. We instantly became good friends.

That was all there was to our home in Company D. All of the platoon sergeants and officers slept in town except for the one who was the Officer of the Day. The captain and company commander, a white Russian with a strong Russian accent, was seldom seen.

Our daily routine was as follows: reveille was at 4:30 a.m., due to the heat. Daytime temperatures could reach 130 degrees, so we did our active training prior to noon. In the afternoon we attended lectures sitting under trees. After dinner and mail call, evenings were usually free unless a night hike or other exercise was scheduled. Although it was hot all summer at Camp Hood, it was tolerable because of the "dry heat," i.e., low humidity.

Mornings began with roll call followed by a visit to the latrine to wash and shave. Showers were usually done at night. If we did not keep clean, we were threatened with being scrubbed with Fels-Naptha soap.

We went to the Mess Hall for breakfast after which we cleaned the barracks, made the bunks, had a brief inspection then fell out for calisthenics that were similar to those we had in high school.

I was strengthened by them at Camp Hood because we did them every day.

We spent the rest of the morning engaged in various training activities: learning the Manual of Arms, Close Order Drill, Hiking, How to Pitch a Tent and Follow a Compass Course, and Rifle, Pistol, and Bayonet Practice.

Lunch and an hour-long siesta were followed by an afternoon of training lectures, including Care and Cleaning of Rifles and other equipment, how to pack a Combat or a Full Field Pack, how to identify Enemy Aircraft, and Memorizing the Rules for Guard Duty.

At the beginning of training, we had to practice making beds without a wrinkle and the use and care of our government-issued (GI) equipment, which included fatigues and dress uniforms, pack, helmet, rifle, bayonet, trench knife, web-belt, canteen, mess-kit, first aid packet, water-purification tablets, shelter-half, tent pole, poncho, entrenching tool (foldable shovel or pick), and footlocker. You can imagine that we spent a lot of time learning how to use and maintain all this gear. Every set of instructions was done "by the numbers"—that is, in a certain US Army order.

Our helmets came in two pieces: the helmet liner was made of plastic with webbing inside that could be adjusted to fit your head and the steel helmet fit on top. Most of the time during training, we wore just the helmet liner.

Once we learned how to clean our rifles, we carried them with us everywhere; however, we were never issued ammunition except on the firing range. Even so, we were taught never to point our weapons at anyone, even without ammunition, unless you planned to shoot them.

Following strict ground rules such as these was the reason I never saw or heard of an accidental shooting in my two-and-a-half years of service.

We also carried our combat packs and inside them we kept our mess kit and, when needed, three boxes of food called K rations. Attached to the outside was an entrenching tool, a foldable shovel that could be turned into a pick, and, under the flap, a poncho for easy access. The bayonet in its scabbard was attached to the right side of the pack where you could get to it with your right hand. I do not know if lefties had theirs on the other side.

We always wore a web belt at our waist. It had pouches all around to carry clips of rifle ammunition. In addition, it had grommet holes along the bottom to attach your canteen and a small medical pack with bandages. If required, one could attach the bayonet or a trench knife to the belt.

Wherever we went during basic training we were loaded down with our helmet, combat pack, rifle, and web belt with all its attachments in order to get used to them and to toughen us up physically.

After a few weeks, we learned to make our full field pack. A single blanket was rolled up around a tent pole and three tent stakes, then rolled inside a tent shelter half to keep the blanket dry. This roll was inserted into the bottom of the combat pack, which could be opened to accommodate it and had straps to keep it in place.

The full field pack was needed for overnight camping. The idea was for two soldiers to pitch their tent together by combining their two shelter halves, tent poles, and stakes; then make their bed by sharing their two blankets. I remember the first time we made these packs and carried them on a hike around the block. That full field pack was heavy and the straps bit into my shoulders. I did not believe I would be able to carry my pack very far. Thirteen weeks later, I carried it twenty miles.

Prior to marching with a rifle, one had to learn the Manual of Arms. A soldier begins this training procedure at "Attention" with his rifle at "Order Arms"—that is, his rifle butt is resting on the ground against his right foot and held near the top of the stock with the right hand. Heels are together with toes slightly apart, stomach pulled in, chest out, chin tucked in, and eyes straight ahead.

Next, he might be ordered to "Port Arms" wherein the rifle is brought up across the front of the body with the right hand and then grabbed with the left hand at the balance point near the trigger guard. From there one can respond to "Shoulder Arms" by moving the right hand to the butt of the rifle while the left places it on the right shoulder. One is now in position to march.

These movements are all learned "by the numbers." While at 'Right Shoulder Arms" if you are given the order to "Order Arms," you follow the reverse procedure by the numbers. While at "Attention" with rifle at "Order

Arms," you are often given the order "At Ease." In this case, you simply take a short step sideways with the left leg, simultaneously moving the right hand and the top of the rifle slightly forward with the butt of the rifle remaining on the ground. In this position, you may relax while remaining in place. "Parade Rest" is similar to "At Ease" except you put the left hand behind your waist and remain at "Attention."

After learning the manual of arms, we practiced Close Order Drill, the army's term for marching. The instructor, a corporal or sergeant, began this instruction by teaching us how to "Dress Right"—that is, to straighten our lines by looking to our right and adjusting our positions until the line was perfectly straight and at the same time adjusting the spacing between each soldier by placing our left hand on our hip so that our elbow touched the next soldier in line. Occasionally we were required to provide a larger spacing by stretching our arm to the left just touching the next soldier with the tip of the hand. Once lined up and spaced evenly, the Instructor looked down each line of soldiers to see that we were in a straight line.

He then taught us how to do "Right and Left Face" so that we were looking at the back of the person ahead of us. Most of the Instructors shouted the words, "Right Hoo" or "Left Hoo" replacing the word Face with Hoo. These strange words might have been used to make sure we heard them, but don't ask me why. The reason for the change was never explained; we just had to get used to each instructor's idiosyncrasies. We were then ordered to begin marching with the command "Forward Harch," always leading off with our left foot. While we were marching, the instructor "Counted Cadence" to control the rate of speed and to keep everyone in step. Each instructor counted cadence using his own unique pronunciation. Many of them gave their commands with a southern drawl since of course many of them were southerners. For example, he might say: Lehft, Riight, Lehft, Riight or Hut, Two, Three Four or Lehft, Lehft leaving out every other step. It did not matter to us, as long as he was loud enough and consistent.

In order to have us stop he would shout "Squaaad Halt." The drawn-out use of the word Squaaad gave us notice that another order was coming, in this case, Halt. This word Halt or something meant to be Halt had to be given while we are on our left foot, so we had time to stop our momentum by taking the required two more steps before stopping.

Eventually we learned to do "Column Left or Right." We had to listen for the "Hoo" or a similar term before we did our turn, always given on the left foot for a left turn and on the right foot for a right turn. Once we heard "Hoo," we took one more step and turned in the direction required. We also learned "By the Right (or Left) Flank March!" a command where everyone in a column does the turn at the same time.

We became proficient at marching. You just had to concentrate and wait for the "Hoo." It is a little like the game, "Simon Says" we learned in Boy Scouts. You must not anticipate the turn until you hear "Hoo." Square dancers understand this because they must not anticipate the next dance step until it is given.

Once the basics of marching were learned, we marched with helmet, rifles, combat packs, etc. everywhere! To train us for hiking long distances the instructors started with several five-mile hikes. These hikes toughened up our bodies especially our feet as we got used to and broke in our new boots. All of these hikes were at a steady pace of 110 or 120 steps per minute; moving along smartly, but not at a pace that was going to kill you.

During these hikes we were usually given orders to "Sling arms," that is, to loosen the sling on our rifle so we could hang the rifle over the back of our right shoulder, holding it there with our right hand on the strap. After "Sling Arms" we were ordered to do "Route Step" which meant we did not have to march in step. Route step made hiking much easier.

As we became experienced hikers, we then took part in a ten-mile "Forced March" which meant we were in a hurry to get somewhere. The pace for the forced march was so fast we were almost running. In addition, we were led by a tall "string bean" of a second lieutenant with long legs, who was cruising along with no difficulty. It was brutal but we did it.

Eventually we advanced to hiking with full field pack. By the time we did the first of these hikes we were in good physical shape and able to handle the extra load and I learned something about myself.

After about a mile or so I was in some sort of cruise control; some would say, "getting a second wind." It seemed that I could go on much further than I had ever imagined. In other words, I discovered that I had a large reserve of stamina. I could lift 'em up and put 'em down and just keep going even if it hurt. That was very comforting to know.

As I mentioned earlier our bayonets were stored in a scabbard attached to the right side of our combat pack so when we were ordered to "Fix bayonets," we reached back with our right hand and pulled it out of the scabbard and inserted it in the slot under the tip of the rifle barrel. Bayonet practice involved only two commands, "short thrust": and "long thrust." To begin these maneuvers, the rifle was held in the port arms position in front of you. A short thrust required one to take a short step forward with the left foot while lowering the rifle to plunge it forward. A long thrust usually followed in which you took a long step forward with the right foot, thrusting again.

When extended in this latter position, our corporal loved to tell us to take away the left hand so that you were holding the bayoneted rifle with only your right arm. We had to hold that position until he told us to return to port arms. It is important to know that when the bayonet is on your rifle, the rifle is no longer balanced at the balance point, so when you remove your left hand, there is a lot of off-balance weight out in front of you. But as I have said we were now in good shape so we could do goofy stuff like that. Bayonet practice turned out to be just more physical exercise.

The rifle range was a good distance away from the barracks, so to practice shooting our rifles we went there in trucks. We had already practised the various firing positions back in the training area. These were called "dry runs." There were three firing positions: prone, sitting, and offhand. In the prone position you lie on the ground and hold the rifle up by leaning on your elbows. This is the steadiest position. In the sitting position you crouch forward with elbows leaning on the legs just in front of the knees. This is uncomfortable but reasonably steady. In the offhand position you stand and support the rifle with your right hand at the trigger area and your left hand forward at the balance point, but in addition you obtain additional support by wrapping the rifle strap around your left arm. This is the most difficult position to keep the rifle on the target. As you take your sight picture the rifle tends to waver a lot.

In each of these positions you must learn to make a "sight picture" by lining up three things: the center of the hole in your rear site and the top of the little stub near the front end of the barrel and the center of the target. All three must be centered at once. This is a challenge if you are not in a good rifle position because just the slightest movement will disturb the alignment.

When ready to fire you take a deep breath, exhale a bit, hold your breath, and squeeze the trigger. Squeezing is the key. If you pull the trigger you are going to jerk the rifle and miss. I would squeeze the trigger ever so slowly while holding the sight picture in alignment, so that when the rifle fired, it just seemed to go off on its own.

At the range there were enforced safety rules. A limited number of soldiers were allowed on the firing line at a time so there would be an instructor for each person. We were given a ten round (bullet) clip of ammunition to insert in the rifle when we were in the firing position; then we would fire all the rounds, one after the other.

We were armed with British, bolt-action Enfield 98 rifles, first designed in 1898, so after each firing we had to pull back the bolt and push it forward to insert another round; consequently, each time we fired we had to take a new sight picture. Incidentally, this was in 1943, and I have always wondered why we did not have the new US Garand M-1 semi-automatic rifle during training. Were there still not enough to supply everyone?

We fired at targets located at two distances, 100 and 500 yards, in each of the three firing positions. My score was around 75 percent—good enough to be called a "marksman," not good enough to be called an "expert" or a "sharpshooter"; however, I was happy with my score because this was my first experience with a rifle.

We were trained on three types of obstacle courses. One involved crawling or creeping on the ground, keeping basically flat under barbed wire, approaching a machine gun that was firing just over-head. You had to keep your rifle close, dragging it along holding the sling in your hand with the barrel over your arm. This had to be done in a way to keep the breech clean so it could be fired. There was a safety feature for this course in which the barrel of the machine gun was supported by a wooden frame to keep the gun from accidently slipping down and killing someone.

Another course involved a hike with only a D ration, a hard chocolate bar, that was supposed to give you energy equivalent to one meal. At some point each GI was separated from the others on the hike, so that each was alone. We were to seek cover as we approached a certain area that in the beginning was not known to us. Mine was a hot dusty route. I remember crawling under a tree to eat my D ration.

At some point a training officer advised me to go in a direction which led to a deep trench. I had to roll over the edge and drop down the side into the trench without being seen. Down in the trench, they checked to see if my rifle was clean enough to fire after all the crawling around. Then I was led to a firing position and told to fire at some targets. The targets were at several distances, so I had to adjust the range settings on my rifle sights. It was fun because I did well, firing at the targets.

On the third obstacle course, we had to cross a creek by pulling ourselves over on a rope. This was done by wrapping our legs at the knees around the rope and pulling with our hands while hanging onto the rope. It was not easy because our combat pack and rifle tried to drag us down. Some guys did not get all the way across. They eventually dropped into the creek and got their feet wet, not me.

Since it was blistering hot in the Texas summer, we were advised to drink water and take salt tablets frequently. I filled my canteen every day before going out to the training fields using a faucet near the latrine After filling my canteen, I made sure to take a drink of water to stay hydrated.

Unfortunately, the water had a foul sulfur taste and while I was drinking, my nose would curl up and the mechanism that makes you want to regurgitate would try to go into action. I never got used to it, but I had to drink. That is one memory I will never forget.

The Mess Hall, our fine dining place, was a large barracks-like building near the 1st platoon's barracks, the furthest from the camp entrance. It was made of wood and covered with tar paper with inside walls of rough, unfinished, unpainted walls and studs. As you entered the door, the serving line was on the right with the kitchen and cook's quarters behind it. All the picnic-like, wooden tables were to the left in two rows with a center aisle.

The food was good. In fact, I enjoyed US Army food throughout my time in the service. Breakfast often included oatmeal or dried cereal plus soft-cooked or scrambled eggs with milk or coffee to drink. Lunch consisted of hot sandwiches, a vegetable and fruit. Dinner was meat and potatoes. I, like everyone else, was hungry every meal and although the meals were satisfying, I never left the mess hall completely full. Most people would associate that feeling as normal for a young growing boy with a "hollow leg." However, for me, this phenomenon did not happen until I was eighteen years old, training at Camp Hood.

I was simply a late bloomer; the fresh air and exercise triggered something within as I started growing up and out. A sense of well-being overcame me as I began doing things I never imagined I could do. I felt good in body, mind, and spirit.

Frequently the cooks served seconds. We particularly wanted seconds of whatever beverage was offered, be it milk, juice or coffee. Early in the meal I drank my glass or cup till it was about half empty, so if seconds were announced, I could quickly down the rest of my drink and then rush up to get seconds. One's cup or plate had to be empty to get seconds. It paid to think ahead in the mess hall.

On Sundays we had most of the day free so one could sleep in, but if you did you might miss breakfast which was great on Sundays. Since there was no big crowd of diners, the cooks had time to prepare fried eggs to order or serve pancakes or waffles. I loved Sunday breakfast.

The greatest joy I experienced while in the army was receiving mail from home. At Camp Hood, this was done every day right after lunch. The mail clerk, a non-com, would sound a bell and everyone would come running. He would call out names of those receiving mail, not always pronouncing them correctly. No matter the mispronunciation, if he had to call your name more than once, you might end up on K. P. If you were a little slow in responding, he would say, "What's the matter? Have you got a time mind?" We all thought that was a stupid remark but still, we knew what he meant.

It was obvious to us recruits that most of our non-commissioned officers like the mail clerk were southerners whose language made them sound like country boys. Since most of the recruits were from the north and had college grade intellects, many developed a feeling of superiority toward the noncoms. However, I thought this was not a very generous attitude since the non-coms were only doing their jobs and when it came to training, they were way ahead of us.

After dinner, we relaxed or went to the Post Exchange (PX) for a Coke or some sundries. We really did not spend much time at the PX. More often, we took showers, cleaned our weapons or whatever, and turned in early. I was ready for bed by nine at the latest because reveille was only seven-and-a-half hours away.

During lectures under shade-trees we were taught how to read a map, use a compass and to identify enemy and Allied airplanes. I was familiar with map reading and the compass from my time in Boy Scouts, having earned the Mapping Merit Badge. At Camp Hood, we were tested by being required to follow a trail guided only by our compass and map.

Airplane identification was taught by use of airplane silhouettes. My youthful interest in model airplanes and magazines provided me with considerable foreknowledge on this subject, as well.

I remember a rather comical experience while sitting cross-legged on the ground during these lectures. Because of the bright sun, we needed to wear sunglasses; consequently, the lecturer could not tell if we had our eyes closed, so an assistant non-com stood in the rear of the group and if he saw a head nodding, he would bounce a pebble off the trainee's helmet to remind him to wake up. That always drew a laugh from the group. Rather resourceful, don't you think?

Another training activity I enjoyed was the Company Field Day, primarily relay races, held for entertainment as well as exercise. I remember Charles Remington and I, the two skinniest guys in the company, winning the piggy-back race.

In another event, pairs of piggy-backers played "king of the hill." I sat on the top of a giant of a soldier and we knocked down all the other competitors. This guy was so strong he would bump into the other players and knock them down. In turn, no one could knock him down and he held my legs so tight, no one could knock me off, so we won!

Sooner or later, a private in the army must take his turn doing chores. One of the most common chores was Kitchen Police. When you were on KP, you were excused from training because it involved a lot of work and took up most of the day and some of the evening. The easy part was setting up and cleaning the tables as well as replenishing the salt, pepper, and sugar dispensers. The more difficult jobs were mopping the floor, washing and drying dishes, and the onerous task of cleaning out the grease trap after every meal.

Once I peeled potatoes for almost 200 soldiers. This job seemed endless. One of the cooks kept checking to see if I was goofing off. Believe me, there was no time to do anything but peel. Working at these tougher jobs in the Texas summer was no fun, because it made you hot and tired.

There was one chore worse than cleaning the grease trap—that was cleaning rifles that had been stored away. Army rifles are stored between wars in a thick, dark brown, greasy material called cosmolene. This material protects the gun metal from rusting and is much like the grease used to lubricate a car. Cleaning rifles meant getting this goop off with not one speck remaining, then oiling them to further protect them as well as ensuring the moving parts would function properly. I cannot imagine anyone ever wearing his clothes again after messing with cosmolene. This was another job that I happily missed having to do.

On Saturday mornings, the officers did a full inspection of your person, barracks, equipment, and rifle. After breakfast, we carried our bunks outside and scrubbed the barracks floor, put everything back and then "policed the area" by lining up and moving forward while picking up all the trash on the ground. Most of us were smart enough to keep the area clean to make policing an easy chore, but smokers were a continuing problem. A smoker, when he was finished with a cigarette, was supposed to "field strip it," which involved tearing the paper off the butt so the left-over tobacco would fly away in the breeze and then rolling the paper between his fingers into almost nothingness and throwing it away or in the trash. Someone always failed to do that, so we had to police the area. While we were policing, several soldiers were scrubbing the garbage cans.

During barracks inspection, the officers inspected our bunks to see that they were super neat with a tight blanket, so tight that if they dropped a dime on them, it would bounce. They also inspected all equipment, including foot lockers, sometimes running a white glove under a portion of the bunk to make sure it was clean. Then we marched off for rifle inspection.

Rifle inspection took a long time because one officer had to inspect each soldier in his platoon of forty-eight men to see if they were clean shaven, with a short haircut, and wore a clean, neat uniform. Heaven forbid that you had a button unbuttoned. Finally, he inspected your rifle. When the officer stood in front of you, you had to quickly bring your rifle to Port Arms and slide back the bolt. The inspecting officer would then grab the rifle from you while you simultaneously let go of it. Then he would put his thumbnail in the bolt area and look down the barrel from the other end to see if the inside was perfectly clean. The light reflecting off his thumbnail allowed him to see clearly throughout the barrel. Pity the soldier who had the slightest smudge or even a piece of lint from his cleaning patch in the rifle barrel.

Everyone stood at attention while the inspection was in process. On one hot Saturday we had our usual inspection before having the weekend off. We were standing in the sun, the inspection seemed to take forever, and I was feeling faint. I managed to get through my rifle inspection. Remember, I was near the end of the line in the third squad of the third platoon and it had been going on for a long time. I told one of the non-coms accompanying the inspecting officer that I was feeling dizzy, so he told me to squat and put my head down and forward. That fixed the problem. Fortunately, that never happened again.

Camp Hood was the home of a large contingent of German prisoners of war. In 1943, they could have been from Africa or perhaps Sicily. Africa was cleared of Germans in May of 1943. Several times, our training exercises took us past their confinement area, which must have been rather large because we could see many of them on parade. Their marching was impressive. They were in perfect step with straight rows and they sang together with one loud, beautiful voice.

Our steps were never perfect, our rows were never straight, and our singing was poor. The best we could do was, "Around her neck she wore a yellow ribbon. She wore it in the springtime and in the month of May, hey, hey, and if you ask her, why the heck she wore it. She wore it for her lover who was far, far away. Far away, she wore it for her lover who was far, far away." That song and "I've been working on the railroad" was about all we sang. We didn't know the rest of the words and we were only singing to pass the time on a hike. Those Germans, on the other hand, were making beautiful music.

Near the end of our sixteen weeks of training we went on the dreaded twenty-mile hike with full field pack. I remember reading about how Stonewall Jackson, during the Shenandoah Valley Campaign in the Civil War, ran circles around the Union soldiers by doing twenty miles and farther every day. Later General Lee sent Jackson's Army on a long, long hike around the Union right flank just prior to the Second Battle of Bull Run. Those southern boys were tough! Now we were going to see how tough we were.

We hiked for eight hours, having a ten-minute break every hour. Those breaks were precious. I learned to immediately sit down and lean against a tree. Lying down was a temptation but it was hard to get up while carrying a large pack. When the command, "Break's over!" was announced, we immediately had to get moving.

On this hike we became victims of a phenomenon I called the "accordion." This occurred because the whole AST battalion was involved, which included four companies, each with four platoons, making the column sixteen platoons long. As we hiked along, the lead platoons would set the pace and if they were going downhill they got way ahead of everybody else, particularly those who might be just starting up the previous hill; therefore, as each company went over that hill, the line would stretch out over a long distance. The officers would then order us to "close up." That meant the platoons toward the rear of the column had to march faster. The farther back you were, the longer and faster you had to move to catch up.

After closing up, inevitably, the column would stretch out again. This accordion-like motion of the column occurred within platoons, as well, of course, though not to the same degree. It was a real problem for those at the rear. Hiking at a steady pace was bearable but alternating between walking and running was no fun at all. Since I was in Company D, the last company in the battalion and in the Third Squad, of company D's Third Platoon, I was fated to be a continuous victim of the "accordion" during the twenty-mile hike. There was nothing I could do but grin and bear it.

Needless to say, I was happy when the hike was over, not only because I had done it and was proud of myself, but I had made it to the end, even though my big toes hurt, probably from blisters and I had not given up and become one of the stragglers or drop-outs that had to be picked up by a Jeep following the hike for that purpose. For me, that would have been embarrassing.

By the way, the Boy Scout in me always carried bandages and tape to correct any discomfort to my feet that might occur on a hike; however, on this hike, I had no chance to do it. Afterward, I made a wonderful toe bandage because, when I took off my boots and socks, I found, as I suspected, both of my big toes were a bloody mess.

The twenty-mile hike completed our thirteen weeks of basic training. Little did we know that we would have to wait at North Camp Hood without much to do for another 3-weeks before we were transported to an as yet unknown college.

Pvt. Herbert Ridyard

That wait did not bother me for I was enjoying life while resting on my laurels. I had done my best and I was proud of and thankful for what I had accomplished. My physical being had been greatly improved. During the three months I had gained around fifteen pounds, mostly muscle and had done many things I never imagined I could do. My rifle scores were decent for a rookie. I could march and hike with the best of them. I found stamina within me that I never knew was there. Clearly, I was ready physically for the life of a soldier. For the first time I felt very good about myself.

Looking forward to college, I felt confident I would be able to do as well in that environment. However, for the moment I would enjoy our reward, a weekend away from camp.

During Saturday's inspection we finally got to hear from our company commander. I do not remember his name. We had been told he was a white Russian. He spoke with a deep Russian accent, telling us we had earned a weekend pass to Waco, Texas. I remember the part where he said, "If you are going to get 'dronk,' please do it in your room and don't disgrace your uniform."

All of us got all "spiffied up" and set off for the train. First, of course I had to report to the Officer of the Day to get my pass. I had never been in his office, so I proceeded to open his screen door to go inside. That was a big mistake. I was told in no uncertain terms that I was supposed to knock first, which I had not done and of course I did not know I had to. No matter, he was going to teach me a lesson. I was ordered to knock and keep on knocking until told to stop. OK, so I knocked and knocked for a long time. I thought I was going to miss the train, but—finally—I was given my pass.

The train ride was ridiculous. The seats were park benches; nothing is too good for the trainees. It was hot so the windows were open, and the hot breeze wafted over us. The breeze was seeded with coal dust. Our train was pulled by an old-fashioned coal-fired locomotive. The restroom was a toilet at one end of the car. There was no privacy screen. It was open to the world. You never totally get used to this kind of stuff in the army, but you are told that combat is going to be much, much worse, so they needed to degrade us ahead of time. Well, that is the theory; however, believe me, none of this training completely prepares you for the reality of combat.

At last, we arrived in Waco. All 1,000 eighteen-year-olds in our battalion had not seen a girl for four months, so we were in great expectation of what was ahead. What we found in this relatively small town was about 50,000 other soldiers. Besides Camp Hood there was the rest of Fort Hood and an Air Force base nearby, so there were lots of soldiers and we all went to the USO canteen, where we found donuts and sodas waiting and lots of other GIs. That was it. There was nothing to do.

We walked around town. The sidewalks were made of wood, as seen in Western movies, so back to the USO we went to sit around and drink sodas. Now in truth there were a few girls manning the USO and there was a jukebox with big band music, which was nice and a half dozen girls who were dancing with some GIs, but the best the rest of us could do was goof around until the evening when it cooled off so we could walk around town again.

The next morning while everyone was sleeping in, I went to the local Methodist church, which I had spotted the previous day. I went early enough for Sunday School and, bingo, there was this neat-looking young girl visiting from Baylor University and no other soldiers in sight. Baylor is sponsored by the Baptists, so she may have been the only Methodist in town. After church there was a dinner to which everyone was invited. There, I got up enough nerve to talk to the girl from Baylor. After the meal we went for a walk downtown and soon she had to be back on campus; that was the last I saw of her.

The moral of this story is: "If you want to meet a nice girl, go to church."

CHAPTER 22

THE UNIVERSITY OF FLORIDA

We completed basic infantry training in early December and were shipped out to places unknown. We were a pretty cocky bunch, quite proud of ourselves. The troop train took us through Louisiana, Mississippi, Alabama, and into Florida, all places I had never been. From the train, the South appeared to be a poor place to live, especially for Black people. When we arrived at the University of Florida, we knew we were lucky. We were in Florida for the winter. Only the wealthy could go to Florida for the winter in those days.

Our new address was Company B, Section M, Murphree Hall, S. C. U. 3418, ASTP, University of Florida, Gainesville, Florida. We were housed in a dormitory. Most of us were in two room suites. I was in one of the larger corner rooms with Charles Remington from Pennsylvania and John Mauro from Connecticut. We each had a desk, bunk bed and a place for clothes.

One of the problems, if you can call it that, was whether to wear our summer cotton uniform, "Suntans," or winter woolen "ODs" (olive drabs). The battalion commander had to make this monumental decision every day because of Florida's variable weather in the wintertime. If that was our biggest problem, you can understand that we were really living "The Life of Riley."

Even better, we were no longer eating in a mess hall but in a cafeteria with pretty much all you could eat. I gained five pounds the first week, now weighed 135 pounds and would remain at that weight until I was married in

1950. Putting on weight was easy not only because of the food but because the only exercise was calisthenics and marching to classes.

Of course, the real purpose for being there was our studies. We had all the classes of a first-semester engineering curriculum: English, History, Math, Physics, Chemistry, and Geography. The subjects were accelerated to only three months per semester, so you know we spent most of our time studying.

We were expected to maintain a B average; thus, at midterm, when I received a warning notice in Physics, I was concerned. I went to see the Physics professor, a kindly, white-haired old gentleman. I was having trouble with ballistic trajectory problems, which I had found intimidating in high school, as well. He noted that I had all As in the lab experiments, reviewed the equations for trajectories, and said, "Put a little more time on Physics."

My real problem was that the tests were all true and false or multiple choice with a time limit. Working against time was always a problem for me. I did well in most subjects given enough time, so I began to use the strategy of doing all the easy problems first and then concentrating on the harder ones; that system worked!

As eighteen-year-olds will do, we found ways to have fun at the University of Florida. Everyone took note of the peculiar antics of Chemistry Professor Anderson. He frequently walked up to the blackboard in a slight crouch and then backed away with a bouncing motion. Outside of class we would imitate his walk, which we called the "Anderson Walk."

One day while marching from class to our dorm, we invented the "Anderson March." Our cadet commander would call out the command, "Anderson . . . March!" We would immediately do a "to the rear march" and then, while marching backward, we began to bounce along. We thought that was a lot of fun until, one day, a battalion officer who seemed to be hiding next to one of the college buildings caught us doing the Anderson March. I don't remember the punishment for that but, it wasn't KP or anything onerous.

I also remember going to church in the nearest town, Gainesville and attending a Saturday afternoon high school football game. One of the teams was called the "Celery Heads." We thought that was hilarious.

At Christmastime we had a few days off so, I decided to visit my brother, John, who was taking basic training at Camp Blanding near Jacksonville. I traveled by train to Jacksonville, then by bus to the camp. I was not sure if they would let me on the base unannounced, but they did. I found John's tent and waited there until he was free from whatever he was doing. The fact that it was a weekend made the visit possible, but he could have been out in the field and I would have missed seeing him. Fortunately, after an hour or so he showed up.

We visited for a short time and I made my way back to school. I do not remember much about the visit, but I was glad to have made the effort. This was 1943 and I would not see or hear from him until I came home from the war in 1946.

Near the end of the semester, we all received a letter dated February 23, 1944, from the War Department terminating our assignment with the ASTP and reassigning us to the Army Ground Forces[1]. We were a part of some 100,000 eighteen-year-olds in the ASTP whose education was abruptly ended and sent to the infantry. The reason stated was, "The time has now come . . . to break the enemy's defenses and force their unconditional surrender. It is necessary to hit them with the full weight of America's manpower. Your intelligence, training, and high qualities of leadership are expected to raise the combat efficiency of divisions and other units."

I remember a newspaper saying it was being done for "the convenience of the government." That seemed a little callous. Whatever the reason, it came as a disappointing shock. We had it "made in the shade" until that moment and we knew it. We also knew a little of what the future held for us, but never did we imagine how bad it would be.

CHAPTER 23

THE 94TH INFANTRY DIVISION
AT CAMP MCCAIN, MISSISSIPPI

O ur battalion of eighteen-year-old GIs traveled by troop train, again destination unknown, in a westerly direction through Florida and Alabama and northwest into northern Mississippi, finally arriving at Camp McCain. As we rode into the railyard, there were some soldiers working among the railcars and along the tracks who gave us new arrivals the usual greeting, "You'll be sorry." This universal putdown would come to us no matter where we traveled.

After being transported by trucks to a large field, our names were called out and we were reloaded onto other trucks and driven to our individual destinations. The only way I can describe what happened is that we were sprinkled among the various units of the 94th Infantry Division. I was never again to see most of my friends from the ASTP. After the war, I had the opportunity to meet up with only a few at 94th Division reunions. One exception, however, was a friend, John Gardy, who was assigned to G Company, which was positioned right next to H Company, where I was dropped off the day of the "sprinkle." When we had some free time, we would see each other at the Post Exchange (PX), and soon became good buddies.

At some point later in my service with the 94th, I learned that our division had been training for over a year and, like many other divisions, the army had been taking some of their trainees and reassigning them to other divisions to fill their roster before going overseas. Apparently, the younger soldiers were selected for this purpose, which caused the average age of the soldiers remaining in the division left behind to rise.

Since the army had a rule that the average age for a division going overseas had to be under a certain number, it follows that the inclusion of us eighteen-year-olds into the 94th went a long way to lowering the 94th 's average age.

After reporting to H Company Headquarters, I was taken to one of the barracks, assigned a bunk bed, and instructed to wait for further orders. At my arrival, most of the men in the company were out on parade. The only one in the barracks was a relatively old southerner named Uncle Leamon. He was quite welcoming, but I wondered why he was not with the others. I thought perhaps he had been on KP.

As we were getting acquainted, the barracks door opened, and a large group of noisy men came charging in. Within seconds, there were crap-games going on at each end of the barracks. I wondered what I had gotten into. Were the rumors true that they were a bunch of ex-jailbirds?

I soon found out that was not so. The army was an amalgam of relatively young men from all over America, some rich, some poor. In our unit there were city folks, farmers, coal miners, lawyers, firemen, gas station attendants, pianists, college boys, Catholics, Protestants, a few Jews, and probably some atheists, northerners, easterners, westerners, and lots of southerners. Thank God for the southerners, because they all knew how to shoot and were also very amiable to be with.

I learned that H Company was a Heavy Weapons Company. Every battalion had three Rifle Companies and a Heavy Weapons Company. We were a part of the Second Battalion. Our battalion's Rifle Companies were designated as E, F, and G. Similarly, the First Battalion was composed of A, B, and C Rifle Companies and D was their Heavy Weapons Co. Our Third Battalion had companies I, K, L, and M. For some unknown reason there was no J company. Our three battalions were part of the 301st Infantry Regiment. The 94th Infantry Division had two other Infantry Regiments, the 302nd and the 376th.

There were many other units in our division. Each company, battalion, and regiment had a small Headquarters Company with one at the division level, as well. Also, there were artillery, engineer, medical, signal (telephone), service (transportation), and ordinance (repair) units in the Division, but I was never familiar with their organizations.

H Company was divided into three platoons: two heavy machine gun and one heavy mortar platoon. I was assigned to the First Platoon, a heavy machine gun platoon. The Second Platoon was similar to ours and the Third Platoon had the 81 mm mortars.

Capt. George T. Caywood, Co. H, 301st Inf. Reg., 94th Inf. Div.

Our Company Commander was Captain George T. Caywood, a giant of a man. His executive officer was First Lieutenant George Farmer. Each platoon had a second lieutenant as a platoon leader but during training we seldom saw any of the lieutenants.

Captain Caywood's lead non-commissioned officer was First Sergeant Roger Keith. Caywood also had a supply sergeant, named Glenn Harvey, and a group of cooks led by Sergeant Thadeus Koziol. These men were all in a unit called Company Headquarters.

Our platoon was led by Platoon Sergeant Milano Parobek, a rather loud-mouthed young man who demanded obedience with threats that he never had to carry out. Everybody tried to do their best to get along with no need for punishment. No one wanted to needlessly spend their weekends on KP.

There were four squads in our platoon with seven men in each. I was part of the third squad. Sergeant John Lyons was our squad leader. Larry Ryan, number-one man in our squad, was the first machine gunner who carried the tripod and had a .45 caliber Colt Pistol as his side-arm in a holster on his web belt. Number-two man in our squad was second gunner, Robert McClain, who carried the 30-caliber water-cooled machine gun (mg), and a 45 for a sidearm. I was assigned as number-three man in our squad, was classified as a Rifleman and an Ammunition Bearer, carried a pack frame with canisters of machine gun ammunition (ammo) and an M1 30-caliber Carbine, a small semi-automatic rifle. Number four and five men in our squad, Vince Lamperella and Jerry Driscoll, had the same job and equipment as me. Our job was to protect the machine gunners and provide their ammo.

Sgt. John J. Lyons, Squad Leader

We were a motley crew. John Lyons was from Massachusetts; he came to the 94th after being dropped from officer training school—bad news for John but good news for us. He was a great leader and person. I liked and respected him and was glad to be in his squad. He treated us decently and fairly, giving directions without screaming like Parobek. Larry Ryan was a friendly, quiet, and competent southern farm boy. Bob McClain was a tall, well-built young coal cracker from West Virginia. He acted like a tough guy and had a rather dirty mouth. He wasn't a bad person; however, I never cared for him that much. Vince Lamparella was considerably older than me, a one-time first sergeant busted to a private for some unknown reason. Later during combat, we two would stand guard and I found him to be very strong and reliable. Jerry Driscoll, much older than most of us, was a ne'er-do-well. He seemed to live to gamble and drink. Additionally, we had a Jeep driver, James Hefner as a member of our squad. We seldom saw him for he was kept busy at the motor pool taking great care of the Jeep. The squad needed a Jeep for long trips to transport the machine gun, tripod, ammo, and water-can used to cool the gun. It also carried a large shovel and pick to help dig in gun positions. It is amazing that I spent a year and a half with these men and never got close to any of them.

The First Platoon was divided into two sections with two machine guns to a section. Staff Sergeant Bill Tornfeldt was the section leader of the third and fourth squads. He was a gentleman and much like Lyons. The squad leader of the fourth squad was Sergeant Colvin, a handsome, blonde young man. His first and second gunners were two strong young southerners, Ezra Britten and Robert Chase. Their ammo bearers and riflemen were a little older than most. I do not remember their names.

Staff Sergeant Clifford Shearer, another great leader, was the Section Leader of the first and second squads. He had two good squad leaders. I do not remember any other names. Obviously, Captain Caywood knew how to pick good leaders.

Training with the 94th while I was there can be divided into two types: first, a repeat of things learned in basic training where we trained as individuals, exercising, use of equipment, marching, pitching tents, digging fox holes and shooting rifles, etc.; second, training as a unit, e.g., how a squad prepares and fires a heavy machine gun.

We repeated the routine five-, ten-, and twenty-mile-hikes, complete with bloody toes, but once again I was able to make a comfortable toe bandage.

We learned to fire our new M1 Carbines using the same method as in basic, i.e., proper position, sighting, holding our breath and squeezing the trigger, but it was different this time for the Carbine was smaller and semi-automatic. We also learned how to fire the 45 mm automatic pistol in case one of us would become the machine gunner, for that would be our new weapon.

I was not happy with my experience in firing the pistol. We were lined up behind various firing stations. When it was my turn, I fired a clip of ammo. The target was quite small with ropes attached for a training non-com to turn the target sideways after a certain amount of time elapsed, thus limiting the amount of time one had to aim. I thought I did very well, but before I could fire again, my pistol was taken away and given to someone in the next line, because the pistol in that line had malfunctioned. I assumed they did that because that line was being held up, so like traffic cops they made our line wait.

The next thing I knew they gave me the "faulty" pistol, which they claimed had been "fixed." I resumed firing that pistol and, after a few shots, I shot the rope on the ground about six feet in front of the target. Firing that "fixed" pistol killed my score. I got a 41 out of a 100. That score is called a "bolo" and went into my record. I never had an occasion in the army to fire a pistol again, so it did not really matter but I do not like to fail at anything, so this episode troubled me for a long time.

After the war, my friend Weston Werst and I both came home with German pistols. He had a Luger and I had (and still have) a P-38. We went up on South Mountain in Bethlehem and shot at tin cans. We both did well. Given a good weapon, I know I can shoot a pistol.

On one of our night-training stints we set up camp just as it began to rain. Sergeant Lyons and I shared a tent by combining our shelter halves and poles. We did not have time to ditch the tent because the rain suddenly turned into a heavy downpour and we were happy to get inside. Sometime during the night, the water flowed into the tent. I remember for the first time sleeping on my hands and knees with my head in my helmet, which rested on the ground. When you are tired, you can put up with almost anything. I had to repeat that sleeping position more than once while in combat.

At daybreak we found that we had pitched our tent in a shallow ditch. I do not know whether the downpour formed the ditch or if it was there in the first place. It was good to get back to our barracks to dry out. Drying out was not going to happen in combat.

Another time while hiking at night we were told to stop, dig in, and stand guard. We had no idea where we were. After digging my fox hole, I went to sleep. We were fortunate that the weather was warm because everyone slept on the ground and not in our holes. In the morning, we found a large snake in one of the holes. Ugh!

While the squad was on guard duty, we took turns guarding and sleeping. With six guys in our squad, two stood guard for two hours while the other four slept. That meant you got to sleep for four hours at a time. I did not know it then, but this was a harbinger of things to come overseas.

Surprise, surprise! We woke up the next morning in a grassy field in which every blade of grass was covered with tiny little red bugs as big as a dot or period called chiggers. They were all over us, had invaded our bodies, started to burrow into our skin and itch like crazy. You never saw such a bunch of sad sacks. We had to tough it out and hike home to our barracks, where we showered and tried to get rid of them. No one, even those who had experienced them before, knew what to do. Some used the end of burning cigarettes to get the chiggers to die or back out of the skin. It was hard to tell which was worse, the chigger or the cigarette burn. Perhaps If we had some sort of salve to put on them it would have helped, but we just had to scratch and hope they died gorging on our blood.

Extensive training as a unit was done on maneuvers in Tennessee, where we lived in the field and participated in attacks on mythical enemies. This involved working as a team to move and set up the machine gun at a moment's notice. It was there I got my first chance to carry the tripod and, later, the machine gun. Because they both weighed about thirty pounds we took turns carrying them. Managing an extra thirty pounds in addition to the rest of my gear was a challenge, but again I was able to do my part. I assume everyone knew that I was not as strong as some of the others, so it was nice to know that the bigger, stronger GIs were willing to take more than their share of the load. It fills me with pride to know I was part of a group of young men with such responsible characters.

While on maneuvers, we had a break in the training. Since our squad was near a farm, we went to visit the family. They seemed poor but were willing to share what they had, which was cornbread and milk. That was the first and only time I ever had milk straight from the cow. No pasteurization! It was warm, watery, and tasted funny. Life is different down on the farm and I was proven to be a city slicker.

As serious training began to wind down, I remember some lighter occurrences that are worth recording. The first involved the two drunks in our platoon, Jerry Driscoll and Joe Kossakowski. Invariably, if they got a weekend pass together, they came back to camp late Sunday night intoxicated. Most of us would be in our bunks, trying to sleep. They came into the barracks stumbling around in the dark, because it was after lights out, arguing about an episode in town and began to insult each other by calling names. When they got off a really good insult, someone in the barracks would encourage them (by now most of us were awake), "Oh, that was a good one." "Hit him again. Hit him while he's down." That remark always drew a big cheer. This would encourage the drunks to retaliate verbally. There were never any blows. They were so drunk they could not hit anyone. Someone always recited Wimpy's famous line from the Popeye comic strip, "Let's you and him fight. I'll hold your coat." The verbal jibes would go on for some time until one of the sergeants would threaten them with KP if they didn't shut up. The drunks would continue to mumble retorts for some time and finally fall asleep.

It was after one of Jerry Driscoll's weekend drinking episodes that he missed reveille on Monday morning (a serious infraction), when I found a Private First Class (PFC) stripe on my bunk. I imagine Jerry missed the last bus back to camp. All I know is he was busted—that is, lost his stripe and I got mine. Someone told me there was a quota on stripes, so someone had to lose one for me to get mine. That's the army way.

On a lighter note, John Gardy, my friend in G company, and I got weekend passes to Memphis, Tennessee. It was exciting to be free from training for a little while. We went by train. I can't remember one thing we did in the big city, but afterward (you guessed it), we met some high school girls on the train on the way back to camp. We had fun talking to them. That was the highlight of the trip. We were easy to please.

Then another welcome break from the routine occurred on the Fourth of July. A group of us were assigned to go to Tupelo, Mississippi, to take part in a parade. We road in a Jeep and waved at the crowd to add to the festivities.

In the summer of 1944, probably around my birthday in July, the first sergeant realized I had been in the army a year and was due a one-week furlough. Off I went by train from Mississippi to Pennsylvania via Washington, DC, and Philadelphia. It was a long, hot overnight trip on a very crowded train with lots of other soldiers, sailors, civilians, etc., most of whom, like me, were carrying duffle bags, which did not fit in the overhead baggage racks.

Coming home was a thrill, with me filling out my brand-new, almost-never-worn Class-A uniform, with an additional fifteen pounds, a store-bought overseas cap trimmed in infantry blue piping, a PFC stripe, a good conduct ribbon, and my marksman rifle badge.

Mom and Dad greeted me with open arms and could not do enough for me. I had some good, home-cooked meals. It is peculiar that, while I was home, my family did not pry me with questions, and I did not say much about the army. It was just nice to be away from it for a while. I never entertained the thought that I might be going overseas and perhaps never coming back and nobody asked. Many thoughts were never expressed. That is the way it was in those days in our family.

I went to visit Beth Wills, my senior prom date whom I had been seeing that final spring before leaving for the army and we had been corresponding.

I had mixed emotions about Beth. During basic training she had sent me a "Dear John" letter. She said she would like to go out with her friends at nursing school. The implication was clear they would be going to dances and other social events. That was a little hard to take, but I certainly had no hold on her.

Still, when I went home, we went to the movies and visited her family, who lived near Pennsylvania Avenue in West Bethlehem. Her mother was friendly enough, but a little reserved with me. At some point I learned that her husband had committed suicide. That remembrance always bothered me when I went to visit. On the other hand, her older sister was always very pleasant. Beyond that, I cannot remember much about the visit. It was a long time ago.

Soon after my return from furlough we were told to get ready to leave Camp McCain. No one said where we were going, but it had to be overseas.

We were given a list of items to pack in our duffel bag, but first we had to lay them out on our bunks for inspection. After packing our duffels, we were given a list of clothing that we were to wear on the trip. These were put aside for the next day, except for our undershorts, which was the only item to be worn. Anything not on the list was to be taken to the supply sergeant to be burned.

I followed these orders except I kept one sock on my right foot because I had a small cut between two of my toes and I was afraid of infection. As I was walking to the latrine, I passed by Captain Caywood, who was sitting on a nearby fence. He asked why I was wearing the sock. I told him the reason and he told me to turn the sock into the supply sergeant. I said: "Yes, sir" and continued walking toward the latrine before going to the supply room. I did not think he would mind my circuitous route. The captain called me back and motioned for me to go directly to the supply sergeant, which I did with much embarrassment. A bon-fire of extra stuff was in progress.

The next day there was a call for volunteers to clean up the latrine. "Volunteers" are obtained by a sergeant calling out, "You, you, and you!" It was no surprise to me that I was selected because of the interaction with the captain.

I was given the job of scrubbing the yellow off the urinals with Naptha soap, a Bon-ami type cleansing powder, and a rag. It was slow going. I ended up having to scrape it off with my fingernails. Afterward, I washed my hands thoroughly, but at mealtime I was not a happy camper. I smelled of urine and ate without much appetite while being careful not to touch my food. I've never forgotten that episode for obvious reasons but mainly because I was reprimanded by the captain, a man I learned to revere.

CHAPTER 24

THE 94ᵀᴴ MOVES OVERSEAS

The 94th Division began leaving Camp McCain on July 23, 1944, traveling by troop train north to Erie, Pennsylvania, where we stopped in a freight yard in the middle of the night for quite a long time. Then we continued east and up into New York State to Camp Shanks just above New York City. All the troops arrived by July 31. Now we felt certain we were heading toward Europe.

Camp Shanks was a staging area for units preparing to embark overseas. We settled into our new barracks and had some special training on how to climb down a rope ladder from a simulated ship, plus some inoculations and a final inspection.

Then we were given an overnight pass to New York City. It was exciting just to see all the sights in the big city but my memories of how we spent our time are now a blur.

On my last evening at Camp Shanks I decided to go to the Post Exchange (PX) and have a beer. Who knew if I was ever coming back? I don't know how it happened, but I was alone when I drank my first and last beer. I thought it tasted awful, but I persisted and finished it. I could not figure out why everyone liked it. When I got up to leave the PX, I could not walk straight. That was a surprise. I felt lucky that no one I knew was there to see me staggering.

We left Camp Shanks on August 4, traveling by train to a New York City dock where we boarded the converted British luxury liner, the Queen

Elizabeth. It took several days to load all 15,000 94thers on that huge troop-ship. And all the while there was a band playing, among other songs, "The Pennsylvania Polka" over and over.

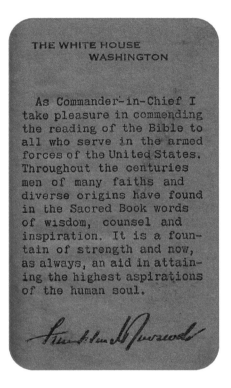

THE WHITE HOUSE
WASHINGTON

As Commander-in-Chief I take pleasure in commending the reading of the Bible to all who serve in the armed forces of the United States. Throughout the centuries men of many faiths and diverse origins have found in the Sacred Book words of wisdom, counsel and inspiration. It is a foun-tain of strength and now, as always, an aid in attain-ing the highest aspirations of the human soul.

President FDR commends reading the Bible

Before boarding we were given diddy-bags by the Red Cross that included toothpaste, a toothbrush, shaving necessities, and a New Testament Bible.[1] I already had one from my church at home, but this one included a wonderful letter from President Franklin D. Roosevelt advising us to read the scriptures.

This would not happen today. I tell this story to remind the reader that I lived in another time. Since then, we have lost something important and can't seem to get it back.

We sailed from the good old USA on August 6, 1944. The Second Battalion, 301st Infantry was assigned to guard duty on the ship, making sure among other things that no one lit a match or smoked while on deck where the light might be spotted by enemy submarines. Because of this responsibility, we were given permanent quarters on the upper deck in state rooms with bunk beds. We even had shower stalls to use if we wanted to wash in saltwater. No one did.

I enjoyed guard duty on deck with its cool breeze giving me the opportunity to observe all the GI activity there. My other station in a hallway looking at the side of a funnel was very boring.

Most of the men on board slept either in the hold or on deck and took turns moving between those two locations. Meals were served twice a day. There were so many men that the chow lines were essentially continuous throughout the day. The food was very plain as prepared and served by the British, who ran the ship.

Fortunately for us the weather was good all the way over and the Queen Elizabeth's speed was so great, submarines could not catch up to it. Even so, the ship tacked back and forth every two to four minutes so that it did not present a steady target.

We arrived in the Firth of Clyde, Scotland on August 11th after just five days at sea. Since there was no docking facility large enough to accommodate this large ship, the 94th Division disembarked from the "Queen" on August 12 by ferry boat into the town of Greenock, Scotland near Glasgow. I knew we were close to Mom's hometown, Clydebank, so when I wrote home, I told Mom that I could see Aunt Annie's window. That was not strictly true, but I knew she would know where I was.

After the local people gave us some food, said "Cheerio," and the children asked, "Some gum, chum?" we boarded a train and headed south through the beautiful countryside of Scotland then England. The hills of Scotland were grand. Although bare of trees, they were covered with heather. England was mostly rolling farms with picturesque fields surrounded by stone walls.

We stopped at a few train stations long enough to receive food from the British civilians. Because we were hungry, we gratefully ate their tasteless, pastry-covered meat pies.

At one station we saw a white English girl escorted by a Negro American soldier. The soldiers in our car who were from the South were shocked and almost went berserk with cursing. It was clear they had never seen that sort of thing before; neither had I. I had never seen such a display of prejudice and was shaken by that incident.

My battalion arrived at an encampment of ten-man tents near the small town of Chippenham (pronounced with a silent "h") in Wiltshire County, southwest England, about eighty miles due west of London. The nearest town of note was Bath, about ten miles to the southwest and the nearest city, Bristol, fifteen miles west on the England's west coast, was located on the south side of the Severn River estuary. It was summertime and very pleasant, so I have good memories of our stay in Chippenham.

The mess-hall was in a Quonset hut, a long building shaped like half of a cylinder sliced down the middle made of curved corrugated sheets of metal. The food was good as usual. We have Captain Caywood to thank for that. He always took good care of his men. Bees were everywhere especially in the jelly jars on the dining tables. The latrines were outdoors and very rustic to say the least. Gross would be more descriptive.

We were there only two weeks and having traveled for three weeks from Mississippi, it was deemed necessary to get us back in shape with daily calisthenics and hiking five, ten, and twenty miles.

One day we went to a demonstration of a "German squad" attacking down-hill which showed how the enemy maneuvered and what their uniforms looked like. A light machine gun manned by two men laid down fire while the rest of the squad took turns running ahead to another position at which point the machine-gunners would move up, always staying in the center, protected by the riflemen.

Next, we saw a display of German infantry weapons and equipment including small arms, rifles and machine guns. I noticed that all the machine guns were stamped with the year 1942. I was visibly upset by this because I knew that our machine gun was from WW I and dated 1917. This was August 1944. We had been at war for almost three years and still using WW I machine guns. I complained about this situation in a letter to my Dad. Our platoon leader, Lieutenant Mulehall, censored my letter and let me know about it in no uncertain terms. I learned that all letters were read by our officers and approved or not with their signature on the outside of the envelope.

There were two other rather exciting events during our stay in Wiltshire. One weekend, three of us ex-ASTPers got together (I'm sure John Gardy was one of them) and visited a pub in Chippenham. There, we met three young girls who were in the Royal Air Force (RAF) and stationed at a nearby RAF base. Later, we went for a walk with them. I think it was the girls' idea because they knew the territory.

We spent a very pleasant afternoon talking to them and listening to their English accent. I'm always impressed with native Englanders and their command of the English language. I do not remember their names or their looks, but one of them sent me a package while I was in France with some practical things like candles.

The other event was our weekend pass to London. We stayed overnight at a hotel reserved for US soldiers. Our first adventure was to see the famous Piccadilly Circus, a large intersection surrounded by buildings with large electric billboards. There we saw the beautiful Shaftesbury Monument with the Statue off Anteros, the Criterion Theater and the London Pavillion. The whole area was covered with soldiers and girls looking for dates.

Eventually, we became hungry, so we bought fish and chips from a vendor, my mother's favorite treat. I was disappointed. The fish was cooked but had little taste. There was no tartar sauce or ketchup. The chips, the English version of french fries, were edible, but they were sliced too thickly and were not crisp. It was one of the blandest meals I'd ever tasted. I could not finish it. Where was McDonald's when we needed it?

We were still wandering the streets of London as the night closed in and heard an air raid siren. The locals paid little attention to it, but we did. Soon, we heard the putt-putt of a German V-bomb engine off in the distance. When the noise of the engine stopped, we knew it was coming down. As soon as we heard an explosion off in the distance, we headed for our hotel.

The V for Vengeance V-1 bomb had wings, was launched from ramps in German-controlled Europe or by aircraft and was powered by a pulsejet. This was the predecessor of today's cruise missile. When the V-1 reached its target area, usually London, the engine stopped and, without power, dropped onto its target. While the putt-putt or buzz of the engine was heard, there was no immediate danger, but when that noise ceased, one knew it was coming down—hopefully not nearby. As long as the Germans were able to launch those bombs, some poor souls in London would meet their demise if they were not in an air raid shelter.

The next evening, the guys in our squad just had to go to a pub. After my experience with my first beer at Camp Shanks I was reluctant, but I did not know anyone else in London, so I stuck with my friends. There I tried a "half and half." I was told it was half beer and half ale and was surprised to find it tasted like root beer, not bad at all. Later, we went to a nice restaurant, where we enjoyed a delicious meal. These are my wartime memories of London. The next day we were back in Chippenham.

On September 4, 1944, the 94th Division began its move to France. Our regiment took a troop train to Southampton and, on September 5, after a twenty-four-hour delay, boarded a ship, either the Neutralia or the Crossbow,[2] and began sailing at night for France.

On the way over, I paid for my indiscretion of complaining in my letter home. The men in our unit were jammed into a large mess room. Lieutenant Mulehall entered the room and announced that he needed volunteers for latrine duty. As was normal practice when seeking volunteers, Mulehall said, "you, you, and you." I knew I was going to get latrine duty from the moment he walked into the room.

The latrine was a large box about fifteen feet long, three feet wide, and about twenty inches high. It straddled the deck from the bulkhead to the ocean side and was canted at an angle because the box was longer than the width of the deck. The top of the box had about eight holes that served as seats for those using it. Both ends of the box were open and it was the latrine orderly's job to use a very long pole with a two-foot piece of wood across the end to periodically shove the smelly human excrement overboard. Obviously, this was long before there existed an Environmental Protection Agency. This was my second brush with authority in the army and I ended up on latrine duty both times.

Crossing the Channel at night was uneventful. We arrived at Utah Beach and were greeted with a scene of desolation and destruction. Visible were more wrecks of landing craft and Liberty ships than a man would care to count. Masts, funnels, bows, and sterns were thrust above the waves at all angles. Nearby were LSTs, LCIs, Liberty ships, freighters, and tankers, waiting to unload. Various smaller craft were plying to and from the shore. Overhead were scores of barrage balloons strategically placed to discourage low-level aircraft attacks.[3]

We began landing on September 6. I remember climbing over the ship's railing onto the rope ladder weighed down with all my gear, including full field pack, rifle over my shoulder, and hanging on for dear life.

About two thirds of the way down I dared a quick look below and realized the ladder curved away from the side of the ship to the landing craft, where the ladder was being held by two men standing in its middle. I also noted that the landing craft was bouncing around because of the waves—up and down, up and down, periodically banging into the side of the ship.

Having no other choice, I continued descending and, as I neared the bottom where the ladder was pulled away from the ship, I could now look through the ladder at the angry water below where the ship and landing craft were banging together. Needless to say, I was one nervous GI.

Fortunately, I was soon over the landing craft and between the two men holding the ladder. I immediately realized there was no way I could step safely onto the rising and falling wobbling deck. My dilemma was solved as they urged me to jump, which I did, and was caught in their arms. From there, I was directed by other seamen to a waiting seat on a bench.

Once the craft was loaded, we motored to the beach and I took my first step onto European soil as thousands of American soldiers had done before me and would do again after me.

PART V

WW II SERVICE OVERSEAS

CHAPTER 25

THE 94ᵀᴴ DEPLOYS TO BRITTANY, FRANCE

The 301ˢᵗ Infantry Regiment landed on Utah beach on D-Day + 92, September 6, 1944[1]. The scene here was chaotic with destroyed bunkers and equipment everywhere. We followed a path marked with signs indicating that mines had been cleared and entered a wooded area where we spent the night. The neighboring fields were littered with smashed gliders used on D-Day to land airborne troops. I have never understood why they were so close to the beach. Maybe the walk to the woods was further from the beach than I thought. The neighboring fields were surrounded by hedgerows, which were not accommodating to gliders trying to find a flat area large enough on which to land. It must have been horrible to be killed or injured on that first day crashing into a hedgerow before you had a chance to fight.

After one night in our pup tents in the woods, we were loaded onto trucks for the long ride from Normandy to Brittany. We passed through many towns that had been in the news during the past few months when the US Army had fought to break out of the Normandy bridgehead, towns like St. Lo and Avranches, with many damaged buildings.

94 th's Route to Brittany, France

On we went through the countryside with its hedgerows surrounding apple orchards. Everywhere we went, the French people greeted us with cheers and apples, about the only things they had in abundance. The next night we stopped in another temporary camp complete with a slit trench latrine. While one of our guys was squatting, a young French girl came over and offered him an apple. Right then we understood what we had been told about the French not being big on modesty. Still, we laughed at the GI's embarrassment.

After arriving at our destination, the 94th Division relieved the Sixth Armored Division[2] and the 83rd Infantry Divisions[3] and then we were spread out along Brittany's Atlantic coast in order to contain the 60,000 German troops in and around their submarine pens in the cities of Lorient and St. Nazaire. Our regiment, the 301st Infantry was positioned in the Lorient sector, the 376th at St. Nazaire and the 302nd in reserve.[4]

Captain Caywood told us that the Germans had retreated into this area with thirty-five battalions of artillery to protect their submarine ports; thus, we were not going to try to capture them.

After the war I learned several reasons why this might have been decided. First, the battle of the Atlantic had essentially been won by our navy using radar and aircraft carriers to locate German subs, which were being sunk at a fearsome rate. Wolf Packs had disappeared from the mid-Atlantic by the summer of 1944. Second, the US Army had captured the ports of Brest and Cherbourg to use them to bring in supplies; however, the Germans destroyed those harbors by sinking ships in them and blowing up harbor facilities. The casualties we received while attacking those ports, to some extent, were for naught. Supplies continued to come across the beaches of Normandy for many months. Finally, after the 94th's arrival in Europe, the British captured the huge port of Antwerp in Belgium that provided a major means of providing supplies for Allied armies and one that was closer to the front line than Normandy.

CHAPTER 26

FIRST COMBAT EXPERIENCES

Six heavy machine-gun squads and four heavy mortar squads from H Company were sent to the front line. Two machine-gun squads, including mine were kept in reserve at Company Headquarters near Pont Scoff, about a mile behind the frontline in a wooded area near a road intersection. The cooks set up their kitchen in a tent under the trees.

After supper, I picked out a spot near a slit trench that was next to a hedge row and told myself, "That's where I will go if any danger occurs." It never entered my mind to dig a foxhole, yet I was moments away from receiving my "baptism of fire."

As the evening shadows gathered, I spread my blanket on my shelter-half near the slit trench. It was a lovely autumn evening, so when I lay down to rest, there was no need to get under the covers.

Suddenly, there were explosions all around me, as the Germans plastered the area with artillery fire. I literally flew from my blanket into that slit trench and pulled my helmet over my head with both hands, trying to climb into it. I was so frightened that I desperately prayed to Jesus to save me and promised I would do anything for Him if He would only save me. I repeated this prayer over and over until the artillery barrage stopped.

Unbelievably, no one was hurt. There were a few holes in the cooks' tent.

You can surely understand that I was useless as a soldier at this time.

It is important to note that I did not recognize until much later how much this prayer affected my future. Eventually, I realized that two significant things occurred immediately following this episode and continued with me the entire time I was in combat.

First, it was the beginning of constant fear—every living, breathing, minute fear that I endured during combat for six months.

Second, it was the beginning of combat in which I was able to perform my duty as a soldier to the best of my ability, regardless of the situation and the ever-present fear.

This was an amazing, incredible turn of events for me! From being useless to useful within the blink of an eye. Because of this experience, my baptism of fire, I believe the Lord answered my prayer by not only saving me, but also by giving me courage for the future.

The next day, everyone started digging holes and cutting down trees to cover them. I dug my first hole, six feet long, three feet deep, and almost two feet wide. Then I cut down my first tree ever and sawed it up into three-foot lengths and covered my hole with layers of them, leaving a hole at one end for an entrance.

That night as we took turns standing guard, a funny episode occurred. I heard one of our guards looking for Jerry Driscoll to take his turn on guard. Because of all the new holes, the guard did not know where Driscoll was located so he went around whispering "Jerry" into each hole. Since the word "Jerry" was also a nickname for the Germans, his call for "Jerry" could have been an alert to the presence of Germans. Of course no one was fooled, but it gave us something to laugh about.

That same day we learned that our battalion had received its first enemy attack, which fortunately was driven off by our artillery. We had been told that it was standard German procedure to attack whenever green troops (that was us) came onto the front line, so we were not surprised.

Sometime later, Julie Horowitz told me with a smile on his face what happened to him that day. He said the Germans were advancing on our company's position. He aimed his carbine at one of them, took his sight picture just as he had learned to do, and squeezed the trigger slowly just as he had been taught to do, and nothing happened . . . because he had forgotten to turn his safety off. Just then our artillery drove the Germans away.

Can you imagine a young Jewish GI missing the opportunity to shoot a German soldier and then smiling about it? That is the way it was for all of us. We were green and we knew it.

After a few days in reserve, our two heavy machinegun squads, led by Captain Caywood, traveled toward the front in Jeeps down a road bordered by hedgerows. Suddenly, there was rifle fire over our heads. The Jeeps pulled to a stop in the middle of the road and we all jumped into a drainage ditch along the opposite side of the road.

Captain Caywood passed an order for each squad to send a man across the road to look over the hedgerow into the wooded area beyond.

Our squad leader, Sergeant Lyons, said, "Who wants to go?" There was dead silence! We were green.

Then Lyons said, "OK, number one has to go."

At that moment Staff Sgt. Shearer one of the machine gun section leaders said, "The captain says don't send the first and second gunners." Lyons said, "OK, number three!" Guess who was number three?

I crawled to the edge of the ditch to Sgt. Shearer who said, "Take your safety off." Good advice! Man, was I green! I ran across the road and, while doing that, I thought about holding my helmet on the end of my rifle to see if anyone would shoot at it. That is something you might see in the movies, but I was not going to do that with the captain and everyone else's eyes on me, so I gingerly peeked over the hedgerow. First, I looked up in the trees for snipers and then all around through the woods and saw nothing. I moved along the hedgerow and looked over at several other places with the same result. The other guy did the same. Seeing no one, we all got back in the Jeeps and moved on. It was concluded that a German patrol behind our lines had fired at us and then skedaddled.

While this was happening to our squad, another H Company unit on Hill 101 sustained its first casualty. It seems that, prior to their arrival on Hill 101, another outfit had been using the church tower on that hill to observe the Germans; consequently, the Germans periodically shelled that hill with 88s to discourage use of the tower. Unfortunately, one of our GIs on Hill 101was wounded while using a slit trench latrine when the German artillery fired on the hill. He called for a medic who came to his aid, but the medic was killed when the next shell came over. War is hell, just as General Sherman remarked long ago.

On our first day on the front line, we set up our two machine guns at the intersection of our hedgerow and a hedgerow on the far side that was perpendicular to ours. There we dug two holes so that one machinegun could fire into the field on the right and the other into the field on the left.

The area immediately behind our machine gun positions was bare of foliage for about fifty feet up a slight slope to the woods in back. When evening approached, we set up our pup tents there but only about ten feet behind the hedgerow and posted guards. I slept in one of the tents with Sergeant Lyons.

Just after daybreak the next morning we were awakened by the sound of rifle fire over our heads. Our tent had a few bullet holes to testify to the closeness of the enemy fire. I have no idea what the other guys in our machine gun section did, but I crawled a mile a minute into the right-hand machine gun hole. I wanted to look through the aperture that our gun was sighted into, but I was afraid, thinking that perhaps the Germans were nearby on the other side of the hedgerow. Seeing several hand grenades sitting on a ledge inside the hole, I took one, went outside the hole and threw it over the hedgerow. Then I went back in the hole to look across the field. I saw no Germans. There was no more enemy rifle fire and none from our side at all. In retrospect, we guessed that the rifle fire came from a German patrol that was looking for information not a fire fight. When had we heard that before?

I do not recall what anyone else did during those few minutes after the German rifle fire, but I have often wondered why our gunners did not come into the machine gun holes like I did. One thing is certain—we never put up our pup tents again. We were still green!

A short time later, some GI I had never seen before came by and asked who threw the grenade and then told us that the Engineers had placed mines in front of our position and did not want them disturbed.

I thought, "Now they tell me!" I kept my mouth shut and no one ever asked me what happened.

Unfortunately, information like the presence of mines in front of us would have been important to know for our own safety if nothing else. Sometimes communications in the army did not make much sense.

After moving to the front line, we took turns standing guard for the first time. The schedule was two hours on and four hours off round the clock. This went on for most of the time that I was in combat, about six months. Our chances of ever getting eight hours sleep were slim to none. In fact, you never even got the four hours' sleep allotted to you because the previous guards woke you about ten minutes ahead of time so you could get ready to take your turn and of course after your two hours on guard you needed some time to stow your equipment and curl up in your blanket roll. Sleep was a precious commodity and you never knew when you might not get any of it.

The critical time for guard duty was during the night. With six men in our squad, two stood guard while the other four slept, thus the sleepers' lives were in the hands of the guards, so we took guard duty seriously.

Most of the times, I stood guard with Vince Lamparella. He was a good soldier and a good buddy. We stood relatively close with our backs to each other, looked over and along the hedgerow and in the rear of our position. We would scan left and right, trying to see any approaching enemy.

It was weird because as you stared into the blackness, your eyes sometimes saw things moving that were not moving at all. Consequently, you had to keep checking certain objects to make certain they were not moving. These objects might be bushes, trees, stumps, or even farm animals which of course did move. We heard stories about jumpy guards who shot cows thinking they were the enemy, to the chagrin of the local farmers. I was fortunate because I never saw the enemy at night.

One night while I was on guard by myself there was a sudden, loud swoosh of air that ended as soon as it began. It startled me but I soon realized it was a flock of birds that had flown off from a huge tree near our hedgerow. An artillery shell passing over makes a similar sound, but the swooshing from shells lasts much longer.

Although we had been online for only a week it seemed we had been through a lot and learned a lot; however, actual combat was in our future and that was a different ball game entirely.

CHAPTER 27

THE REST OF THE STORY IN BRITTANY

Most of the rest of the 94th time in Brittany was restricted to patrols by the rifle companies and maneuvers to improve their positions. Heavy Weapons Units such as ours spent much of the time with guard duty and improving gun positions with minimal enemy contact.

As Autumn days grew shorter the chill in the air became rather nippy. The powers that be found a solution to this growing problem. A group of us of us were trucked to an abandoned German Officers' Training Facility near the French coast to obtain materials to build huts along the hedgerows. These buildings were prefabricated so the walls came apart as readily as they were put together.

I remember how beautiful the location of that facility was, set on a hill overlooking the Atlantic Ocean. The picturesque view included rock arches which extended out into the water, a scene, artists would die for.

We gathered a few small panels and some two-by-fours and headed back to our hedgerow.

Then the fun began. Everyone in the squad wanted to get into the construction of our new "home" after weeks of boredom standing guard. With some hammers and nails we built a frame for a hut up against the hedgerow that would sleep six with a shed roof sloping down and away from the top of the hedgerow. We then cut and nailed pieces of the panels for the roof and sides. At one end was a small window for air circulation; the other side was open but covered with a shelter-half. It was a little crude but as best could be done with the limited tools and materials in hand.

The fun part involved Tom Sawyer style, encouragement for those working. Since there were not enough tools to go around, the spectators "ooohed" and "aaahed" at the workmanship being demonstrated by the volunteer workers. For example, "Boy, he's done this before. Look at that he put that nail right in the center, well, almost, anyway. Oops, he bent the top of the nail. What can you expect from a rookie builder? Take it easy on him—it might have been a faulty nail. Come on, he doesn't know a nail from his rear end, etc." This banter was followed by an occasional response from a worker, "If you think you can do better here's the hammer."

As I have mentioned before, the Third and Fourth Squads were a team, officially called a Machine gun Section, so we were always close together. One day one of the second gunners in the fourth squad, a well-built young southern boy, got so drunk he started fooling around, threw his helmet up in the air, and shot at it with his 45-caliber pistol. Shortly thereafter Capt. Caywood heard of the incident and put him on Company Punishment. His punishment was to dig a hole sixteen-by-sixteen-by-sixteen feet. Of course, we all pitched in to help.

We had two ex-coal miners in our group. Bob McClain in our squad was one of them. They taught us a lot about digging holes. When we were finished, that hole was a perfect square with straight and true sides. To dig the sides, a series of vertical grooves about two feet apart were inscribed using the pointed end of the pick, and then with the wedge-shaped end, a digger would start at the top and scrape down between the grooves. The dirt just crumbled down, easy as pie. We finished the hole in one day and covered it with log beams. On top of the beams, panels from the German camp were laid and then covered with dirt and branches for camouflage. This became our new sleeping quarters.

A short distance behind our position was a French farmhouse. Word got around that one could get cider there, so when I was not on guard duty, I went to visit this place. The house was one story with a thatched roof. Next to it was a shed of some kind with a few animals and a garden with a small fence. A short distance away was a small one-story barn. These buildings were in the center of an apple orchard surrounded by hedgerows.

The farmer was in the barn serving a few other GIs, so I wandered over and saw for the first time an apple press with a huge screw crushing the apples. The mash or remains of the crushed apples was ugly-looking stuff, but issuing from it was a small stream of clear liquid. It appeared they never bothered to clean up the mash but just threw more apples into it. Whatever procedure they used it apparently did the job because there were small barrels of cider stacked everywhere.

I had already learned from other GIs that *cidre doux* (sweet cider) was free, but the hard cider was not. In fact, the cider in most of the barrels was hard cider being fermented into Calvados, a popular French alcoholic beverage. GIs in Brittany soon began drinking it because it was the only hard liquor readily available.

I preferred the sweet cider, so I asked for a canteen full and was obliged. I do not remember how the transaction was accomplished. I had two years of French in high school that was of no help at all. Hand waving and finger pointing seemed to work. Over time most of the squad visited the barn for cider.

One night in late autumn as the weather turned chilly, a bottle of Calvados showed up on the hedgerow at our guard post. Calvados, as I have described earlier, is made from apples and is basically hard cider. I had been told it was good for keeping you warm, so one night I took a drink. Whoa! I felt this warm feeling come over my body and permeate all my extremities. The next day I was jokingly accused of using up the supply of Calvados. It was not true for I was smart enough to know the damage almost pure alcohol can do to your body, but if that story made the guys laugh, that was all right by me.

Several months later, on another cold night, Jerry Driscoll got in trouble when he became drunk on guard duty. I only heard this story second-hand so I cannot vouch for any of the details. It seems that Driscoll got drunk and someone reported it to Battalion Headquarters. As the story goes, Captain Caywood saved his neck by putting him in an open Jeep on a very cold night and drove him up and down the road behind the lines until he sobered up, then took him to Battalion Headquarters where he was reprimanded, given Company Punishment and lost his PFC stripe, again. He was lucky that Caywood helped him because getting drunk on guard duty was a serious offense.

One afternoon I made another foray for sweet cider. This time I met the very pretty farmer's daughter. In the process of getting more cidre doux, I tried to strike up a conversation with her. I learned her name was Louisette. I must have used the Tarzan finger pointing technique, "Me, Tarzan. You, Jane" and it worked. This was also the time when I learned the importance of knowing the foreign words for "speak slowly" in French–that would be, "parler lentement." The French speak way too fast and they string together words with an undulating voice. I managed to get Louisette to slow down her words and was able to understand some of what she was saying. I must have made an impression because I was invited back the next day.

Unfortunately, the next day, Louisette had to pick beets from their garden with her father, so I helped pick beets. They were ugly looking beets. Maybe they were for the pigs? I did not see her again after that because we were moved to a new position. After I told the guys in the squad that I had a date with the farmer's daughter and ended up picking beets, I got a lot of razzing.

In addition to digging holes, we were repeatedly moved to new locations. The officers must have done this to keep us from getting bored and sloppy. Quite often when we moved, the officers would not be satisfied to let us take over the previous unit's holes. They figured they could improve our defenses by rearranging our gun position and foxholes; consequently, moving meant digging.

One of these new locations was Hill 101, where we had suffered our first casualty. The Germans periodically shelled this area, sometimes with 88s; hence, we were in great danger.

One evening, Sergeant Lyons and I were on guard duty. We were standing up against a hedgerow that was perpendicular to the front line. Someone had dug an L-shaped pocket into the hedgerow; consequently, we were protected reasonably well except for our heads which had to be exposed to look for enemy movements. Suddenly our area came under artillery fire. Sometimes this preceded an attack, so we could not just duck for cover; we had to be more vigilant. That is when I heard my first German 88 artillery shell explode nearby. Whizz-bang! was all I heard. Because of its high velocity there was no forewarning swish. GIs commonly remarked that if you heard the whizz-bang, you were probably still alive. I also remember hearing GIs say, "If one of those shells has your number on it, there's nothing you could do about it." Such was conversation on the front lines.

During our stint on guard duty, it began to rain. After being relieved, Lyons and I found water in our wide but shallow slit trench dug next to the hedgerow. Our hole was covered with large branches giving some protection from the cold and enemy fire but was not waterproof. We crawled into our hole and crouched on our hands and knees in about an inch of water with our heads resting in our upside-down helmets.

We were prepared to spend the night that way because we did not want to be outside on hill 101. The GIs in the next hole were dry because they had put shelter-halves over their hole and when they heard us grumbling, they invited us to join them. We crawled in with two or three others. There was just enough room for everyone, but it was tight. I ended up lying on my back which was a problem because I preferred to sleep on my right side, but I could not move and was uncomfortable. In addition, there were raindrops falling on my helmet, ping, ping, ping. I think I have heard that called "Chinese water torture." I tried to move to get out of the way of the drops to no avail. Eventually, I dozed off. GIs learn to do that anywhere, anytime.

The next day was beautiful and I was about to go on an adventure. Our section staff sergeant, Bill Tornfeldt, asked me to join him while he checked our defenses and observation post. These defenses included trip wires all around us, set to warn us if anyone tried to sneak up on our position. Unfortunately, there was the danger that we would accidentally set them off ourselves.

To understand a trip wire, one must understand how a grenade operates. A grenade is made with a firing mechanism or "firing pin," which screws into the center of the grenade. Surrounding the firing pin is a charge of explosive to be set off by the firing pin. This charge is surrounded by an outside metal covering which is grooved to make sure it breaks into multiple pieces when the grenade explodes thus causing damage in all directions to anyone or anything nearby.

There is a "handle" that curves to fit down the side of the grenade. This handle is attached at the top to the firing pin keeping it from firing. The handle is kept in place by a safety ring that has a cotter pin used to connect the handle to the firing pin and the grenade housing. There is also a spring under the top of the handle to eject the handle when it is released.

Prior to throwing the grenade, one holds the grenade handle down against the side of the grenade. Then one pulls out the safety ring and its attached cotter pin. The grenade will not go off as long as you hold the handle in place. Once you throw the grenade the handle is ejected by its spring releasing the firing pin that ignites the charge after a ten-second delay.

A trip wire is made by unscrewing the center portion of the grenade which contains just the firing pin and safety ring. The firing pin assembly is tied with fishing line to a tree a foot or so from the ground. Another piece of fishing line is tied to the safety ring and stretched across to another tree. The fishing line is hard to see in the daylight and impossible to see in the dark. If the enemy walks between those two trees, they will stretch the string and pull out the safety ring, thus setting off the firing pin which will make a loud noise, alerting sentries to the enemy's presence. The firing pin is not a real danger to anyone unless they are close to it when it fires. To make sure that no one is injured during the day, a second safety is inserted in the firing pin.

Tornfeldt and I walked around the area in daylight to make sure the trip wires were in place and that the safeties were set. As we completed our rounds, Tornfeldt headed to the edge of Hill 101, where we had an observation post. I was following him about two feet behind and several feet to his right. Suddenly I spotted a trip wire in the brush just in front of Tornfeldt and I called, "Stop!" Tornfeldt froze with his leg inches from a trip wire. He was several feet from the firing pin so I do not know whether it would have hurt him, but it was not worth taking a chance to find out. He checked the firing pin to see if the second safety was in place. I do not remember if it was. In any case I had kept Tornfeldt from possible injury and from having to replace the trip wire if it had exploded.

Arriving at the observation post, we took turns looking through binoculars in the direction of the enemy and down the almost vertical side of the hill. We could see a few German soldiers going in and out of sight at the base of the hill. I assume they had a dugout there. They seemed to be eating for they had something resembling mess-kits. No, we did not shoot at them or drop a grenade, even though it would have been easy to do. I do not really know why, but it was not up to us to make those decisions. As you are aware, we were there to contain them, not start our own private war.

In addition, if we had shot at them, those 88s would have answered our fire and the observation post had no protection; consequently, we let sleeping dogs lie.

I have made it clear that fear was ever present in my mind. I knew at any moment an artillery shell could land on top of or near me. That was a fact of life in war. However, with the help of the "Holy Spirit" I was given courage, to be able to function as a soldier despite my fear.

In addition to the Holy Spirit, there were human morale boosters that supported me at the front, including the closeness of my "buddies." I had the feeling that they needed me as well as I needed them. Certainly, there was the need to work together to do our jobs but there was also camaraderie as we frequently discussed our situation among ourselves including the fear and hardships we faced and shared together. We joked about most of these problems. That was good medicine.

Letters from home were another major morale booster. I wrote home every chance I had and receiving mail from home was a blessing. The army made sure we had V-mail, a form with space to write on one side and for the address on the other. A V-mail could be folded into an envelope making them very convenient to carry. They were just the right size for letter writing when we had time on our hands and easy to stow away in case we might need to move on with little notice.

V-mails were important to the army mail system as well, because they were readily reduced in size to minimize weight on the mail planes. However, I also carried a small note pad and envelopes for other more extended writing occasions. There was no need for stamps because our postage was free.

From time to time, we would also receive packages from home. Most times there were goodies in them that we shared even if by the time we received them, they were reduced to crumbs.

And then there were those wonderful gifts from Mom. She knit and sent me olive drab items of clothing like wool sox, the same color as my GI knit cap. I received several pairs of her sox and they were a blessing during the winter. She also made me an olive drab, wool, Balaclava helmet, your basic ski mask, although back then I had never heard of a ski mask. There was one slight problem with the Balaclava since they covered your ears, a no-no on guard duty; otherwise, they too were a blessing in very cold weather.

A raise in pay could have been a morale booster if you knew about it. My Soldier's Individual Pay Record Book tells me that, "it should be retained on my person at all times." I still have it and it looks like it went through the war, but I do not remember carrying it. In the book, it says it was issued on July 2, 1944. That was about a month before we went overseas.

The title of the booklet is on the middle of the front cover and on the bottom of the cover it has an official designation, W. D., A.G.O., Form No. 28, March 26, 1942. Inside there are five lines under the heading, Changes Affecting Pay Status. These lines are listed and discussed below:

1. "CL E ALOT $35.00 COMM 1SEPT/44."

   I have to assume this entry occurred the day I was called into Active Service on July 28, 1943 when I began receiving $35 per month. Since I did not receive my Pay Record book until July 2, 1944, the company clerk had some catching up to do, hence the strange date of entry, September 1, 1944, the date we left the UK for France. If that sounds peculiar to you, it does to me, too.

2. "Expert Inf. Pay from May 9, 1944."

   There is no indication of the amount paid and I never knew there was Expert Infantry pay. The date corresponds to a time when I was assigned to H Co. of the 94th Division in Camp McCain, Miss. and the 94th received the Expert Infantry Commendation.

3. "Cl E ALMT Inc. to $50.00 Comm Nov. 1, 1944"

   This pay raise to $50.00 per month was given to me about two months after our arrival in Brittany, France from the U. K. I have to assume it was due to our being overseas or in combat. Why they waited two months to begin the pay raise is inexplicable to me.

4. "Due C. I. B. Pay from Oct. 1, 1944."

   C.I.B. undoubtedly stands for Combat Infantry Badge but there is no indication of the amount paid. The date, Oct. 1, 1944 is approximately one month after we landed in Europe. That makes sense.

5. "CRE ALMT Inc to $60.00 Comm Feb. 1, 1945."

   Another undefined increase in pay that occurred at the beginning of February,1945 and happened as our Battalion was preparing to attack the German village of Sinz.
   For completeness, on the adjoining page it is indicated that I was insured for $10,000.00.

Considering the fact that we were at war, pay raises were of little consideration, but in the long run they must be counted as positive recognitions of our service. The pay increase from $35 per month to $50 is a whopping 43 percent increase. The second increase, from $50 to $60, is a 20 percent increase, again a significant amount.

Compared to the fact that we were putting our lives on the line in combat the raises meant nothing. I had enlisted to do my best to serve my country come what may. If I survived the war then the pay raises including the ones that were not defined in dollars and cents, would certainly be of interest.

At some point, our battalion was placed in Regimental Reserve and given a rest from front-line duties for about a week. We lived in a tent camp near the large town of Rennes. I have only a few memories of this time. I do not remember the camp or its facilities except that we had a shower. I do not count this one as a real shower because here is what happened. There was this semi-open booth. I really do not know what to call it. I was only there a few minutes. We stood in line with no clothes on. When it was my turn, they told me I had only a few minutes of water. First, an over-head gadget doused a little water on me. Then I tried to soap up, wash and get rinsed. Unfortunately, there was not enough time to get soaped before they doused me with the rinse water. It was a joke. You would have to like a cold-water shower outside in October to call this a shower. It was ridiculous! Why did they bother?

Several of the members of our squad went to a French restaurant for dinner or whatever. We got whatever. The place was crowded with GIs, but we could not read the menu and the restaurant owner (there was no waiter) could care less.

I had two years of French and I knew "poisson" meant fish and "pain" was bread. That was it. The restaurant had neither one. I think the other guys had some wine. I do not remember getting anything except ticked off at the owner who was no help at all. He spent the whole time we were there, talking to a couple of Frenchies. No wonder they lost to the Germans. This visit to a restaurant took a close second place to the non-shower.

There was only one bright spot about our stay in Rennes. We were given the opportunity to go to Communion. As it turned out, on the very day picked for Communion the Protestant chaplain became ill so we were told the Catholic chaplain would allow Protestants to come to his service through special dispensation. I went, even though I was not happy with the thought that I needed dispensation to take Communion. However, all the Catholic GIs thought it was great that we could be with them and they welcomed us. That made it especially nice.

The priest held the service in an open field. It was in Latin but although we did not understand the lingo, it was clearly Communion and I was happy to partake. The good news is that everyone I knew went to Communion. That was uplifting too.

After our time in the rest area, we were moved to another hedgerow and sleeping in another hut somebody else had constructed. It was a little bigger but was not ventilated as well as the previous one. As the nights grew colder the hut seemed warm enough but that was because there was no window to let in the chill.

One night I woke up feeling nauseous. I got up and went outside. I soon felt better. This happened once more before I figured out that, with all the guys sleeping together, we were not getting enough oxygen. We solved the problem by making sure the tarp over the door was not completely closed.

A few day later, we had some real excitement. While I was on guard duty in the morning, I heard a band playing. Lo and behold along came a group of men led by a small band playing "La Marseillaise" and, what's more, they were marching on the wrong side of the hedgerow, the German side. We all ducked down and thought for sure the Germans were going to fire artillery at us, all the time, laughing at these French soldiers. Fortunately, the Germans paid no mind.

We soon learned they were members of the Free French resistance sent to fill in holes in our lines. It would have been nice if someone had told us they were coming.

They were a rag tag bunch if I ever saw one, having no uniforms but bits and pieces of US uniforms with their emblem, the Fleur de Lis. We greeted them warmly and talked with their leader, a handsome young man who spoke a little English.

One day one of their men came to me while I was on guard duty. He showed me a grenade in one hand and the safety pin in the other. Since I was on guard duty, I sent him to Sergeant Lyons, who helped him put the safety pin back in the grenade. That was a little scary, but it worked out all right. Over time, more and more FFI joined the 94th Division so that we were able to extend our line all the way to Auxerre, southeast of Paris.[1]

The Germans occupied that part of France south of this line, until the US invasion of southern France by our Sixth Army drove them out of France and across the German border. Brother John was a tank driver during that invasion.

On Thanksgiving Day we had a turkey dinner with all the trimmings prepared by our cooks. It was delicious. The Germans would have given up right then if they knew we could bring that food overseas for the whole army. Not only that but they served the FFI guys turkey dinner as well. Unfortunately, something went wrong; we were told that the FFI got the "GIs" (diarrhea) from that dinner.

Speaking of food, one of my favorite meals overseas happened on a cold wintry day. After weeks of K rations, our cooks brought hot food to a place just behind the line. We took turns going back there for the meal. I remember there were pork chops and mashed potatoes, but my favorite part of the menu was the bread.

Our cooks made a deal with a French bakery that was given some of our flour in return for some French bread. I have never tasted bread so good. For all I know it could have been sourdough bread, which I had never heard of, but it was unbelievably good. You might consider the fact that I was cold and hungry, but I enjoyed that bread like none other, then or since.

After the war at one of our division reunions, one of our cooks told me how they had gone to pick up the bread in a Jeep with no bags to carry it, so they'd carried the loaves in their hands and tucked them under their arms to get them back to their kitchen.

At Christmas, we were still in the hedgerows near Lorient doing not much of anything but guard duty. To celebrate Christmas, we found a five-foot-tall spruce tree nearby and decorated it with bits of paper and string. Someone made a Star for the top, out of a tin can. We sang a few Christmas carols, had another great turkey dinner and felt lonesome for home. For me, feeling lonesome for home sometimes meant wondering how much time out of my life was being wasted by that idiot Hitler and the Japs who were the reason I was in the army, overseas, and away from home.

In the middle of December, we received a copy of the *Stars and Stripes*², a small newspaper published by the US Army. It contained some startling news about a German offensive against the US First Army in Belgium. I remember only one small paragraph of the news that said the 106th Infantry Division had lost 15,000 casualties—that was a whole division. I was surprised they did not keep that debacle secret. In addition to the great loss, it had to be a great embarrassment to the US Army. Of course, it was not totally true. After the war, I learned that two of the 106th Division's Regiments, say 6,000 men, had surrendered. Even so this was the greatest loss ever sustained by the US Army.

After that, we received no further news on the battle that was to be called "The Battle of the Bulge," and we did not know when or how we would be involved.

CHAPTER 28

SUMMARY OF THE BATTLE
OF THE BULGE

Since the Battle of the Bulge was to be part of the 94th Division's future, it will be helpful to understand the German's rationale for starting it and how it ultimately failed.

After the Allied forces broke out of the hedgerow country in Normandy in August 1944, most of the Germans retreated to their Siegfied Line defenses along the border of Germany. I say most, because the British were held up in Holland because of the many rivers, dikes and lowlands that provided easy defenses for the Germans. Also, General Patton's 3rd Army was held up by the Germans who manned the French forts of the Maginot Line. After some time passed, Patton had to almost stop because gasoline for his tanks were allocated to the planned Allied offensive in Holland, "Market Garden." This was a combined US and British Army attack with the objective of crossing the Rhine River at a bridge in Arnhem, Holland. The battle plan required British paratroopers to seize a bridgehead across the Rhine while two US Paratroop Divisions, the 101st and 82nd, seized key bridges on the 55-mile road to Arnhem so that a British armored column could travel north and cross the Rhine in 3 days.

The Market Garden battle is sometimes called "A bridge too far" because of two major failures. First, the British paratroopers landed northwest of Arnhem, but only a small contingent of them were able to seize the bridge before German re-enforcements re-captured the bridge. Second, the British army driving north through Holland took nine days instead of three to get there.

Meanwhile, during the fall, the Germans spent their time building their border defenses so that when the Americans tried to move into Germany through the Hurtgen Forest, several US infantry divisions lost a lot of men in the bitter fighting.

As winter approached the Allied High Command thought the Germans were exhausted, so they moved the American 28th and the 4th Infantry Divisions from the Hurtgen Forest to rest in the "quiet sector" of the Ardennes Forest in Luxembourg. They were supported by one battalion of the 9th Armored Division.

The northern portion of the Ardennes in Belgium was held by the 99th Infantry Division, just arrived, about 5 weeks before, from the states and the experienced 2nd Infantry Division positioned south of the 99th. Thus the 60 to 70-mile Ardennes front was protected by only four Allied infantry divisions and a battalion of armor.

Unbeknownst to the Allied generals, the Germans had been planning a major offensive since early Fall against this lightly manned Belgium-Luxembourg line. The Germans planned to push through Belgium to the coast and capture the only Allied supply port at Antwerp, Belgium. This attack would separate the British in Holland from the Americans in Belgium and perhaps cause them to sue for a separate peace.

This was not just a pipe dream. The Germans had done it before two times: Once against the Allies in WW I and in 1940 against the French.

Meanwhile, true to their belief that the Germans were beaten, on December 13, 1944, just three days prior to the German attack, the Allied High Command made a colossal blunder by moving the experienced 2nd Infantry Division north to invade Germany at Aachen and replaced it with another new Infantry Division, the 106th, just overseas from the states.

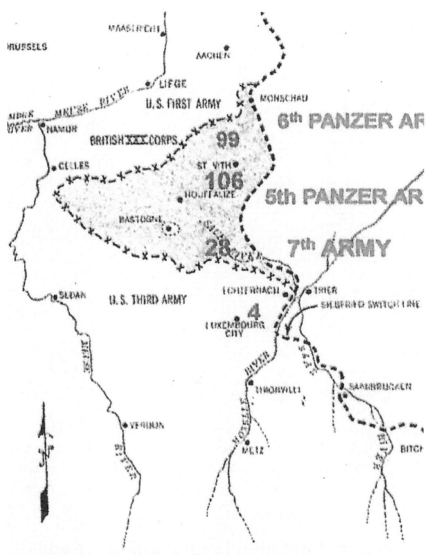

Opposing Forces on Day One of the Battle of the Bulge

While preparing for the attack, the Germans assembled three armies, two of them Panzer (armored) armies with a total of twenty-eight divisions against our four infantry divisions and an armored battalion, almost a 7 to 1 advantage.

Along the northern portion of the line, the Germans had the Sixth Panzer Army which included four Panzer divisions and five infantry divisions. In the middle they had the Fifth Panzer Army which included five Panzer divisions and six infantry divisions. And in the south, they had the Seventh Army with eight infantry divisions (two of these were parachute divisions). The Seventh Army was there to protect the southern flank of the Panzer Armies thrusting into Belgium and Luxembourg.

The German offensive started with a tremendous barrage from over 1,000 artillery pieces, at 5:30 a.m., on December 16, 1944. Surprise was on their side. It took about two days for US General Eisenhower to realize this was not just a spoiling attack. In the center the Germans immediately surrounded two regiments of the 106th Inf. Division, who had only been on the line three days by capturing the town of Schoenberg that provided the only river crossing in the 106th rear. After a few days of fighting, they surrendered. This was the greatest defeat ever suffered in the history of the US Army and an embarrassment to the leadership of the Allied European Theater Operation (ETO).

The US reacted by sending a Task Force of the Seventh Armored Division from the north to the town of St. Vith to block the advance of the Sixth Panzer Army. The Seventh Armored together with the reserve regiment of the 106th Infantry Division and stragglers from other units held St. Vith for several days, retreating only when they were about to be surrounded.

Further north the US 99th Div. gave a good account of themselves, killing many attacking Germans during the first few days. This included the I & R Platoon of the 99th's 394th Regiment that was sent to fill a gap in the line at Lanzerath.[2] They were quickly re-enforced by the 2nd Infantry Division that called off their attack on Aachen and moved south to help the 99th. Units of the 99th and 2nd held the Germans at the twin villages of Krinkelt and Rocherath until the bulk of the men in these divisions could retreat to prepared positions on Elsenborn Ridge. These US troops held the Elsenborn Line for the rest of the battle. Since the 6th Panzer Army could not budge the American from Elsenborn, they went around them, only to find the US

1ˢᵗ Infantry Division, brought from Holland, in their way. After trying to battle their way forward against the 1ˢᵗ Division the 6ᵗʰ Panzer Army side-stepped again.

This pattern of American units fighting and retreating and fighting again delayed the German advance almost everywhere in the Battle of the Bulge. Meanwhile, US Engineering Battalions began to blow up bridges along the Panzer Divisions' routes. All these delays gave the US time to bring more divisions from other sectors to block the Germans.

In Luxembourg in the Southern Ardennes the 28ᵗʰ and the 4ᵗʰ Infantry Divisions were told to stand and fight; consequently, the Germans' Fifth Panzer army suffered huge losses for the first few days. Eventually the Germans bypassed the 28ᵗʰ Division strongpoints, overwhelming them and forcing the 28th to retreat in disarray.

This sacrifice by the 28ᵗʰ gave Eisenhower time to bring the US 10ᵗʰ Armored Division and the 101ˢᵗ Airborne Division to the town of Bastogne, a multi road junction, that lay in the path of the 5ᵗʰ Panzer Army. The 10ᵗʰ Armored Div. lost a lot of tanks and men trying to slow down the Germans. It was this one division against a whole German Panzer army (no contest). Meanwhile the 101ˢᵗ Airborne had time to prepare their defenses around Bastogne and try as they might the Germans could not budge them. After some delay the Germans surrounded Bastogne and kept on driving west.

In the middle of these horrendous battles the Allied generals met to see what could be done. The re-enforcements readily available to Eisenhower had already been pulled out of their rest areas and thrown into the battle. The 101ˢᵗ Airborne Div. at Bastogne in opposition to the Fifth Panzer Army and the 82ⁿᵈ Airborne Div. near the Salm River in opposition to the Sixth Panzer Army.

Now the question for the Allied Command was what do we do next? Since the Germans were trying to split the Allied troops in the north from those in the south. Eisenhower decided to split his command by giving the British commander, General Montgomery control of the troops in the north and General Bradley control of those in the south. Most American Commanders were not happy with this arrangement, but it was done.

When Eisenhower asked for ways to immediately counterattack the Germans, General Patton said he could move his Third Army north in two or three days and relieve Bastogne. The other generals looked at him in disbelief, but Eisenhower said go to it but take your time. This decision was made on December 19. Patton relieved the Bastogne on the December 26.

By this time the German Sixth Panzer Army had passed over the Salm River and the Ambleve River and had reached the Ourthe River. Along the way they were opposed by the US 30th Inf. Div., 82 Airborne Div., 3rd Armored Div., the 84th Inf. Div. and others. The American forces in this area continuously increased, blocking every road and blowing up every bridge in front of the Germans advance so they were slowed down trying to find an open road west.

Eventually, the Germans ran out of gas, literally. By December 28, the German advance had been stopped. The US lost 4,000 killed in this portion of the battle. The Allies then began to push the Germans back to their border from whence they had started. It would be almost five more weeks until January 28, 1945, before the Germans would be pushed back to their original positions at the cost of 15,000 more US soldiers' lives.

CHAPTER 29

THE 94ᵀᴴ IS ON THE MOVE

When the Battle of the Bulge (BOB) started the Commanding Officers of the 94th Infantry Division thought that they would be called to assist in the fight; after all the 94th had considerable combat experience. However, when the new 11th Armored Division arrived in France from England, they were rushed directly into the BOB. The reason for this was that it was quicker to move them straight to the BOB than to take the time to move them to our area and make the switch with the 94th. An unfortunate tragedy changed this situation.

On Christmas Eve, December 24, 1944, His Majesties Transport, the Leopoldville[1], one of the ships bringing the 66th Infantry Division across the English Channel to France was torpedoed by the Germans with the loss of 784 enlisted men and fourteen officers. Because of this tragedy it was decided to have the 66th division relieve the 94th. The 66th started to move into our positions on December 26 at the very time the Third Army was relieving Bastogne.

Around New Year's Day, 1945, the 94th's ground troops boarded WW I French, forty men or eight horses boxcars in Chateaubriant and Pluay on trains headed northeast to Reims,[2] France, some 350 miles away and 125 miles northeast of Paris. The trip seemed to take forever but it was only three days.

The boxcars were smaller than those in the US. They had just enough room for us to lie down next to each other. A layer of straw on the floor plus all those warm bodies provided some warmth and comfort, but we had to leave the boxcar door partly open to provide enough ventilation. Of course, it was January so perhaps the word "warmth" is not quite appropriate.

One night while we were sleeping, one of the guys got up to urinate at the only place available, out the door of the moving train. Because we were so crowded, he could not avoid stepping on people to get to the door; consequently, there was some loud grumbling as someone asked, using colorful language, "What in the world are you doing?" He said in a loud plaintive voice, "I have to pee." That brought a burst of laughter that ended the griping.

This trip reminded me of a phenomenon in the army that allows GIs to sleep anywhere and anytime they get a chance. I have already told you about sleeping on hands and knees in a flooded foxhole. During a hike when GIs get a ten-minute break, they immediately plop on the ground and get a nine-minute catnap. It is not surprising that we had no trouble sleeping on the floor of that boxcar except for GIs needing to pee.

During the day we ate our K-rations and made coffee using little Nescafe packets provided in the ration box. We heated the water from our canteens in our canteen cups using our small gasoline stove. It took quite a while to make coffee for all forty of us. Drinking the coffee was also a challenge because our metal cups were hot from the stove. Our gloves saved us from having burnt hands, but we had difficulty touching our lips to the hot cup. Letting the coffee cool off was not an option for GIs wanting to get warm insides so I learned to slurp the coffee while barely touching the lip of the cup. The rolling of the boxcar helped this process as I timed the roll of the boxcar with my slurps. Boy did that coffee ever taste good and warm me up!

During the three-day trip the train stopped from time to time for no apparent reason. Most GIs jumped off the train to stretch and some to relieve themselves in the brush nearby. That was a concern because the train would suddenly blow its whistle and start moving shortly after that. All of us trying to climb back in the car by the one short ladder took considerable time; fortunately, the train moved ever so slowly while starting out so that everyone made it on board. There was always a lot of cheering as the last guy was pulled on board. No one wanted to be left behind; consequently, I did not get off very often.

Our regiment, the 301st detrained in Reims, France on January 5, 1945, and was immediately loaded onto trucks because we were given an urgent mission to relieve the 90th Division.[3] As a matter of fact, the situation was so dire in Belgium that two regiments of the 90th Division had already left the German Siegfried line south of Luxembourg for Belgium, leaving only one of their regiments to hold the line until our arrival. As a result, we took off on a wild truck ride to the rescue. On a proverbial cold day in hell, we left Reims at 1:00 p.m., traveling across France on trucks with no canvass cover, no lights, and no stopping for thirteen straight hours arriving in Germany the next morning at two o'clock.

During the daylight hours we talked, joked and took in the countryside. There was one funny episode when one of the guys had to relieve himself over the tail gate. Two of his buddies (we were all buddies) held him by his arms as he sat on the tailgate with his bare rear-end over the back of the truck. Well don't you know the truck stopped in the middle of a village much to his embarrassment. Everyone laughed.

Then we came upon two very sobering sites. One was the huge WW I cemetery near Verdun. The crosses, row upon row, upon row, seemed endless. Later we saw, along the side of the road, a long row of KIA's in body bags piled up three bodies high like cord wood. There was no more joking after that.

As darkness closed in, the non-stop ride continued, the air grew colder approaching zero. Conversation ceased as we tried to tough it out. We huddled together on wooden fold-down benches on either side of the truck. Piled in the middle of the truck was everyone's full field pack.

Our uniforms were all that kept us from freezing. Mine included long-johns, winter wool uniform, a pullover sweater, field jacket, scarf, all under my heavy woolen overcoat, balaclava helmet (ski-mask) knitted by Mom and my GI wool cap under my helmet liner & helmet. Gloves on my hands were both stuffed inside my coat pockets and two pair of socks (one pair knit by Mom) both inside my combat boots.

Even with all these clothes we were still cold, especially our feet because the floor of the truck was covered by a sheet of steel, which really felt like a floor of ice. All we could do was stamp our feet and wiggle our toes to no effect.

Wedged shoulder to shoulder in these cramped positions did not help our circulation although it did provide some body warmth and helped shield the wind blowing around us. There is no doubt that was the coldest I have ever been, and my toes were partially frozen.

Our misery ended at two o'clock in the morning when the trucks stopped in the little German village of Eft. We were all stiff and, because of that, I stayed in the truck and helped hand off the packs to those who climbed down onto the icy, cobble-stone road. Last off the truck, I found Captain Caywood holding a presumably lost pack over his head asking whose it was. I was embarrassed to say it was mine. He of course did not know that I had been trying to be helpful when somebody else unloaded my pack. When I said it was mine, he dropped it from on high (he was a big man) and I was just able to catch it without slipping and falling on the ice.

Our squad caught a real break since we were to remain in Company reserve that night. Totally exhausted, we slept soundly with all our clothes on, curled up on the floor of a German house. There was of course no heat but at least we were out of the wind. Those who had to go to the front line faced another type of misery. I could not imagine having to be ready to fight in the condition we were in.

Letter Home—January 9, 1945

Dear Mom and Dad,

Sorry, I haven't been able to write as much as I would like. It's been mighty cold and we've had plenty snow. The snow is mighty cold on the feet. We have to rub our toes to keep the blood circulating. I guess things can't get much tougher.

I'm still making out OK, regardless of conditions. I got rid of the head cold I had. That woolen cap you sent did the trick. I saved it till I really needed it.

I also put on a pair of woolen sox that came in an envelope. They saved the day as they were warm on the one night I will never forget for the rest of my life. It was bitter.

Things are going well and much the same as usual. Have you heard anything on Weston? Mail is scarce. Let me know the local news.

I'm doing my best sweating out these cold months. Don't worry about me. I'm learning to take more than I ever thought possible. Someday I'll be able to sit back and laugh at all this. That's one consolation.

I'll write again when I get the chance. Please keep writing even though it doesn't come to me regularly. So long for now.

Love, Herbert

CHAPTER 30

THE 94TH ATTACKS

T he 94th's attacks on the German Siegfried Line Defenses are summarize here with just enough detail to give the reader a feel for what went on in WW II in the area in which I fought. This summary is based primarily on the History of the 94th Infantry Division in World War II[1] as edited by Lieutenant Laurence G. Byrnes, Washington Infantry Journal Press Inc., 1948, as well as my memory of events when I was present and comments by 94th veterans either at 94th Division Reunions or other WW II veterans' meetings. For a more detailed description of the 94th attacks, please refer to the 94th Divisions' History indicated above.

Only those present during these various battles can understand how terrible the horrors of war were and witnessed how many young Americans gave their lives, suffered wounds and disabilities in achieving victory. It is my hope that my story will help future generations understand why our veterans have earned our deepest gratitude and greatest honor.

The 94th moves into the Siegfried Switch Line.

After arriving by truck convoy from Reims on the morning of January 7th, the 301st Infantry Regiment of the 94th Infantry Division relieved the 358th Infantry of the 90th Division. The 94th's 376th Infantry Regiment continued from Reims by train arriving on the 8th and relieved the US 3rd Cavalry Reconnaissance Squadron.

The 301st was positioned on the right side of the front and the 376th positioned on the left with its left flank abutting the Moselle River. The 302nd Infantry Regiment of the 94th was temporarily assigned to support a secondary defense line along the Meuse River and then moved to join the 94th on January 10, and placed in Reserve. Although I did not know it at that time, on the right flank of the 301st was the 95th Infantry Division. My high school friend, Pfc. Weston Werst, was a member of that division.

The Triangle

The Siegfried Switch Line that the 94th faced was just inside the German border with France. This12-mile-long defense line formed one leg of a triangle with the Moselle River that flowed from France into Germany forming another leg about eight miles long perpendicular to the Switch Line at its left end. The third leg of the triangle was formed by the Saar River that flowed from the right end of the Switch Line to the Moselle, emptying into it at the eight miles point from the Switch Line. Pythagoras theorem tells us that the leg of the triangle along the Saar was about fifteen miles long. It was the 94th's job to reduce this Triangle.

It is worth noting that the Main Siegfried Line was behind the Saar; consequently, to make serious progress in this area the 94th was going to have to penetrate the Triangle of the Siegfried Switch Line and then cross the Saar River and drive through the Main Siegfried Line. That was a huge challenge for a single infantry division. Incidentally, prior to the arrival of the 94th, the 90th Infantry Division had tried to penetrate the Siegfried Switch Line but had been turned back.

The Siegfried Switch Line

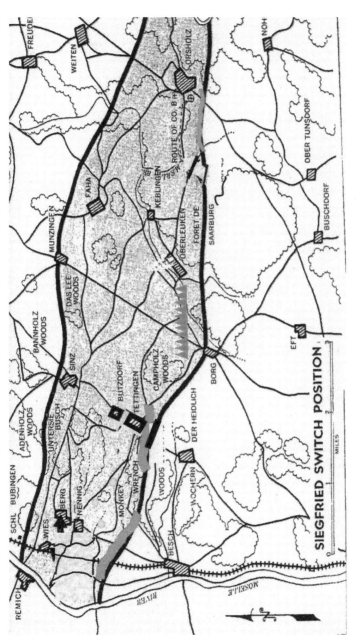

The Siegfried Switch Line

The 12-mile-long defensive area facing the 94th was two to three miles wide at places and included a 10-foot- deep tank trap ditch at its front. Behind the ditch was a line of dragon's teeth that was composed of several rows of staggered, three-foot-high concrete pyramids designed to hang up tracked vehicles so their treads could not get traction.

Behind these frontline defenses were twelve fortified villages distributed throughout the Triangle and each one was full of German soldiers. Between the villages were numerous concrete pillboxes of different sizes and designs manned by German troops from the villages. Strategically placed among these manned defenses were minefields protecting the approaches to them.

The tank ditches and dragon's teeth were not serious impediments to our forces once our Infantry was able to penetrate them because our Engineers either bridged them or used bulldozers to fill them in where necessary. The German soldiers in the villages and pillboxes backed up by German artillery on the hill behind their lines were the real problem.

A major advantage for the Germans was that they held the high ground of the Borg-Munzingen-Ridge at the rear of their defensive area requiring the 94th's troops to maneuver only at night. This was an especially difficult, one-sided problem until the 94th discovered it could observe the Germans' daylight movements as well, from the hills on the other side of the Moselle.

Tettingen[2]

Although the German advances during the first few weeks of the Battle of the Bulge were stopped near the end of December, the Battle of the Bulge continued until the 28th of January, while the Allies eliminated the German penetrations by pushing them back to their original positions, a difficult, time consuming effort that would take a month. Consequently, it was decided by the 3rd Army Commander that the 94th should not get involved in any major fighting. Therefore, our division was restricted to battalion-sized attacks. Our Division Commander, General Maloney decided to proceed with these attacks after about a week of reconnaissance patrols.

The First Battalion of the 376th Regiment was assigned the first attack on January 14, 1944 against the village of Tettingen, located about two and a half miles east of the Moselle. After an early morning artillery barrage the GIs crossed the tank ditch and the dragon's teeth, and attacked with A Company on the left of town and C Company on the right. The town was taken within an hour with twenty-three prisoners captured.

The regimental commander decided to exploit this attack by pushing ahead to the next town, Butzdorf. This additional attack was quickly organized and soon Butzdorf also was captured as well as the "half-way house" between Tettingen and Butzdorf. A one-mile salient was made into the Switch Line and the Germans had to retaliate.

That very night a battalion of the German 416th Infantry Division attacked the Tettingen and Butzdorf salient from the west side.[3] The GIs called for artillery and mortar support mowing down many of the attackers. Enemy troops entered Tettingen, but the GIs were able to drive them out. Some 300 of the 400 attackers were either killed, wounded, or captured, quite a victory for the young 94th's soldiers.

Nennig[4]

One day following the capture of Tettingen, the Third Battalion, 376th Regiment was assigned to capture Nennig, Weis, and Berg, three villages near the Moselle River west of Tettingen. Our engineers were able to clear mines from a path along the Moselle and the GIs of K Company followed it at night. They then had to wade through some freezing streams slowing them down and making them late getting to the jump-off point at dawn, so a smoke screen had to be laid down to hide their movement. In the confusion caused by the smoke, K Company attacked Nennig from the rear which turned out to be to their advantage, allowing them to capture the town easily, taking many prisoners.

Unfortunately, one of K Company's platoons got lost and attacked the village of Weis by mistake, suffering many casualties. L Company subsequently attacked and captured Weis after laying down an artillery barrage.

L Company's Third Platoon then captured the village of Berg and its castle. A German counterattack was repulsed with the loss of sixty of the 100 or so attackers. Charles Remington, my buddy from basic training was one of the heroes who repulsed that counterattack.

These attacks by the Third Battalion, 376th made another deep salient into the Siegfried Switch Line; consequently, the Germans repeatedly counterattacked over the next few days but were driven off sustaining heavy losses.

Meanwhile the Second Battalion[5] secured the area between Tettingen and Nennig capturing several pill boxes and made contacts with units from the First and Third Battalions while undergoing continuous artillery barrages and repulsing numerous counterattacks.

German Counterattack at Tettingen

Because of the 94th's penetrations into the Triangle the German Commander called for help and was re-enforced by units from the German's Eleventh Panzer Division. While this was going on, the 302nd Infantry Regiment relieved the 376th Regiment in both Nennig and Tettingen.

On the morning of January 20th soon after the 302nd was in position, the Eleventh Panzer Division attacked the Tettingen-Butzdorf area[6]. The initial attacks were directed at Butzdorf where the GIs fought valiantly but eventually were forced to abandon that village.

The Panzers then attacked Tettingen. The GIs were ready for them and mowed down the German Grenadiers. Simultaneously the German tanks blasted the town as they roamed the streets firing at GI occupied houses. The GIs responded by firing bazookas from cellar windows, knocking out many German tanks.

Encounter at the Aid Station

During this battle our platoon was moved to Tettingen as potential reinforcements.[7] Standing knee-deep in snow the GIs in our machine-gun platoon were spread out in an open field just behind Tettingen.

None of us knew what lay ahead that day. All I knew was that I was not feeling well. While standing in the snow I came down with a case of diarrhea. I went some distance away and did what was necessary. Returning to my squad, I reported to its leader that I was not feeling well. I received permission to go to an Aid Station in the rear of the village where a Medic gave me some paregoric, a WW II version of Imodium, and told me to lie down on a cot. I lay there for about half an hour until I began to feel better.

During this time, I realized the Aid Station contained mostly wounded German prisoners. One of them asked me for a cigarette by simply saying, "Cigaretten?"

I was stunned speechless. A feeling of tightness occurred in my throat as I was seized with indignation. I did not smoke, nor did I carry cigarettes, but even if I had some cigarettes, I certainly would not have given any to that German soldier. Here was the enemy, someone who had recently been trying to kill our guys, and he wanted a cigarette from me!

At last, I found my voice and mumbled one of the few German words I knew, "Nix." I was surprised at my reaction. I had no idea I had that much hate in my heart and as a result I have never forgotten that two-word conversation, "Cigaretten?"

"Nix!"

Returning to my unit, I learned that the Germans had been driven out of Tettingen without the need for our platoon. With sighs of gratitude, we returned to our previous position in a reserve area.

Orscholz

On January 19, the 1ˢᵗ Battalion of our 301ˢᵗ Regiment was chosen to make the next attack on the village of Orscholz[7] on the far-right flank of our division's position. The 2ⁿᵈ Battalion 301ˢᵗ placed Company H on the left of the 1ˢᵗ battalion to guard their flank.

In the middle of the night our machine gun section was taken to the top of a snow-covered hill and ordered to dig in. We used small charges of explosives to break through the frozen crust of the ground. We then dug holes for the machine guns and foxholes for the riflemen. My hole was some distance down the slope of the hill. I noticed that it was relatively warm down in that hole simply because I was out of the wind.

There was nothing down that hillside but beautiful smooth snow as far as the eye could see. Far to the right there was a forest. We took turns on guard and when off guard duty we stayed in a stone house behind the top of the hill. We never saw the enemy. Early in the morning we heard a cacophony of noise on the right of our position from the battle being waged at Orscholz. We could hear screaming, shouting, rifle, machine gun and artillery fire but we had no idea what was happening.

Later our captain related that the First Battalion's Company B was able to sneak into the vicinity of Orscholz, but Company A ran into a German minefield and was unable to support Company B's attack.

The mine explosions alerted the Germans and as the battle progressed, Company A was decimated after which Company B was surrounded. Those who were left surrendered. It was a first-class debacle. Captain Caywood reported that the First Battalion's commander was relieved of his command because he would not keep attacking. Our division history says he was killed by artillery fire. Who knows?

Sometime later our Captain also told us that General Patton was not happy about the surrender of Company B. Patton brought all the officers of our regiment together and told them that there would be no more surprise attacks. The next time we attacked there would be a large artillery barrage with corps as well as division artillery, airplanes and everything else that could be mustered to assist the attackers.

Letter Home—January 22, 1945
"Germany"

Dear Mom and Dad,

Hello, folks! Notice the new title. At least we are not going backwards. They allowed us to say a few things and our location in Germany is one of them. I cannot say exactly where of course but we are in General Patton's Third Army on the western front. I saw in the Stars and Stripes where the Russians are in Germany in the eastern front. We are hoping they finish this thing soon.

As usual this is not much fun and I say a prayer as each day passes. I'm doing my best. Combat is not anything like you read in the papers. They talk in miles and towns and generals and armies. I don't worry about who is winning what and why; with me it's "are my sox dry, did I get a letter today or is the ground hard to dig in?"

Well, take it easy back there. I'm OK. I'm in good spirits. We can still laugh at most everything, so do not worry. Love, Herbert

The 11th Panzer Attacks Nennig

On January 21, the Eleventh Panzer attacked Nennig,[8] capturing half of the town as well as Weis and Berg. The Second Battalion of the 376th Regiment was brought forward to help clear Nennig of the Germans.

At this point, the XX Corps sent an Armored Battalion from the US Eighth Armored Division to assist the 94th, but only for forty-eight hours. Together with the 94th they recaptured all the ground lost to the Eleventh Panzer Division. This was an enormous help because the Germans had tanks while the 94th did not.

Sinz

On January 25[9] a combination of units from the 302nd and 376th Regiments began an attack from the vicinity of Monkey Wrench Woods located between Nennig and Tettingen with the objective of attacking the village of Sinz[9]. The Third Battalion 376th received heavy casualties from German minefields necessitating its withdrawal. My friend Charles Remington, acting as lead scout for his platoon, managed to extricate himself from the minefield after mines went off behind him by retracing his footsteps in the snow.

The First Battalion 376th replaced the Third Battalion and side by side with the Second Battalion 302nd cleared the area south of the Nennig-Sinz road and across from Untersie Busch where the Germans had three tanks and some infantry. The Eighth Armored came down the Nennig-Sinz road battled with the Germans in Untersie Busch knocking out all three German tanks with the loss of seven of their own. The 376th then stormed across the road and captured Untersie Busch. The way was now clear for an attack on Sinz the next morning.

At this time the Third Battalion 376th replaced the First Battalion in Untersie Busche. German artillery hit the 3rd Bn. as it was moving up and Charles Remington, my pal, was wounded in the foot. He hopped a mile to the aid station with the help of another wounded soldier.

As the 376th and the 302nd were about to attack Sinz with the 376th on the left and the 302nd on the right, the Germans attacked Untersie Busche so only the Second Battalion 302nd was able to attack Sinz. It was at this point that the 8th Armored Unit was sent back to Corps control. The 302nd GIs got into Sinz but had to withdraw, burning houses behind them to block the Germans' pursuit.

The 94th's Troops are rearranged.

With the loss of the 8th Armored Division's Task Force, the commander of the 94th decided to rearrange his units while making plans for future operations. Therefore, on January 31, 1945, the 301st Infantry Regiment took over the left side of the front and the 302nd was positioned on the right with the 376th in reserve.[10]

The 3rd Bn. of the 301st was placed on the left of the 301st 's area including the villages of Weis, Berg and Nennig and the Second Battalion, the one I was in, was positioned on the right including the villages of Butzdorf and Tettingen. The 1st Bn. was placed in reserve below Berg.

The next major operation called for the Second Battalion 301st to seize Sinz and Bannholz Woods behind Sinz. But prior to that the First Battalion 301st was to capture Schloss (castle) Bubingen on January 28, which they did. This Schloss had been a German Observation Post and launch point for numerous counterattacks.

Also, Campholz Woods[11] located just west of Tettingen, that contained pillboxes, anti-tank ditches and dragon's teeth had to be taken to remove it from being used against the 94th during future operations. This task was assigned to C Company, 302nd Inf. Reg. but before the operation was completed, E, F, and G Companies of the Second Battalion became involved.

Letter Home—January 27, 1945
"Germany"

Dear Mom and Dad,

Well, it snows and it snows and then it snows again. Great life! It rains all fall and snows all winter. January is almost gone; however, maybe it will be dry next month before it rains all spring.

Do not worry about me being out in the cold too much. I live in a house at present and we have a stove to keep the room warm. No use living outside when there is a German house available.

It's not hard being a doughboy if you have a warm place to sleep. Of course, we never know where we will be from one day to the next and when you do sleep out, the hole you dig for protection keeps you out of the wind and is warmer than sleeping on the top of the ground.

There is a good half a foot of snow on the ground and I do not relish sleeping out at all, but then there is a war on isn't there. When this happens, I've got two blankets which I fold in my sleeping bag. The bag with its water-repellent cover and wool liner is equivalent to two more blankets. We always sleep with all our clothes on, so we keep this side of freezing.

As it is now, sleeping inside a house, I do not even use blankets. We keep the stove going with German coal and German wood. No sign of scorched earth here.

I had a letter from you dated January 8. Glad to know everyone is well. I am the same. I hope Tom writes me. I do not want to send a letter to Corsica if his APO has changed. I haven't received an answer from John yet. I hope to soon. Yes, I had a package from the MacKays sometime before Christmas. I mentioned it then. Maybe my letter went down to Davy Jones.

We are having steak for dinner so I must close now. If there is anything you want to know, then just ask. I can always give you a yes or no although I cannot tell you myself. I'm okay. I just shaved. I feel good. So long for now.

Love, Herbert.

PS: We were issued hoods which cover our head, neck, and chest and new boots and thick socks.

CHAPTER 31

PRELUDE TO THE BATTLE FOR SINZ

Pfc Herb Ridyard's Personal Story

Precious Lord take my hand, lead me on, let me stand,

I am tired, I am weak, I am worn;
Thru the storm, thru the night, lead me on to the light:
Take my hand, Precious Lord, lead me home.

The 94th Division was determined to capture the fortified village of Sinz and the area just beyond called Bannholz Woods. The rearrangement of the regiments was done in such a way that the 2nd Battalion, 301st was in position to carry out the attack, their first attack, my first attack.

Our Battalion Commander, Colonel Francis H. Dohs' plan of attack, a plan of which I had no knowledge at the time, was that G Company would move along the Sinz-Bubingen Road and assault Sinz while F Company jumped off from Untersie Busche, crossed the open ground to the west of Sinz and attacked Bannholz Woods located behind Sinz. E Company would be held in reserve[1].

In preparing for the attack our Division History tells us that E Company of the Second Battalion was moved into Untersie Busche just north of the Sinz-Bubingen Road and to the west of Sinz. F Company was to replace E Company the night before the attack. The first and second squads of H

Company's first heavy machine gun platoon were assigned to support F Company in the Untersie Busche area, while the third and fourth squads were moved to the wooded hill southwest of Sinz.[2] By now the reader should know that yours truly was in the third squad.

Without any knowledge of what was planned or why, I quite vividly remember our move to the hill near Sinz. We had been on the right flank of the division for weeks, ever since the Orsholz battle, at a town called Buschdorf, not to be confused with Butzdorf. Then on the last day of January 1945, H Company's third and fourth machine gun quads were loaded on a truck and transported to an area south of Nennig where we got off, retrieved our equipment and began marching in columns of two, north to Nennig. It was a lovely evening with a light snow falling. At another time and place it would be described as heavenly.

We entered the Siegfried Switch Line by crossing a small bridge over the tank ditch and then hiked along a passageway through the multiple rows of dragon's teeth.

After a short march we entered the village of Nennig. The stone buildings showed the battle scars of bullets and artillery shells. Walls were pock marked, windows were smashed and in some cases roofs and walls had collapsed. Any thoughts of beauty were put aside.

We came to a road intersection and turned right, parallel to the front line. On our left next to the road was a steep embankment just below several stone houses. The embankment was covered with a row of dead German soldiers who were obviously gunned down during one of the many recent, failed German counterattacks[3] intended to retake the town.

Although shocked by this scene, we had no time to dwell on it, and continued to march about a mile out of town where we left the road and turned right crossing into a foot-deep, snow covered field. We then moved single file into a wooded area where it was necessary to follow the GI in front of you. Wandering off the trail could take you into a minefield. As we hiked up-hill the footing was treacherous, because under the snow, the ground was covered with branches, rocks and other forest debris. In spite of my best efforts, I tripped and fell forward into the snow. As I tried to recover my footing, I discovered I had tripped over a dead German soldier buried in the snow, an unforgettable shock for a nineteen-year-old and one remembered to this day.

Eventually we reached the top of the hill, the position we would occupy for several days. From the edge of the woods the ground dropped off steeply. We could see the village of Sinz below. It was a scene from hell! Fires were burning in the portion of the town nearest to us and a US Army Tank and a Jeep were burning part way down the hill. I thought, "Who is winning this war anyway? "

We had no way of knowing what had happened prior to our arrival upon the scene, but in hindsight it must have resulted from the Second Battalion 302nd's aborted attack[4]. The US Army tank was most likely one from the Eighth Armored Division.

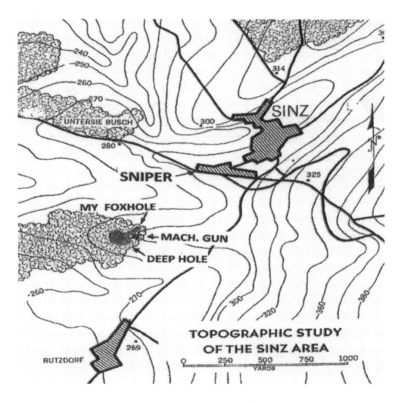

Our MG Position Near Sinz

In the forest at the top of the hill just inside the tree-line, we found two holes already dug, next to each other and covered with logs. Each hole was big enough for four men. With six men per squad and two men per squad on guard duty around the clock, these were perfect sites for our two squads. The fourth squad took over the hole facing the front, the third squad took over the dugout at the rear. The logs formed a common roof over the two depressions but there was a dirt partition between them. I never saw inside the other hole but ours had German ammo boxes for a floor with 88 mm lettering on them. It appeared that Germans had dug these holes. We never took the time to look in the boxes, we just assumed they were empty. Do not laugh. We were happy to get in that hole out of the cold and have a dry floor to lie down on.

Quickly we settled into the usual around the clock guard duty, two men at a time, two hours-on, four-off. Sgt. Lyons assigned Ryan to guard with McLain, Lamparella with yours truly and Lyons stood guard duty with that ne'er do well, Driscoll. I told you before that Lyons was a good guy.

Our squad stood guard at our machine gun position that was about six feet from our hole. The gun was dug into the side of a huge crater-like hole about 6 feet from the tree line at the edge of the hill. I never liked this position because there was no protection for our backs in case a mortar shell dropped into the crater.

Later, Platoon Leader Lieutenant Walter Mulhall raised an issue that the gun position was too far from the edge of the hill. However, because it was freezing and the place was covered with snow, we wanted no part in moving and digging in the gun at another spot.

When not on guard, we spent time in the hole eating, sleeping, and shooting the bull. We had K rations for breakfast, dinner and supper. Each box of rations resembled a Cracker-jack box containing a small tuna fish sized can as the main entrée. These cans contained scrambled eggs and ham for breakfast, cheese for dinner, and hash for supper. The rest of the box contained several crackers, a cookie for dessert, small packages of powdered coffee, chocolate, lemonade to drink, and a small pack of cigarettes. My cigarettes were traded for candy. We also had some "D" rations, a very hard chocolate bar.

Overtime I learned that if I felt constipated, I ate some hash and if my bowels were a little loose the cheese took care of it. I wondered if our rations were designed that way.

Because our squad was assigned a Jeep with a trailer, we were able to carry extra equipment not available to the rifle companies. Consequently, we always had a small gasoline stove to heat up cans of food after piercing them with a small GI can opener. Our favorite drink, hot coffee, was made in canteen cups, then enjoyed with a "D" bar as a tasty dessert after softening it over the stove. The heating of rations one at a time for each person was time consuming, so you can imagine we spent a lot of time on meals.

Even with two soldiers on guard duty at all times, it was tight sleeping in the holes; however, the tight quarters proved to be a good thing because the combined body heat helped keep us warm. Waking or sleeping we wore all our clothing and shared our blankets.

Standing guard on that snowy hill was a different matter. It was extremely cold outside, especially at night. Guards were sure to be bundled up to withstand the frigid temperature while keeping alert for the entire two-hour shift. The period of two hours seemed to last forever until we were able to crawl back into our hole.

Guard duty consisted of visually scanning the surroundings by rotating one's head back and forth, looking and listening, listening and looking, for the enemy who might try to sneak up on us at any moment. It was very tedious. I found myself counting to 100 over and over and over to pass the time.

One night on guard duty I was contemplating the situation. We did not know where any other GIs were located. There did not seem to be anybody around but us, not on the right nor on the left. No one ever told us anything. We never saw Capt. Caywood, Lieutenant Mullhall or Platoon Sergeant Parobek while we were stationed on that hill.

During the day there was some smoke laid on the hill far off to the right. We heard rifle fire in that direction, but who was firing? We had no idea. This lack of information started to get to me.

I began to wonder, "How did Mrs. Ridyard's little boy Herbert end up on the front line with no one between him and the enemy? There are only twelve of us here to hold this hill, to do or die in this forsaken place. I know there are at least 13 million servicemen in uniform. Where are they all?" If you think I was feeling sorry for myself, you would be right; however, there was nothing to be done about it but to soldier on.

During daylight hours a German sniper in one of the houses in Sinz started taking potshots at us. We could see an open window in one of the nearest houses but never saw the sniper. Wherever he was, he apparently had a clear view of our position. I do not know whether the fourth squad had a problem with him, but every time one of us got out of our hole during the daytime, the sniper shot at us. When it was my turn to go on guard duty, I would brace myself on the edge of the hole and throw myself out and over to the crater in a flash of movement keeping low to the ground. It was only a matter of feet to the crater. As I moved, I heard the snap of a rifle bullet as it passed by, at least four different times.

Don't ask why we never dug a trench between our hole and the crater. In hindsight that would have been the smart thing to do, but a trench would have exposed our hole to shrapnel coming from that direction. Some thought and effort on how to dig a zig-zag trench would possibly have solved the problem.

For some unknown reason, we never even discussed means of retaliating against the sniper. We obviously did not want to start our own private war.

One day we learned by phone that Staff Sergeant Bill Tornfeldt, our section leader, was coming to see us. Yes, we had phones especially when we were in a position for more than a few days, thanks to the busy US Army wiremen. "Windy three" was our phone's call sign.

Tornfeldt was supposedly coming to tell us about Lieutenant Mulhall's decision to move our squad's machine gun position toward the front edge of the hill, so that we would have a better field of fire if the Germans attacked up the hill. On the other hand, we thought moving it there would expose us to observation by the Germans. We did not like that idea.

We were worried about Tornfeldt's visit because he might not know the danger presented by the sniper. He had never been to our position; therefore, we kept constant watch for him, looking over the edge of the hole back toward the rear of the woods in the direction Tornfeldt would be coming. When we saw him coming, we all yelled, "Get down! Get down!" Tornfeldt started running and took a belly flopper slide in the snow. When his face came over the edge of our hole, he wore a big grin and said, "Lieutenant Mulhall has been shot.[5] We don't have to move the machine gun." We all cheered.

I have fond memories of that moment, partially because on the frontline you need a certain sense of humor that no one else can appreciate and partially because I never really liked Lt. Mulhall for putting me on latrine duty back on the ship crossing the channel.

We later learned that Mulhall had been wounded in the arm, your basic "million-dollar wound" that could get you sent to the rear or perhaps home—in either case, potentially saving your life. Everyone wanted one of those.

A day or two after we arrived at our snowy position on the hill above Sinz, the powers that be came up with a great idea. In spite, of every precaution, frostbite and trench foot took their toll in casualties among the frontline GIs. Consequently, each company was ordered to set up rest-houses in their area where, each night, one man from each squad could go to get dry socks and shoes, hot food, warm blankets, and a night's rest in a cellar not right on the front line.[6]

Unbeknownst to us, the powers that be also knew that the 94th was battling the Germans over in Campholz Woods[7] and it was taking longer than planned. This was the reason for our staying put until that battle ended before we initiated our attack on Sinz. That also accounted for the smoke screen seen off to our right. They just loved to keep us in the dark.

In our squad, Sergeant Lyons chose Ryan and Mclain to go back to the rest area for the first two nights. The third night, February 4, was my turn. As I reached Company's headquarters in Wochern after walking back through the woods, I met First Sergeant Roger Keith who simply said, "You're getting a special break. You have been chosen to get a forty-eight-hour rest." The next thing I knew I was on a truck with a bunch of other guys and driven many miles to the rear.

We arrived at a large facility, probably a French Army camp, and were taken to a large tent with showers. After surrendering all my clothes, I was able to get my one and only hot shower in eight months of combat. After a dusting of a disinfectant (possibly DDT), new uniforms were issued. Later, I would get my clean uniform back. I know because it had my name sewn in it.

Then I was sent to a huge mess hall where I had a wonderful hot meal and the largest dish of ice cream and apple pie I had ever seen. We all slept on cots with warm blankets in a barracks-like building with no guard duty, nor the fear of enemy mortars or artillery. It was like heaven except that I was not comfortable on the cot. Believe it or not after months of it, I preferred sleeping on the ground.

The next day I had a haircut and shave from a real barber, three more square meals, entertainment by a USO show, time to write letters and just relax. It was soon time to board the trucks for the ride back to the front.

As a little side story, one of the letters I wrote was to Doctor Jenny Werst. I needed to write to her because my high school friend Weston Werst, a private in the 95th Infantry Division who had been wounded and was recuperating in England, had written two letters to me saying that his mother would not believe him when he told her he was OK. Therefore, I wrote a brief letter explaining that I was happy that Weston was feeling better. I included Weston's letters confirming what I was saying.

Weston's story is worth repeating here for historical reasons if nothing else. Weston's Regiment was attacking the fortresses at Metz, France, when he was wounded by shrapnel in the back of his head. One of his buddies pulled him into a hole until the medics came to take care of him. He traveled on one of four litters mounted on a Jeep with three other wounded soldiers. The patient above Wes was bleeding and his blood dripped down on Weston's chest. When they reached the 95th Division Clearing Hospital, Weston received immediate attention because he was thought to have a chest wound.

After operating on his head wound, Weston was found to be blind, paralyzed and suffering from a bad headache. He was transferred to a French hospital in Paris for a few weeks and then sent to England. There, a nurse tried to get him to move his legs by having two medical orderlies hold him upright while she moved his legs, all to no avail. Can you imagine what was going through his mind as he suffered from his wound. I can't.

Days later, a new doctor examined Weston in a darkened room, looking into his eyes with a small flashlight. Weston told me after the war that the doctor simply said, "They didn't get it all out." He then pulled the stitches out, releasing a lot of fluid. Weston's headache felt better immediately. A subsequent operation removed more shrapnel and Weston eyesight was restored and his paralysis healed, a true medical miracle.

That evening, February 6, 1945, I arrived at H Company headquarters in Wochern which was about a mile and a half behind our machine gun position on the hill above Sinz. To my surprise, G Company was lined up on the cobblestone street. Almost immediately I caught sight of my friend John Gardy whom I had not seen for eight months, ever since we left Camp McCain, Mississippi.

John was carrying a huge rectangular communication's radio on his back. He was obviously his Platoon Leader's Radioman. After shaking hands, he informed me they were going to attack Sinz in the morning. He was smiling but he was obviously scared (who wouldn't be) for he said, "I am going to have to be Superman to survive this." Then, for safekeeping he gave his Mickey Mouse wristwatch to a mutual friend, a company clerk in G Company who would not be involved in the attack. That was the last time I saw John Gardy. Two days later he was listed as Missing in Action. It breaks my heart to think about it.

Back in Camp McCain when they split up our ASTP battalion, I had no idea how fortunate I was to be assigned to H Company rather than a rifle company; that is, companies E, F, and G in our battalion. Until the attack on Sinz I did not realize that the rifle companies would be the first sent to seize enemy positions followed by the heavy weapons company moving into those positions to help repel the inevitable German counterattack.

Prior to this time no one had explained this to me. Possibly the men who had been with H Company for a year before I joined, knew about this procedure but it was never discussed in my presence. Do not let me mislead you. H Company personnel encountered enough danger to last a lifetime, but it was not the same for us as it was for the riflemen who had to cross the open fields to reach their objectives and who had to capture houses with the enemy inside firing at them.

CHAPTER 32

THE BATTLE FOR SINZ

Pfc Herb Ridyard's Personal Story Continues.

had never been in an attack. I have told you about the many battles in which the various 94th battalions were engaged during January 1945. The Battle of the Bulge was officially over but no matter, in the days ahead, the war was about to get more personal for me. Would I measure up?

After saying hello and goodbye to John, I reported to First Sergeant Roger Keith. He assigned two replacements to me and directed me to take them to Milano Parobek, my platoon sergeant who was now platoon leader replacing Lieutenant Mulhall, who had been wounded.

This assignment would lead to an entirely new role for me in H Company. I would not return to my squad again until the war in Europe was almost over. The change from ammo bearer to guide was probably not planned. I just happened to be available after my return from the rest area and I filled a need.

Keith said I should follow the white tape through the woods. It would lead me to Parobek's hole. The white tapes were put there by the engineers to mark the path they had cleared of mines.

I thought there would be two parallel white tapes marking the sides of the path. There was only one! Oh Baby! What do I do now? Well, when in doubt, improvise. I told the two new guys to follow me and keep as close to the tape as they could. Eventually, I found Parobek's hole. It was huge like a small room and covered with logs. I wondered who dug it?

I had not seen that loudmouth Parobek since we had gone overseas. He never came near our positions at the front. It appeared to me he was looking out for number one. Perhaps I did not understand his role in the Platoon, just like so many other things in the army.

Parobek welcomed me and thanked me for the two replacements. He had been expecting them. I could see he had a phone, so he knew what was going on. Parobek then gave me a portable battery-operated radio called a Walkie-Talkie, high tech for those days. I had never seen one before, so he showed me how to operate it and made certain I understood. I started to warm up to him.

Then he instructed me to report to the Second Platoon's leader and be his guide. I would find him on the hill near Sinz where I had been before, only further back in the woods. "Simply follow the phone wire," he said. I never asked him, "What's a guide?"

As I left Parobek's hole, I found that it was raining and had turned pitch dark in the woods. Wonderful! What if an artillery shell had shattered the wire? Lucky for me it had not. I also wondered if the second platoon had trigger-happy guards on duty, for I had not been given the password.

Quickly donning my poncho, I climbed up the hill and through the woods with one hand sliding along the phone wire, my rifle and radio over my other shoulder. Since vision in that dark and rainy night was no more than a foot or so in front of me it was little wonder that I accidently fell into a hole, fortunately with no injury. I continued to the top of the hill and found the Second Platoon hunkered down in their ponchos. The idiots had not posted guards.

The wire led me straight to the platoon leader's tent. I reported to him and let him know I was to be his guide. He welcomed me in a friendly manner, appearing to me to be a nice guy.

I regret I do not remember his name. We seldom saw our platoon leaders back in the States. They seemed to keep their distance. Perhaps that was part of the mystique of rank they had been taught. I did not know my own platoon leader, Lieutenant Mulhall, well at all and certainly did not know any of the other platoon leaders. You can see this is not like it is in the movies.

The 2nd Platoon was located a good distance away from the edge of the woods where our squad had been located previously. I wondered if they were still there (in fact they were not). Time passed quickly that night. Early in the morning of February 7, our artillery started to bombard Sinz. We could hear the outgoing swishes of the shells overhead. It must be H-hour for the attack.

At the sound of the artillery, the lieutenant told his men to seek cover because he knew the Germans would return fire. He and I and the others lay down in a shallow ditch. Fortunately, the German artillery passed over our heads, looking for GIs somewhere else, but a piece of shrapnel did land near me. It must have traveled a long distance because it hit the ground with little impact and when I picked it up it did not feel hot. Its energy was spent.

I showed it to the Lieutenant and he immediately reacted and said we need to find better protection. I told him that I knew where there were some holes near the forward edge of the woods. He said, "Let's go". He and the rest of the GIs followed me through the woods. We stumbled around a bit until I found the edge of the woods where it was not so dark. I kept going in the general direction of the tip of the forest. I found my hole by falling into it. I was getting good at falling into holes and not getting hurt. Fortunately for us my 1st Platoon buddies were no longer there. Later I learned they had been moved to Untersie Busche.

The Lieutenant, two others and I crept into the hole. The other members of the Second Platoon hid in the large crater hole or wherever they could find protection.

We huddled together in this rather well protected spot and heard someone talking in the next hole. It became obvious that an artillery observer was using that hole. He seemed to know a lot about what was happening for we heard him say G Company was making progress with their attack in the town, but some portion of F Company, assigned to attack Bannholz Woods beyond Sinz, had been pinned down in the open ground before they reached Bannholz.

Suddenly, I received a message on my Walkie Talkie. Whoever it was, told me to come to the edge of the woods. I crawled over as fast as I could. When I got there, I was told to look for a blackened building at the edge of town nearest me. I looked, saw it and said, "Yes, I see it." The voice said, "That's where you are supposed to come." I immediately returned to our hole and told the lieutenant that we were supposed to come to the blackened building on the edge of town.

The lieutenant ordered everyone to load up their machine guns and other equipment and follow us into town. I led the way down the right side of the hill. The rain had melted the snow, so we were on firm frozen ground. As we neared the blackened building, I noticed some black boxes here and there sitting on top of the ground. I turned to the lieutenant and said, "Those things look like mines." I imagined that the mines had been buried in the snow but now were completely exposed. The lieutenant ordered his men to line up and follow us. I led them through the minefield and soon we were all in the blackened building which turned out to be a barn with stone walls.

The young man who called me, came over, and said, "You were not supposed to come until night-time." I recognized his face but not his name and recalled that he was a member of the Second Platoon. My first thought was that I had made a big blunder.

Seeing that Captain Caywood was right next to me, I faced him and said, "Sir, I brought the second platoon." Without a word to me, Caywood immediately turned to our battalion commander, Colonel Dohs, and said, "Colonel I have four more machine-guns." Colonel Dohs said to him, "Get them in position." It was obvious to me that they were pleased to have four more machine guns to defend the town.

Thinking back over the situation I believe this was one of the luckiest days of my life. That idiot from the second platoon had said, "That's where you are supposed to come." He left out "Wait until nighttime."

Think about it. If we had come at night, we probably would not have seen the minefield and what if the rain had not melted the snow. I do not want to think about that too much.

Miscommunications during a battle are sometimes called the fog of war.

Some would say we were saved by dumb luck, but not me. I give full credit to the Holy Spirit!

If you still think it was just luck, consider these additional facts. An hour or so earlier, the German artillery stopped F Company in an open field. Why did that same artillery not see us coming down that hill in broad daylight, lined up in single file, a tactical no-no? And where was that pesky sniper or one of his buddies? Perhaps G Company was keeping them busy? Thank you, Holy Spirit.

Captain Caywood ask me to stay with him. He planned to use me as his Runner or in laymen's terms, messenger. I followed him to the basement of the house next door where Second Battalion Headquarters was located. At last I was in a place where I would know what was going on!

This house was one of the few on the south side of Sinz-Bubingen Road. Almost all of the village was on the north side of the road toward the German lines. There was only one main street through the center of the village. It was perpendicular to Sinz-Bubingen and it ran all the way through town to the German positions in Bannholz Woods.

At this point in my story a brief account of the battle for Sinz is in order to help the reader understand what was happening around me on that first day of the battle. My account is a composite of what I overheard from the artillery observer on the hill above Sinz, what I heard in battalion headquarters and from veterans at 94th reunions and as recorded in the history of the 94th Infantry Division in WW II.[1]

The pre-dawn artillery fire sent the Germans into their basements and gave the GIs cover. As planned G Company attacked with one platoon along the Bubingen-Sinz Road parallel to the front and another down the tank-trap ditch parallel to the front. They entered the town in the same area on the southwest corner of Sinz, using standard tactics of tossing grenades into windows or doorways before entering each building, all the time dodging machine gun and rifle fire from enemy snipers. This approach garnered many prisoners.

According to a friend in G Company, early in the fighting a young German soldier shot one of G Company's sergeants and then tried to surrender. The sergeant's squad members were angry and did not give him that option.

A good friend, Tom Smith, involved in the attack, says his squad took a number of prisoners from one house and he asked them, "Wo ist Officier?" The prisoners said, "In den Kellern." Tom asked the Germans in the cellar to surrender and they refused, so they threw some grenades into the basement and out came the Germans with their hands up, not exactly like the supermen the Germans were touted to be.

As time passed, the battle intensified and G Company's progress was slowed. They had to call in artillery on each individual house before attacking it. Consequently, the battalion commander added E Company to the attack.

E Company approached Sinz up a draw that lay along the left (west) side of town and attacked the buildings at the far end of town, thus getting in the rear of the Germans that were holding up G Company By the end of the day both companies cleared all the German houses except for one at the far end of town. Hundreds of prisoners were taken at the cost of many young GIs.

The battalion commander ordered his men to capture that last house. The GIs were ready to attack from a house across the street when suddenly they were attacked by the Germans firing Panzerfausts (German bazookas) which killed a number of GIs. The US attack was postponed until the next morning, wherein the GIs found that the Germans had withdrawn from the house.

F Company had a more difficult time[2] because they had to attack across a large field west of Sinz, uphill with little cover. The reports I heard from the artillery observer in the next hole was that they were pinned down in that open field by German weapons. However, the truth is that some of F Company's men indeed entered their objective, Bannholz Woods, and were making progress clearing a part of the woods when German tanks counterattacked. F Company bazooka men tried to disable the tanks, but their rounds bounced off the tanks and soon they were ordered to withdraw.

Unfortunately, some men from F Company did not receive the order to withdraw so they spent much of the day hiding in the woods because the Germans and their tanks were everywhere. It was cold and they suffered greatly as they lay in the mud and ice water not daring to move for fear of being discovered. Unfortunately, the F Company men who had returned to Untersie Busche mistakenly said that any Americans still in Bannholz were dead; consequently, 94th artillery pounded the woods making things worse for our men still there. After dark the GIs managed to crawl past German guards and returned to Untersie Busche.

On the evening of the first day in Sinz, Captain Caywood asked me to see if the Second Platoon machine gunners were OK. It was dark as I made my way down the right or east side of Sinz to the house where they were located.

On my way I heard a frightening sound. The Germans were firing artillery shells at Sinz. Some of the shells had the usual "swish-swish" sound as they traveled through the air but there was also a weird, clanging, vibrating sound as some of the shells came over and when they hit their target there was a huge explosive "carrump," louder than any I had ever heard. I learned later that these weapons were multiple rockets the GIs called "Screaming Meemies." To me, they sounded like a giant had taken two pieces of railroad track and banged them together thus producing this strange clanging, vibrating noise. It is funny what your imagination will come up with. The good news is that they missed me and I was able to get into the second platoon's basement where I was told that everybody was OK. On my return trip, I heard more Screaming Meemies that missed me once again so that I was able to give the captain the good news.

That night before I retired into my blankets, I heard the officers making plans for continuing the attack on Bannholz Woods.[3] Four groups of twenty-five men each were to attack Bannholz from Sinz, supported by six tank destroyers. The four groups were to enter the woods during the night from the side nearest Sinz, dig in and destroy the German tanks with "Bangalore Torpedoes." The group on the left (nearest Sinz) was composed of 94th Commandos. On their right was a group from E Company and further on to the right were two groups from G Company They were the furthest from Sinz. My friend John Gardy was in one of G Company's groups as Lieutenant Christiansen's radio operator.

The commandos had two tank destroyers with them, but one was knocked out by a mortar. When they learned that tanks were advancing in their rear to cut them off, their tank destroyer with some infantry men clinging to its side pulled out of the woods. The other commandos withdrew as well.

The men of E Company were outflanked by the Germans, so they abandoned their tank destroyers and withdrew from the woods.

In the north part of the woods the two tank destroyers supporting G Company were destroyed by German tanks. I heard G Company's platoon leader, Lieutenant Christiansen asked to be allowed to withdraw because his position was becoming untenable[4], but Colonel Dohs ordered him to side-step his position. Then Christiansen reported that the tanks were moving along the line of GI foxholes and shooting into them[5]. The Germans killed or captured all these men. John Gardy, who probably helped Lieutenant Christiansen send those messages, was listed as missing in action.

One of the tank destroyer officers came to second battalion headquarters in the cellar where I was and reported what had happened. I think our regimental commander, Colonel Hagerty was present to hear his story. He said the German tanks came behind the US tank destroyers and destroyed all six of them. That was not entirely true, but in effect it was.

Second Bannholz was a disaster for our battalion. I remember hearing someone say at that time, "The only men that survived, ran away." Listening to all these communications in the cellar, I still did not know first-hand how bad it was. Later when we were in reserve, I heard more of the details. It seemed to me that once we knew there were a number of German tanks in Bannholz, we should have called off the attack. I think John Gardy died needlessly.

Sometime during the morning Captain Caywood asked me to go to Untersie Busche and see how the First platoon machine gunners were doing. He told me when I got to the woods, I would see a knocked out German tank and just beyond it I would find our H Company men.

I went upstairs and out the front of the house and saw and heard the German artillery shelling the Sinz-Bubingen road that I had to travel. The shelling was clearly intended to keep us off that main supply road. There was no question that I had to go. One does not say no to a captain.

I could see a low stone wall about a foot and a half high on the right side of the road, the side facing the Germans. That would be my only cover for quite a distance. Open ground lay on the other side of the wall all the way up to Bannholz Woods allowing the enemy to observe the road. Down the road beyond the wall and the open area was a German house where I could hide if I was able to make it that far.

Waiting until I heard a shell explode, I ran in a crouch about thirty feet as fast as I could and hit the dirt close to the base of the wall. Shells kept coming over periodically. I waited for another one to explode, tensed up and prepared to run. As soon as the next one exploded, I ran another thirty feet and hit the dirt near the wall. Then I waited for the next shell to explode and ran another distance and hit the dirt again. I repeated this process a number of times, finally reaching the distant house. Fortunately, I received no rifle fire.

I felt somewhat safe hidden from view behind the German house, but I was greeted by a horrible sight. Several dead Germans were lying in a shallow hole in front of the house. They were cut up, mangled and covered with huge blotches of blood. It was such a horrible mess that it is no wonder I do not remember how many Germans were there. They smelled awful, a sick sweet smell. I quickly decided that I had to get away from there and lost no time in doing just that.

Moving on down the road to the woods, I passed the knocked out German tank and soon found a small bunker with Sergeant Colvin inside. This bunker was a simple log cabin-like structure about three logs high. Bunkers of this type are used in areas where the ground is too hard to dig or, as in this case, the water table was too high to allow digging down more than a foot. They are covered with logs to prevent tree bursts from raining shrapnel down onto the GIs.

I crawled inside Sergeant Colvin's bunker and told him my mission. He told me everyone was all right. I did not stay around to find out for myself. I could not see anyone else as Colvin was in the rear of the woods and the other members of the platoon were undoubtedly at the front edge of the woods. I could have gone further to see my buddies in the third squad, but I did not want to take a chance of being shot by my own men or members of F Company, so I decided to get back with my news for the captain.

That of course, meant going back through the artillery shelling along the road, which I promptly did in the manner previously described. The captain was pleased to hear the good news. He did not question my message, so I settled down to rest on the cellar floor.

Suddenly, one of the officers in our cellar announced, "The Germans are getting ready to attack. All riflemen, outside!" A few other riflemen and I ran up the stairs. I went out the front door, where I could see across the street there was a wall on my left with fields beyond; to the right were some stone houses on both sides of the street leading through the village. I presumed that E and G Company men were in those houses.

Our building was set back about ten feet from the road. The building on my left jutted out to the edge of the street. I decided that house would give me better cover and a better view of the open field.

Moving toward that building, I saw an abandoned German machine gun lying on the ground. It had a stock like those on a rifle with a circular magazine on top. Initially I thought I could use it against the Germans but then realizing I did not know how I gave up that idea and moved quickly into the neighboring house. It was most likely a good thing I did not try to use it as the sound of that gun would have been recognized as German by our GIs and I could have been mistaken for the enemy.

In the house, I was alone, I have no idea where the others went and I feared looking out the window because I rationalized, if I could see the enemy, they could see me. However, I did look in spite of my thoughts and had a good view across the street, over the wall and up the field all the way to Bannholz Woods. I thought of repositioning myself across the street to take a firing position behind the wall. There I would have had a better view but no cover from German artillery. I stayed put.

Suddenly I saw the Germans pouring out of the woods running from left to right toward the far end of Sinz. When they were about halfway there our artillery exploded amongst them. It was devastating. Sooner than one could imagine, the attack was over. The remaining Germans ran back into the woods. The whole episode could not have lasted more than five minutes from the time we were ordered outside until the attack was over. My brain had been racing and the adrenaline was pumping but now I felt relief.

Soon thereafter, on February 9, or perhaps early the next day, our battalion was relieved by the Second Battalion, 376th Infantry Regiment. As we withdrew west along the Sinz-Bubingen Road toward Nennig, I recall seeing GIs from that battalion crouching in the ditch along the side of the road.

We were trucked to the town of Veckring, France, about twenty miles behind the lines. There we were billeted in a French Army Camp in buildings with marble floors. Since it was the middle of the night and we were very tired we simply lay down on the cold hard floor with all our clothes on and attempted to sleep.

We no sooner began to relax when a doctor came into the room in the dark and began to examine our feet. I suspect he or his assistant had a flashlight, but I do not remember seeing one. We were ordered to remove our boots and socks as he moved from soldier to soldier, checking feet. When he came to me, he took my pulse just behind my ankles. I do not remember the doctor saying anything so when he moved on to the next GI, I put my boots back on and went to sleep.

The next day we had time to wash up and relax. It was a sunny day. H Company had a meeting with Captain Caywood. There was a critique of the battle for Sinz and some discussion of the failure of our bazookas against the German tanks.

Later that day I was summoned to Captain Caywood's headquarters. Several of the sergeants were there. I remember one of their faces but not his name. He was smiling and he said that Captain Caywood's Recon Sergeant had been wounded. Captain Caywood asked if I would like to be recon sergeant. I was about to say yes, when we were interrupted by a Medic at the door who said that Private Ridyard was to report to the Aid Station. I asked Captain Caywood if I had to go. He simply nodded yes.

I was escorted to another building and told to sit on a marble bench in a large room, to take off my boots and socks and wait, which I did. It was very cold in the room, especially on the marble surface, so I laid my socks on the floor with my feet on top to protect them from the frigid floor. I sat there for a long time.

A sergeant wearing a Red Cross armband came along and asked what I was doing there. I replied, "I was told to sit here and wait." He left without saying anything. I continued to sit there. Finally, after another interminable period of time, a doctor showed up and examined my feet.

He did not ask me how I felt or if I had a problem. As a matter of fact, I do not think he said anything. He left me sitting there. Soon however, two medical orderlies came and carried me into an ambulance.

I have felt bummed out about that situation, ever since it happened, for more than one reason. First, because I was not given a choice in any of the proceedings. The truth is, my big toes had been somewhat numb, ever since that cold, thirteen-hour truck ride from Reims to Germany six weeks ago, but I had been very active on my feet, felt no serious discomfort walking and was able to do my best in performing my duties. If I had been given a chance to discuss this with the doctor, I would have at least been able to describe how I felt. And wouldn't it have been great to hear his reason for sending me to the hospital? Instead, I received total silence.

Second, the way the medics treated me by having me sit waiting with bare feet in that freezing cold building for over an hour was downright stupid. I am sure that was a major contributor to the Doctor sending me to the hospital. I was also stupid for sitting there without covering up.

Third, I lost my chance to be recon sergeant. I believe Captain Caywood recognized that I had done a good job as guide for the second platoon and as his Runner and that these performances led him to choose me to help him in the future while he was doing reconnaissance to select positions for his machine guns and mortars. Taking a line from Marlon Brando in the movie *The Waterfront*, "I coulda been a contender." I coulda been a recon sergeant.

Finally, having expressed my ill feelings concerning my treatment by the US Medical Corps, I have to own up to the fact, that the unnamed doctor I criticized, may very well have saved my life by taking me out of combat and I owe him my thanks.

Remembering that back in September during my baptism of fire when I prayed to the Lord to save me, perhaps the Holy Spirit was still working the problem.

CHAPTER 33

HOSPITALIZED

On February 10, 1945, the ambulance took me to a US Army hospital in Thionville, France, about thirty miles from the front. Signs on the walls indicated this medical unit was trained for chemical or gas casualties of which there were none. Most casualties like mine were due to frost bitten toes called Trench Foot.

I was provided a pair of pajamas and assigned a bed. The medical orderlies were very cordial but made it clear we were to stay off our feet. Most of the time was spent lying in bed reading and sleeping. The orderlies brought us our meals plus juice and snacks between meals.

The frost bite was treated several times a day with simple repetitive exercises that involved hanging our feet over the side of the bed for a few minutes, then on the bed, followed by up on the wall. Obviously, this was to stimulate blood circulation in our feet.

I'm not certain how long I was in the Thionville Hospital, perhaps three weeks. As our condition improved, we were permitted to visit the town and attend a play at a theater.

PERSONAL EFFECTS

Inventory of Personal Effects

5 April 1945
(Date)

Subject: Inventory of Personal Effects of:

Ridyard	**Herbert**		**Pfc**	**13193892**
(Last Name)	(First Name)	(Init)	(Rank)	(ASN)

To: Effects Quartermaster, ComZ, Depot Q-290, Folembray, France.

The above named individual of **Co H, 301 Inf, 94 Inf Div**
(Unit)
was reported **hospd** about **13 Feb** 1945.

Designated beneficiary_____

* *

Inventory of Effects

Wallet
membership cards & paper clippings
snapshots
2 94 patches
indent bracelet
religious book
german book
sewing bok

Money in the amount of **none** has been turned in to W.A.Cayer,
Lt. Col..FD (Finance O)
SN 211-019 . Form WDFD 38 inclosed.
I certify that the above items constitute all of the effects
secured by me, of the above named individual and that they were
forwarded to the Effects Depot by **truck** on _____1945.

US Military Cemetery:

ED IN B. ROSENZWEIG
1st Lt, QMC
94 Inf Div GRO

Pfc Herbert Ridyard's Personal Effects

When I entered the hospital in Thionville and was given pajamas to wear, I had no idea what happened to my uniform or the stuff I had in my pockets and did not particularly care, out of sight out of mind. When I returned to "normal," my uniform was returned clean as new but the stuff in my pockets was apparently sent to an Effects Depot by the Quartermaster Corps. Months later, they would be returned to me with a document listing my personal effects. As you can imagine my personal effects were not much to write home about. I don't remember anyone explaining to me what was going on. This was either another one of the many lack of communication episodes during my time in the army or else I just don't remember. The good news is that the US MILITARY CEMETERY item on the form is blank.

During the first week of March I was transferred to a convalescence hospital at Jarny-Conflans, France. To my surprise I found the rest of the third squad and others from our platoon were already there. Sergeant Lyons greeted me with open arms.

For some reason we never discussed why we were hospitalized. I do not think any of the group had been wounded so I assumed they all had trench foot, like me. You may recall I found Sergeant Colvin in a small log bunker in Untersie Busche because the highwater table prevented digging a foxhole. The rest of my squad was in that area also.

Our stay at this hospital was also about three weeks. Each morning we did some physical training, but otherwise there was little to do. I recall the weather was mild so most of the time was spent out of doors sitting on a hillside watching trains being assembled in the nearby trainyard. The yard had an incline to allow selected railroad cars to roll downhill by gravity along one of the various tracks to form a train. As they rolled into the car in front of them and locked together, there was a huge bang which became the excitement for the day.

The only other activity was the weekly medical inspection. Everyone lined up in a large building as the Doctor of the Day inspected us and determined if we were fit enough to return to duty. No one in his right mind wanted to go back to the front line so for several weeks we were relieved when it did not happen. Then came the magic day when it was announced that all of us would be given a chit saying, "Return to duty."

It was then Kosikowski made his hilarious plea, which he had been planning for weeks. He claimed he had a pain. When the doctor asked, "Where?" Kosikowski said, "Up and right" meaning the area of his heart. His direction for the pain never made sense to me, but it did not matter because his ploy did not work. Scary as the receipt of the RTDs was, Kosikowski's antics gave us a big laugh.

Meanwhile communications from my folks at home came to a halt, an unhappy situation and they began to receive letters marked "Hospitalized" and "Returned to Writers." It was clear that the mail system did not know where I was. That must have been upsetting to Mom and Dad. Hopefully, my letters to home gave them some assurance that I was all right although in the hospital.

My parents' letter marked "Hospitalized, Return to Writer"

In order to return to duty, we were sent to a Replacement Depot, sometimes referred to as a Repo-Depo, which would facilitate our move back to the 94th Division. We arrived there around the beginning of April but did not return to our outfit until April 25, when the war in Europe was almost over. The Army can hurry up when it needs to or take its good old time when it wants.

As I began writing this story, I must admit I had no memory of the Replacement Depot; however, in checking dates for my time in the two hospitals, I looked through the box of my letters home during WW II that my parents had saved for me and found six referring to the Replacement Depot. Memories sometimes do funny things.

According to my letters, when I got to the Repo-Depo, I thought I would have a speedy return to my outfit but was disappointed day after day. I was there long enough to have three passes, one to a large town with church services on Easter Day and time to enjoy an Easter Dinner with a juicy steak in a café. One would think that would be remembered.

I was able to read books, listen to a radio in the dayroom, and see movies from the US. This place resembled a resort.

Finally, I was given a seat on a train taking me home so to speak. It turned out to be a long ride. We traveled through France and Germany all the way to Cologne, Germany, where we stopped for the night. Cologne showed signs of severe damage due to our bombers. Some resourceful GI left the train and found an abandoned wine cellar and was generous with champagne.

The next day the train turned around, went back to France and headed north through Luxembourg and Belgium, finally turning east, crossing the Rhine River into the Ruhr region of Germany, delivering us to the little town of Mettmann, where Company H was now located.

CHAPTER 34

OCCUPATION DUTY IN METTMANN, GERMANY

The 94th Division moved from Krefeld across the Rhine river, because it was to perform occupation duty in the Dusseldorf Sector[1]. There the three Regiments were assigned the following areas of occupation: the 302nd Regiment, the city of Dusseldorf, the 376th Regiment, Wuppertal and the 301st Regiment, Mettmann. This movement was completed by April 25, 1945.

In these areas the 94th was responsible for the following: military government, security, foot, motorized and aerial patrols, curfew and travel restrictions, salvage of abandoned arms and equipment and caring for prisoners of war and displaced persons. Because prisoners of war were a danger to the German populace, US soldiers were assigned to guard German civilians. In addition, every residence was entered and searched for weapons, uniforms, Nazi flags and decorations, radio transmitters, binoculars, cameras, propagandic material and other pertinent contraband[2].

As a special function of the US Military Government, the 94th was required to identify Nazi party members, remove them from positions of authority and to oversee the organization of local governments with non-party members.

Another major task was to provide and protect food supplies for German civilians, displaced persons, both German and freed prisoners of war as well as US troops.

All these duties were to be carried out while obeying the Non-Fraternization Laws imposed by the US Military Government, one of the standing orders I found difficult to obey.

Searching German Houses

As the division was embarking on these assignments, I appeared upon the scene in Mettmann, was shown to my billets and immediately put to work searching German houses.[3] The procedure was as follows: one of our Sergeants along with several privates walked to the house to be searched and knocked on the door. When the occupant opened the door, the Sergeant read him or her the US military government Proclamation allowing us to search the premises. We then entered, the occupant obtained the bundle of keys, usually kept in the kitchen, and led us to each room where he or she would open each closet or dresser drawer with the appropriate key. We would physically look through everything therein.

Normally while searching we would spread out through the house, so the key holder was kept busy going ahead of us to open doors, etc. I found some interesting things during these searches. There was a magazine called "The Untermenchen" lying on a small bedroom table that showed the ugliest, dirtiest Jewish and Russian individuals you can imagine on the front page as well as the inside pages, along with the hovels they lived in. The accompanying story then proceeded to compare them with portraits of handsome, blonde German soldiers. The bias presented to the reader was so obvious it was laughable. Such propagandic lies could only be effective if they were all one was ever exposed to.

The same approach is found in modern day news presentations, day after day, when referring to current presiding heads of state, as biased news correspondents display their hate for the opposing party.

Another interesting item I found in a bedroom dresser drawer was a lovely little wooden box with a set of about twenty small Hitler Youth awards, each with a swastika symbol on it. The girl's parent, who was showing me around, said they were her daughter's, obviously hoping I would not take them, but of course it was necessary that I carry out my orders.

The last item that made an impression on me was a clothesline in the attic shown to me by the woman of another house. Hanging there were pieces of a German uniform taken apart at the seams. The woman explained her intentions were to make clothes for her *kinder* (children). I had to let that pass without question. I felt she deserved credit for being thrifty.

When we returned to our billets after the first day of searching, I was surprised to find one of the beds piled high with contraband from our searches. There were uniforms, weapons, Nazi flags, cameras, etc. I did not know whether any of this stuff was to be returned to the owners. Little did I know in my naiveté, all of the "contraband" would soon turn into "booty."

Over time I sent home two Zeiss Icon cameras, A Walther P-38 pistol with holster, a bolt action Mauser rifle, a small Hitler Youth knife, a belt with shoulder strap attached to a small caliber pistol, and a large Nazi flag.

Guarding Germans

After searching a number of homes, some of us were assigned to guard duty at the following places: the bakery, the butcher shop, and the potato warehouse plus a Jeep patrol of the surrounding farms. Normally, I had a regular, early morning and afternoon shift at the bakery, but once or twice I went on the Jeep patrol.

I observed that the Jeep patrollers had become familiar with the farmers on their route, a smart thing to do to protect themselves, since the patrollers needed to distinguish between the good guys and the bad.

During my visits to one of the farmhouses I found myself speaking to a little girl who was able to speak English quite well. She made a point of telling me that she enjoyed reading American cowboy books and proceeded to show me her books. I was taken aback somewhat because my familiarity with cowboys came from Hollywood movies. I assured her I thought her books were nice. What else could I say? Especially since I was not sure that I should be speaking to her at all.

The bakery that I guarded was a rather large building where the family lived on the second floor. My guard post was a small parking lot adjacent to the right side of the bakery. When I arrived early in the morning it was covered with cigarette butts from the night-time guards, but not to worry, an elderly German was always present, busy gathering the butts, stripping them and storing the tobacco in his pouch.

The bakery was located along a main road entering the town and I had an additional duty to stop vehicles and inspect their passes. The German words I needed to use to ask for the pass were quite long and difficult for me to pronounce. The drivers gave me peculiar looks when I asked my question, so I would repeat the question with a slight change in pronunciation several times. Usually they got my message, showed me their pass and I waved them on. They could have shown me a ticket to the circus and I would have waved them on. I needed some instructions in this department but that never happened.

From time to time a Jeep with an American army officer and his driver stopped near my post. The officer got out, crossed the street, entered a large building that looked like a factory and later came out and drove away, never making contact with me. I wondered what was going on. I began calling it the mystery Jeep.

On one of my free days, I either walked or perhaps rode the trolley to downtown Mettmann. During my sightseeing trip, I began to learn some of the German language by reading the signs on the various civic and other prominent buildings and was surprised that I could understand many of the German words except for one building called the Rathaus. Somehow, I learned that it was the townhall. I thought that was appropriate and was smiling to myself when two pretty, young German girls asked me where such and such was located. I use the term such and such because I had no idea what they were talking about, so I told them to go inside the Rathaus and ask. They in turn did not understand what I was saying so I kept trying to explain. Suddenly I felt a tap on my shoulder. I turned around and found Captain Caywood behind me. OK, so I was caught red handed fraternizing through no fault of my own. He asked me what was going on. I told him simply and honestly that the girls were looking for directions. He said, "Tell them to read the signs". I was and am still thankful that he did not give me a hard time. He was too nice a man to do that.

The War was Over for Me

On May 8, Victory in Europe Day (VE-Day), the war in Europe was officially over and there was a celebration, I think. However, I cannot remember one thing that happened that wonderful day, the day we had been waiting for, it seemed, a lifetime.

The next morning one of the Sergeants woke me up about 5:30 in the morning and asked if I minded taking an extra turn at guard duty because so many of the members of our unit were under the weather from the celebration. I did not drink and had not been out in the melee, so it was not a problem for me; I told him I was happy to help out.

Early that morning I took my first turn at guarding the butcher shop. The weather outside was lovely and I was enjoying my solitude when a little old German man came walking up the cobblestone street. When he reached my station, he said, "Guten Morgen." I was stunned . . . speechless and could not respond. I was overcome by the same feeling I had when that wounded German soldier asked me for a cigaretten. The war was not over for me.

The next morning, I was on guard duty again. Same time, same place, the same little old German man came walking up the cobblestone street and said, "Guten Morgen." And I responded, "Good morning." Two words that changed my life. The war was over for me.

I never felt enmity for the Germans from that moment on. I, of course, will always remember the awful things the Nazis did in this world. But it was and still is a wonderful feeling that came over me and has stayed with me. I dream about my time in the service but never have a nightmare as some returning vets have. I will always believe that the Holy Spirit sent that little old German man to me. Thank you, Jesus!

Seventy-five years after the war, I began to read my letters home (kept for me by my mother) in order to help me date the events in my memoirs. Most of my letters written during the conflict reflect the utter dislike I had for the Germans. Then one day I came across these paragraphs in a letter dated May 26, 1945, just eighteen days after the war was over. You can tell my heart had changed.

"The Germans know they are at fault, but they were tied hand and foot by the Nazis, as was demonstrated by the concentration camps. They can now only shake their fists at Hitler and say swine. The German people must stand with shame on their faces because Hitler and his thugs drove the ideas of Nazism into their youth and their SS Corps, who ran the army.

In every house we searched, we saw photos of brothers, sons, and fathers. We asked where is so and so now. The answers were a devastating three: killed, missing, or prisoner. It's difficult to imagine. There is no doubt about it. All these people aren't Nazis. When an elderly man breaks down and cries when speaking of his only son who died a month ago, you can tell Germans have hearts. They touched mine.

It is absolutely too big for my small brain to imagine that so many men have died. Practically all of the little children I have seen are fatherless. All the young women are husbandless. The Germans are more than defeated. Their civilian population is heart-broken and desolate. Tears cannot bring back their men and eyes are red with tears in Germany because of their hopeless situation."

One day I felt considerable discomfort in my gums and was given permission to visit one of the battalion dentists. He cleaned my teeth and painstakingly treated my gums with some compound containing arsenic that made my gums feel much better. When I returned to my unit, I told our first sergeant that the dentist said the whole battalion had trench mouth. Captain Caywood immediately ordered us to return to using mess kits instead of china plates and standard GI cleanup methods. I visited the dentist several more times for treatments as required and thought I had put trench mouth behind me.

Elfriede Fincke

Occupation duties continued day after day through May and into June. Boredom began to set in and we heard rumor after rumor that we might be going home—or not—for a short furlough or maybe straight to the Pacific to fight in the CBI. Into this dull routine entered Elfriede Fincke, the baker's daughter. She appeared at the window above the bakery's parking lot one day and began to chat with me while I was on guard duty. The first thing I learned was that she had been working in Nuremburg. That was a warning sign for me, because I knew that's where Hitler gave his orations to all those

SS soldiers in the huge Nuremburg Sports Plaza. In my mind there was a high possibility Elfriede had worked for the Nazis.

Elfriede knew a few words of English and, after almost eight weeks in Mettmann, I had picked up some key German words; consequently, I was somewhat conversant in German. Day after day speaking with Elfriede, I was able to improve my German. I found it was much easier than learning la français from Mrs. Mumbauer at Liberty High.

After about a week of speaking with Elfriede, she invited me to come to dinner. That was a challenge. Fraternization was *verboten*, but like a dummy, I accepted the invitation. I went back to our compound, dressed up, and returned to the bakery. I rang the doorbell and was ushered up the stairs to the foyer, where I hung up my cap and stood my rifle in the coat rack. I then entered what I took to be the living room and was introduced to the family. To protect myself I told a lie and said my mother came from Leipzig. I picked the name Leipzig out of the air knowing it was quite some distance from Mettmann.

The father and mother left the room and I was left with Elfriede and her aunt. Her aunt began to serenade us by playing the organ. Elfriede joined her on the flute. I noticed they were playing Lutheran hymns, so I sang along when I recognized the tune. Soon we were invited to dinner.

We all sat around a modest-sized table. I do not remember for sure if grace was said but I think it was. The dinner included a boiled egg, a small portion of cabbage, and a piece of black bread. I knew the Germans were eating "ersatz" bread that had a sawdust filler, but this bread on a baker's table was certainly not ersatz. The meal was so meager, I was ashamed to eat it and felt sorry for the family.

After dinner, we all returned to the living room, except for the Mutter, and there was more organ music with Elfriede playing flute using the breath from her nose. I supposed that was meant to be funny. They were laughing, but it did not hit me that way. In the middle of this gaiety, the doorbell rang. That was a shock to me. My rifle was in the foyer. Suddenly, this stupid visit became scary.

Elfriede answered the door and ushered three young girls through the archway into the living room. All three gave the Nazi salute before they realized I was there. The family was embarrassed. I should have left at that point, but I just sat there. I do not remember much after that. I could not wait to leave.

The next day while on guard duty, I asked Elfriede what was going on in the building across the street. She said they were selling silverware. I told her I would like to buy some, so she arranged with one of her girlfriends who worked there, to have me go there when there were no officers present. After guard duty, I returned to the bakery.

Elfriede's girlfriend came to the window of the building across the street and signaled to Elfriede that the coast was clear. It was interesting that the girl across the street was one of those who had come to the dinner the night before and given the Heil Hitler salute.

I crossed over and entered the building to buy two sets of silverware made in Solingen with an Olympic monogram. They were inexpensive. Since I thought that silverware was made of silver, I felt I had a bargain and planned to mail them home to Mom. I already said I was naïve—that's a nice word for stupid. Years later after I was married and was using the "silverware," my wife, Nancy Lou, informed me that our knives and forks were made of stainless steel, very handsome looking but not silver.

Retuning to my billets, I was surprised to hear that we were moving to Czechoslovakia. This news added urgency to getting the silverware to the GI post office. I never saw Elfriede again, which in the long run was fortunate because I should have never gone to that dinner. I was lucky I did not get caught breaking the non-fraternization laws.

CHAPTER 35

OCCUPATION DUTY
IN CZECHOSLOVAKIA

We boarded the boxcars in the middle of June 1945, and left Düsseldorf headed for Czechoslovakia. The first day we traveled east to Kassell, the next day south to Frankfurt, then southeast through Wurzburg to Nuremburg, from there to Passau and on the fifth and last day, to Pilsen, Czechoslovakia.[1]

We traveled through an amazing contrast of scenery, the beauty of three rivers: the Rhine, the Main, and the Danube, the peaceful farmlands of Bavaria, the majestic mountains of Austria in the distance, and the hillsides of Czechoslovakia's Sudetenland. Today one would pay a fortune for that trip.

However, the large cities of Dortmund, Kassell, Frankfurt, Wurzburg, and Nuremberg were ghost towns with not one house having a roof, a window, or a floor. Just battered walls with holes left where window frames once were.

Such destruction was also seen in the railroad yards where smashed freight cars were piled on top of one another. Huge engines were blown in two. The US Air Corps helped turn Hitler's dream of a Thousand Year Third Reich into a nightmare.

Can you imagine untold numbers of German women and children riding in open flat cars, going to homes from which they fled, homes that are no longer there, in towns now completely destroyed? The Germans have paid plenty for this war; that is, the small fry have paid. I wonder if the big shots, the Krupps and the Thyssens, have paid?

Someone, looking out for us, stopped the train next to the Nuremberg Sports Plaza, the place where many times, Hitler regaled thousands of his party members and his SS Troops with his oratory and they responded with the Nazi salute, Heil Hitler. The opportunity to see this landmark would not come again.

Like everyone else, I climbed up to the podium where Hitler stood. It felt weird standing there because it was so huge, big enough, it seemed, for a million people. It scared me to think that so many Germans once stood here and saluted one man. One GI said, "Boy, when der Führer looked out on his audience, no wonder he got big ideas."

I had seen a picture of the Sports Plaza in *Life Magazine* with a GI giving the Nazi salute in front of the huge swastika symbol that looked down on the plaza. That symbol was gone, blown apart probably by a US tank. The bricks that formed the swastika were now scattered for hundreds of yards all over the bleachers and stone steps. This evil place was now deserted and gave one the feeling of a haunted house.

In mockery of its past, I, too, gave the Heil Hitler salute, stepped down from the podium and left for the train, bending down to pick up souvenirs: a piece of stone from the stadium steps and a piece of metal from the wreath that once surrounded the Swastika.

Although our train stopped in Pilsen, our company was taken to 94th Headquarters in Strackonice for a short time and I remember the following incident there. Two of us were on guard duty at a street corner in the city. Along came a group of about fifteen teenagers walking up the other side yakking back and forth, having fun. The only problem was that it was almost two hours after curfew. I yelled across the street, "Raus," which means *scram*; however, they either ignored me or did not hear me. I yelled again to no avail, so I shot my rifle in the air; that got their attention. They took off in a hurry.

The next thing I knew a US Army Military Police (MP) Jeep pulled up to my guard post and one of the MPs wanted to know who fired the rifle. I told him it was me and my reason for doing so. The MP said I must come with him. I replied that I was on guard duty. He pointed to his stripes indicating he outranked me, so I acquiesced and went with him. During the Jeep ride, I learned that firing rifles was forbidden because the MPs were having trouble distinguishing US rifles from those of snipers. I did not know that and was afraid I would be punished.

When we arrived at battalion headquarters, Captain Caywood was already there and had secured my release. My guard duty buddy must have alerted him to my predicament. Caywood's only comment to me was that I should not have left my guard post. End of story.

Blatna

Soon after arriving in Czechoslovakia, our company was billeted in a large Sokol in the village of Blatna. I guessed that Sokol meant social hall, but seventy-five years later, Google told me that Sokol was an all-age gymnastic movement begun in Czechoslovakia that spread to all countries in Eastern Europe, based on the principle of a sound mind in a sound body through lectures and exercise.

We used their gym for sleeping and eating quarters, enjoyed playing volleyball with the local Czech youngsters, swam in the outdoor swimming pool, and danced in the adjoining dance hall. Our tallest, most athletic GIs gave the Czech boys and girls a battle in volleyball, but the Czechs usually won because, after years of practice, they had the technique down pat. I joined in when the competition was not so fierce.

Our hosts loved music and played recordings of American songs for us, but they had only a few and the repetitious music became annoying. How long can you stand hearing, "Singing in the Rain" over and over?

They also hosted dances where the parents allowed GIs to dance with young Czech girls and the adults joined in, as well. I attended two of these affairs, but since I could not dance a polka, I quit.

I also attended a dinner at the home of Radia, one of the girl volleyball players. The food was delicious. The Czechs love to put caraway seeds in their rolls and desserts. The only problem was that, at the dinner, I had to sit next to an old-timer, perhaps the girl's grandfather, who leaned over to me every few minutes and said, "Stalin nix gut."

Since my trench mouth had returned during the train trip, I began taking a series of penicillin shots in Blatna and my problem disappeared. In addition to this good news, two recruits, Workman and Trilli, from my hometown Bethlehem, arrived, and I had fun getting to know them.

June turned into July and on the Fourth, our battalion marched in a parade for General Harmon in Pilsen.[2] While there, we saw a Jack Benny show with Martha Tilden singing.

Cesky Krumlov

On July 21, we moved to our final destination in Czechoslovakia, Cesky Krumlov. Moving to relieve the 26th Infantry Division was the whole idea for the 94th coming there. The 26th was persona non grata to the Czechs because their GIs were taking German girls to Czech dances. The Czechs hated Germans.[3]

Our camp at Krumlov consisted of two parallel rows of barracks separated by a narrow parade ground with Company Headquarters and a mess hall across from each other at one end, and at the other, a latrine and shower. An interesting feature of the barracks was that some of the rooms were slightly below ground level. Even so, they were roomy enough for a squad. In addition, there was a Displaced Persons Camp[8] close by Company Headquarters where we stood guard.

There were a lot of changes in our unit while we were in Krumlov. I was now an instrument corporal in a room with a medic and the mail clerk, next to Company Headquarters. Captain Caywood left us to go to Third Army Headquarters, where he was given a new command and we received a new captain. We called him "The Brow" because of his large forehead.

He treated us as if we were in basic training. The men revolted by leaving the mess hall every time the captain entered. The captain was smart enough to call for a meeting to let the GIs get things off their chests. After that, things settled down and the situation improved.

Accused

In order to appease the Czechs, our new captain was ordered to restore the non-fraternization rules to the 94th units in or near Krumlov, even though these rules had been discontinued elsewhere some time earlier. This he did by assembling everyone in H Company at lunch time in the mess hall and giving a direct order to the group. It was my understanding that if a direct order is disobeyed one can be court martialed. The only problem for me was that I was on guard duty at the DP camp when the direct order was given.

After dinner, I left the mess hall as usual, dipped my mess kit into the cleansing water cans, said "Hi" to the German girls attending their clean-up duties and, as luck would have it, the captain, unbeknownst to me, was directly behind me. Well, you would have thought the world had come to an end. I was ordered to report to Company Headquarters.

There, First Sergeant Roger Keith told me quietly that the captain was going to make an example of me. I was in deep trouble and scared to death.

The captain asked if I had heard his direct order at lunch time (or something to that effect). I said, "No, sir. I was on guard duty." He asked Sgt. Keith to see if the order was passed down by my squad leader. After some time passed, I assume he found out that that had not happened. I was too shaken up to remember what went on afterward. Presumably, I was then given the direct order with regard to non-fraternization, but that's not in my memory bank.

I was off the hook, but not a happy camper. I had done my best during combat, serving my country as best I knew how. It is scary to think I could have received a dishonorable discharge over saying hi.

Good Times and Bad Times

Since that incident, I began enjoying the nice weather and cool evenings, trounced the sergeants in volleyball 15 to 8, and went for a swim for an hour to cool off, then relaxed and tried to get a nice tan.

We had an opportunity to see an entertaining USO show that had a tap dancer, juggler, banjo player, a husband-and-wife team who sang while playing crazy instruments, and a very good magician. That was the sixth show I had seen while in Europe.

We also had plenty to read: *Colliers, Saturday Evening Post, Coronet* and pocket novels; however, I liked the *Stars and Stripes* newspaper the best because it gave us the news without pulling any punches.

On July 17, the 301st Infantry Regiment assembled in Strackonice, where General George Patton landed in a light plane and reviewed our regiment riding in a Jeep.[11] Afterward, he gave a talk where he said the US Army would have to be the firemen of the world to keep the peace.

Toward the end of July, we were given the onerous job of loading 2,000 German displaced persons, mostly women and children, on a train returning them to Bavaria. This whole idea was instigated by the Czechs, who, hating the Germans, simply ordered the Germans out of the Sudetenland, bag and baggage.

Our duty was to load them into open boxcars like cattle. Some of the children were hardly old enough to walk. There were old women carrying bundles that would break some men's backs. It was a rotten crime. You should have seen the women keel over as the hot burning sun hit them while they sat waiting for the loading to take place.

We tried to make them as comfortable as possible. All the while the Czech soldiers stole their watches and jewelry. I hid some of their jewels on me until they got on the train where the Czechs could not get to them.

One girl who spoke better English than me helped me by interpreting the questions of people in my group. I asked her where her hat was as I knew the train would be slow and sun torturous. She said, "I have none, surely they will have tops on the cars as we have babies with us." I said, "I'm afraid not." She said with a sad smile, "The Czechs don't like us very much, do they?" I replied, "No."

You can understand why I became upset, seeing women and children being pushed around, especially by the Czechs, and I was ashamed that I was a part of it. I didn't care if a baby was German, Czech, Polish, or whatever, it did not deserve to be punished. These Europeans were too thick-headed to be humane to their fellowmen.

Soon after the Sudeten Germans were expelled, we saw the other side of the coin, so to speak. A group of Jewish people arrived at our camp from

Buchenwald. That was a shock for me and a reminder of Hitler's evil ways. Our lieutenant took a blanket from each building in the DP camp and gave them to the Jews because they had nothing. These people did not want to eat or sleep until they could get as far away as they could from anything German.

Time marches on and soon it was August. Summertime, when the living is easy. I enjoyed peanut butter and crackers as well as a package of soap and razor blades from home. Also, the Wesley Methodist Church's Servicemen' s Guild sent me stamps in a holder. It was nice to be appreciated. Besides that, the chow here had been improving.

I was able to enjoy a Bob Hope show and then we put on our own company party. I was part of the entertainment, singing a solo "This Heart of Mine." In addition, I felt good, and was getting plenty of fresh air and exercise by participating in sports.

On top of all that, I received a pass to the 94th's Rest Center in Pilsen, staying at a big hotel, where I could sleep in and eat in a beautiful dining room, dance in the beer lounge, and wash, bathe, and shave in a modern bathroom. Close by was a Red Cross Club that served coffee and donuts at all hours. The next day I went to see two more shows, The Great John L, and an exhibition by the heavyweight Billy Conn.

On August 16, Victory in Japan Day, we had another parade, this time in Prague, for General Harmon, CG of the 22nd Corps.

At the camp, it was hot the last week of August, so we were given the opportunity to go to school in the mornings four days a week. I studied Physics from 8 to 10 a.m., and German from 10 to 12. It was not difficult schoolwork, and I felt I was bettering myself for the future. In the afternoon, we played volleyball then went swimming and added to our suntans. Life in the army did not get much better than that.

Non-coms and High-pointers

In the first week of September, all men with sixty-five points and over went to Pilsen to join the 8th Armored Division and began their journey home. The 8th Armored, who had gathered High Pointers from several different divisions, provided leadership for the trip.

We lost our first sergeant, Roger Keith, and all three of the squad leaders in the twenty-nine men that left our unit. Tech Sgt. John Lyons, my squad leader, was among them. I really hated to see him go. He was the shrewdest thinker I had ever met and was always ready with a good joke when the going got rough. Whenever I had a problem, he would say, "See your squad leader." I could open up to him; he never failed to give me good advice. Also, if we were in a tight spot, he would use his judgment to get us out of it. We had a party for the over 65ers and the "Voice" Ridyard sang three solos. You should have heard me on "Sentimental Journey."

It was hard to lose a good friend when there were so few remaining. Of the battalion of kids who left Florida to go to Camp McCain, I cannot name five who were still around. Fortunately, the two boys from home with whom I continued to pal around were well liked and made me feel proud of them.

Since the subject of points for going home would be the main topic of interest during the rest of my time in occupation, let me describe how it worked. After V-E Day, the army devised a system to determine the order in which GI's were to go home. The higher the number of points, the sooner an individual would go home. The system was easy enough for each person to sum up his own score.

Each soldier received one point for every month in service up to V-E Day, May 8, 1945, one point for every month overseas, five points for every campaign he took part in and five points for every special award such as a Bronze Star.

For example, this is how I determined my own point score. Before beginning, I needed to know two dates: the date I was called up to active duty, which was July 28, 1943, and the date I went overseas, August 6, 1944. One could count only full months. Thus far, I had twenty-nine months—or twenty-nine points. To that score I included four campaigns, a Bronze Star and a Combat Infantry Badge at five points each for another thirty points making a total of fifty-nine.

Furlough to the United Kingdom

I finally won a furlough, but it was to Marseille, France, so I traded with another fellow for a trip to the United Kingdom. Willie Kraft, our mail clerk, went with me because he said the rest of the guys going to the UK were just going to London to drink their time away.

We left Krumlov by train in the middle of September, toured Paris for a day, then crossed the channel on the US troop ship, Marine Wolf. The crossing was a little rough, but I found a place to sit on some life preservers on the forward top deck, watched the horizon and snoozed. Willie and I took the train to London and spent the first night in the Red Cross Club before setting off the next morning on the Glasgow Express and arriving in Glasgow at 7 p.m.

We had an interesting ride because two British officers in our cabin jousted verbally about the scenery. The English officer bragged about the beauty of the English countryside with its rolling hills and small farms surrounded by stone walls. The Scottish officer responded, "But you wouldn't use the term grandeur, as you would in describing the Scottish scenery."

Willie and I spent the evening checking out the main drag, Sauchiehall Street, in downtown Glasgow, and then cleaned up and slept in the Red Cross Hotel. We didn't want to move in on Aunt Bella, my mom's oldest and favorite sister, during the evening.

The next morning we went to Aunt Bella's on the Balloch bus and walked up Kilbowie Road to Bannerman St. The apartment building adjoining Bella's had been destroyed, presumably by a German bomb.

Aunt Bella was home alone preparing the noon meal for her daughters, Isa and Maggie. She greeted us warmly and was just as nice as can be. It is no wonder she was my mother's favorite sister. Her daughters came in soon afterward for their noon-time break from the Singer sewing machine factory.

We enjoyed the evening meal at Bella's, which she announced was special from the US, Spam, which wasn't truly special, but her sharing it with us was special. That night we stayed at Bella's, and since there was no heat, she put hot water bottles at the foot of our beds.

The next day, Aunt Bella took us to Aunt Annie in Dalmuir, showing us where Mom had lived on Livingston Street and the place where my brothers were born at Agamemnon Street. Annie had a guest, Minnie Cretsor, who seemed to have been a friend of Uncle Willie, who at that time lived in Staten Island, NY.

Bella then took us to Uncle Robert's at the top of Kilbowie Road. We were to stay there so I gave my ration card to his wife, Aunt Minnie Barnett. There, I met her daughter, Cousin May, and the next day, May's husband, Alec.

The following day, Uncle Robert, Aunt Annie, and little Jimmie McLean took us to Uncle John's home. I learned that his prefab home came from the US to replace the one destroyed during the war. Aunt Bella, Minnie Cretsor, Isa, and Maggie were already there. We met John's wife, Aunt Effie, and my cousins Tina and Isabel, and Tina's husband. Uncle Jimmy McLean arrived later after getting off work.

Now the pattern was set, everywhere we went, most of the family would also come and we would have a party. Aunt Effie had a lovely table set and we had a nice time. We were given dishes of cookies while Scottish jokes flew, thick and fast. They had a piano, so Willie Kraft helped with the festivities by playing.

That night we slept at Uncle Robert's in a soft, comfortable bed. Aunt Minnie had stayed home with May and our bed was all set for us. The next day, Saturday, we were to go to Loch Lomond, but it rained, so we returned to Robert's after retrieving our bags from Glasgow. There, we met Alec, May's husband. He showed us some pictures as taking photos was his hobby.

Uncle Robert treated us to a movie at The La Scala, a huge theater on Kilbowie. All during our stay with Aunt Minnie, she made us right at home, serving us delicious meals.

In the evening, we went to Aunt Bella's for tea and dinner and met Uncle Joe. He had a laugh just like Uncle James in America. Aunt Annie's and Uncle Robert's families were there. We had a great time. Incidentally, everyone felt badly about Cousin John Barnett, Uncle James's son, having been killed in action.

On Sunday we slept in until 11:30 a.m., and then went for a walk along the boulevard toward Duntocher and up the hill, where we could look down on the Clyde Valley. We saw where all the houses were destroyed on the hill above the Singer Sewing Machine Co. and how it had not been touched, but a lot of schools and churches had been hit.

In the evening, Bill and I went to the Red Cross in Glasgow where there was a dance. Bill played a few songs and I tried to sing, but to my embarrassment, forgot my lines to the song.

Monday afternoon, Jimmie McLean took us to Fairhill Park to see Queen's Park and Thistle play soccer in a Glasgow Cup 0-to-0 tie. I will always remember that game because one of the players, Geekie, was exceptionally good. He could dribble the ball between the opposing player's legs. Unfortunately, one of the fans behind me, who was obviously drunk, kept cheering for Geekie annoyingly, over and over.

When we returned home, we found that everyone thought we should have gone to another game where the Rangers lost to Clyde 4 to 3 because there was more scoring. Little Jimmie was sad because his team the Rangers was leading at halftime 3 to 1 and lost 4 to 3. Jimmie's sad face reminded me how I felt when Allentown High whipped Bethlehem High. That night, we had another party at Uncle Robert's after dinner at Annie's.

Tuesday morning, Aunt Annie, Uncle Jimmie, Minnie Cretsor, and Uncle Robert took us to Balloch and we saw Loch Lomond Park and drank tea at the castle. It was another lovely day.

In the evening, Aunt Bella and Uncle Robert took us to Uncle Robert's daughter Edith's home, where we met her husband and two daughters. He was a joiner and ship's cabinetmaker and showed us his homemade furniture, which was beautiful. Another party or tea ensued.

Aunt Minnie made us sandwiches and Aunt Minnie, Bella, Aunt Annie, Uncle Jimmie, and Minnie Cretsor saw us onto the train at Glasgow on Wednesday, where we said our goodbyes after one of the most memorable trips I ever took.

We traveled by train through Preston, Wigan, and then to Golborne, where I found my father's sister, Aunt Annie Ridyard, at home on Leith Street and stayed with her overnight, meeting Uncle James Ridyard in the morning when he came home from work. There are two odd things that have stuck in my mind about that visit. When we arrived, it appeared to me they were installing electricity. That seemed strange this late in the century. I never understood what was going on. I also noted that, when Uncle James was stoking the potbelly stove in the kitchen, he bent over from the hips without bending his knees, just like my father did. Since then I have supposed that was a miner's trait. Another one of my life's little mysteries.

Annie and James were very pleasant people and were kind to us, but much more reserved than my Scottish relatives.

We took the train to London only to find that shipments to Southampton were cancelled. To pass the time we saw a play, *A Bell for Adano*, which was wonderful. We looked over the sights in London and saw another play, *GI Joe*, at the London Pavillion near Piccadilly Circus. Then we had dinner with a Mr. Sycamow, a businessman in the Ministry of Food and a friend of Ernie Bevin, whom we had seen on the way to Glasgow. Last but not least, we saw Shakespeare's *Henry V*, a classic and beautiful play.

After a rather smooth channel crossing, we rode the train for three days to the Third Army Leave Center in Nuremberg. There, we called for our ride back to Krumlov. We found the Leave Center clean and the food good and served by German waitresses while an orchestra played American music. Then we saw a movie called *Music for Millions* with Jose Iturbi and passed the time listening to Claude Passeau beat Detroit 3 to 0 in the World Series. The next night I fell asleep while listening to World Series Game 6 with the Cubs having two on base and losing 1 to 0. The next day I learned the Cubs had beaten Detroit 8 to 7.

Waiting to Go Home

Back home in Krumlov in early October, I had a nice surprise when all of my personal belongings left behind at the hospital were returned to me. They included my good wallet, pictures, ID bracelet, prayer book from church, and a souvenir from Brittany.

On another happy note, I learned that a new Czech army crew had begun guarding the DP camp, allowing many of us to have more free time.

I also learned that men over thirty-five years old and those with over sixty-three points had gone home; Workman, Trilli, and others with forty-five points and below were getting ready to leave for other occupation duties. I began to feel sorry for myself again because half of our company was gone. We soon would be left with men having points between fifty-five and sixty-three, including me, with fifty-nine, a total of only forty-five men.

It seemed strange that so many men were leaving and the newspapers kept telling us that Seventy Pointers would be home in November, and Sixty Pointers in December. And then I heard that Ninety Pointers were still in France living in tents in muddy fields waiting for ships. I wished someone would tell me what was really going on.

Mail Clerk

It isn't like I was not busy. I had a new job, mail clerk. It was good because I got to think for myself and there were so many things to do. My day consisted of shaving, cleaning my room, the mail room, and desk, readdressing the mail because letters kept coming for those who had moved out, grabbing a cup of coffee in town at the Red Cross Library and Coffee Shop, sorting the new mail, typing up the outgoing letters, and delivering the incoming letters.

In the middle of all that, we began to get more men. We now had men from the 79th, 80th, 83rd, and 90th Infantry and from the 4th, 8th, 9th, 11th, and 16th Armored in our camp with fifty to sixty-five points waiting to go home. I began to hope that when we had enough men, we would be sent somewhere, anywhere, just so we got out of Czechoslovakia. Any move nearer home would be welcome.

Of course, every time we got another fifty men or so, I had to make a new mail roster. This happened quite often. Also, I had located all the men who had left us and was in the process of making a new locator file. Someday I hoped to get caught up with all this paperwork and to be able to settle down to the nice, easy job this was supposed to be.

Just when I was almost up to date, the powers that be came up with a new regulation, vis a vis, after this month we would only be able to send home in money orders that we drew from our pay. That meant we were forced into something I called Black Market Month. Everyone was getting rid of their extra money: gambling winnings or illegal sales of cigarettes or candy, etc. Consequently, I had to make several extra trips to the APO with money orders.

In the mornings, I worked on odds and ends, wrapped packages, looked up addresses, and made rosters. All the real mail work was done in the afternoon.

Once a week I had to go by truck to the Division APO in Strackonice with packages and, twice a month, with money orders. Those were all-day seventy-mile trips there and back. Fortunately, my assistant took over when I was away.

We had half a foot of snow to usher in November, but we drove to the APO anyway with a large amount of money—$6,402.79—for money orders. For the third time in a row, I came out to the penny, but it was a cold ride. My feet were numb most of the way.

The fourth trip to the APO in five days developed into a problem as we ran out of gas in a snowstorm just three miles short of the seventy-mile distance needed to get there. The driver and I took off on foot. Czechoslovakia can be very barren and deserted up in those mountains when you are looking for another human being. Luckily for us, we did not have to go far to find gas.

As you can see, most of the time, we delivered money order applications and paid for them. Occasionally, we had to take packages; however, one of those times we forgot it was Armistice Day and no one was there, so back we went again the next day and had to deal with another snowstorm. That night, I went to bed early, read a book and kept warm.

When I had free time, I no longer went to movies or the USO shows in town because all my buddies had gone and there was no pleasure in going alone. Reading was my main relaxation. On Saturdays, I walked to town for a ten-cent shave and a haircut, where I teased the girl that put the shaving cream on me, but otherwise I did not go to town.

The silver lining in my days near the end of my time in Czechoslovakia was that, early in the morning, two little German boys about twelve or thirteen years old clomped into my room with their hobnailed boots. They cleaned and swept my room, hauled away the ashes, and filled the coal box with coal. For those chores, they were satisfied when I gave them a piece of candy. Tell that to your grandchildren.

Although we had heard rumor after rumor, week after week, the latest was that we were going to join the 80th Infantry Division in Germany next month. Thanksgiving, November 23, 1945, came and went and we were still there. And then it happened. I was told to pack my duffel bag because we were going to leave good old Czechoslovakia on Monday, November 26. Goodbye and good riddance. We were to join the 80th Infantry Division and we were on our way home at last.

CHAPTER 36

GOING HOME, GOING HOME, I'M JUST GOING HOME

We arrived in Aschaffensburg after a two-and-a-half-day trip by 40 et 8 otherwise known as a boxcar, my sixth trip in that manner. If nothing else I could make a living as a hobo when I got home or just claim the boxcar ride record.

We were billeted in a tent city just outside of Aschaffensburg, which is thirty miles from Frankfurt-am-Mainz. The whole 80th Infantry Division was billeted over an old German airfield. The GIs that made up the division were composed of fifty-six-to-sixty-four pointers from almost every outfit in the 3rd Army. I slept in a tent that had fourteen cots, each having a sleeping bag with five blankets, so I was warm at night even though the weather was nippy in the day and cold at night.

There was no drilling or training, only two roll calls a day and plans to review our records to make sure they were straight; otherwise, there was nothing to do. Fortunately, I had two detective novels.

However, to my chagrin, a few days after arriving, they ordered those of us from other divisions to sew the 80th Division on the left shoulder of our Ike Jackets and I had to move my 94th Division patch to the right shoulder. We were now officially coming home with the 80th Division after serving twenty-one months with the 94th. That did not seem right to me.

To break up the monotony we took a truck ride to Aschaffensburg to a Red Cross Club that had a band, stayed for two hours, and returned to camp.

There were no lights, just candles in our tents, so most of our time was spent reading, joking, arguing, or shooting the bull. Speaking of bull, one fellow, a staff sergeant from the 9th Armored Division, said he crossed the Remagen bridgehead on the first day. An 80th Division GI said they captured Sinz. I told him the Germans must have taken it back because our battalion had captured it, too. Before bedtime we heard an Italian boy from Colorado play his accordion for an hour and then we went to sleep.

I was given the job of mail clerk because no one else had any experience. While there, we received about seventy-five letters, but none for me. I had to re-address all of them to other divisions. My own address was now: Pfc. Herbert W. Ridyard, ASN 13193892, 317th Infantry Reg., APO 80, c/o PM New York, NY.

Out of the blue we were restricted to camp and told the 80th Division was assigned to Camp Herbert Tareyton at LeHavre. We were given boxcar numbers, mine was number twenty. All these orders were a good indication that we would soon be on the move.

We left Aschaffensburg on the fourteenth and I had my seventh boxcar ride, arriving in Le Havre two and a half days later on the sixteenth. Herbert Tareyton was another tent city named for a cigarette. Other camps at LeHavre were called Camel, Chesterfield Lucky Strike, Phillip Morris, and Pall Mall. Our tents had six cots, one stove per tent, and a cement floor. The camp had seven movies. We lived in the movies. There were almost a dozen Red Cross Clubs and Service Centers with free coffee and donuts. Ice cream and Cokes cost only a few francs. Unfortunately, as soon as we arrived, they told us we would be leaving in forty-eight hours, so we changed our francs to US coinage; consequently, we were broke. The forty-eight hours turned into two weeks of boredom until we received word to pack up, we were going home.

The US Vassar Victory, a brand-new troop ship, left Le Havre on December 30 with a group of happy GIs. We spent the first night of the ten-day trip sailing through the choppy English Channel. I remember being wakened early the next morning in my bunk, the second one from the bottom of the stack, and assigned to kitchen duty.

When the chow bell sounded, we fed a boatload of hungry soldiers soft boiled eggs that were not cooked properly. Those eggs, together with a night of sailing through channel waters, turned into a disaster. Everyone except those of us in the kitchen was seasick. People were throwing up everywhere.

By the time the kitchen staff had the opportunity to eat, we were in the Atlantic with smoother sailing; we had oatmeal for breakfast that went down easier on our stomachs.

I personally enjoyed the entire trip, out on deck every day in beautiful weather, clambering around wherever I was allowed to go. I especially enjoyed looking over the fantail at the rudder as the stern rose up and down like an elevator.

Since that trip I have read stories about Liberty ships bringing GIs home that dangerously foundered in heavy seas. Liberty ships were for carrying cargo and therefore had boxy hulls to maximize cargo space, making them less seaworthy. That was not my experience.

This wonderful trip on the Vassar Victory came to a happy ending as we entered the magic waters of New York harbor and were thrilled to see the Statue of Liberty in all its glory. Once we were ashore it would be only a short time until we were home, home at last.

Disembarking on January 9, 1946, those from Pennsylvania took a trip on a train to Fort Indiantown Gap, northeast of Harrisburg. There, we had a brief physical and waited several days while our Honorable Discharge Papers were prepared and presented to us on January 13, 1946.

I remember being interviewed for the Separation Qualification Record, a document supplementing the discharge. It included records of my high school education listing the fact that I took Academic Courses and the various types of subjects involved. It also included a record of my jobs in the army: Basic Training, Rifleman, Ammunition Bearer and Messenger. Unfortunately, it had no record of me as a mail clerk.

The captain conducting the interview began to focus on the messenger aspect. He was obviously trying to help me use this document to obtain a job in civilian life and I thank him for trying because there was little in my service as a rifleman or ammunition bearer that was related to civilian occupations. This is what he entered into my record:

Messenger 675 - Was Platoon Runner carrying messages between squads on front lines; recorded messages in logbook and kept records of messages carried between squads; accompanied officers on reconnaissance concerning bivouacs for men. Also carried verbal orders, commands, and messages. This embellishment of my service was appreciated. He obviously knew more than I did about a messenger's job.

My discharge complete, I was chatting with some of the others in the barracks when in came my high school friend, Weston Werst. He told me he was in the next barracks and had met some 94thers who'd told him I was next door. What a coincidence! I thought because of his wounds, he would have been home well before me. We immediately started reminiscing. I don't remember what we talked about. It was just fun to be together.

Another trip on a train to Bethlehem and a bus ride and I was walking up Hottle Avenue with my duffel bag over my shoulder, knocking on the door of residence 1432 and home at last in the arms of my parents.

What a wonderful feeling for a twenty-year-old who had done his best. The battlefields were silent and far away and two-and-a-half years of service were over. A new phase of my life was about to begin.

AFTERWORD

A fter coming home from my military service during WW II, I immediately focused on entering Lehigh University under the GI Bill of
Rights, which provided the following benefits for veterans seeking
an education:

The government will pay up to $500 a year for tuition, fees, and books
at any recognized private or public approved education or training institute.
Courses must be initiated no later than two years after discharge or the end of
the war, whichever is later, and no training will be given after seven years after
the termination of the war. Uncle Sam will further pay a subsistence allow-
ance of $50 a month plus $25 for dependents for those who return to school.

While waiting to enter school or trying to find employment, veterans like
myself were already receiving $50 a month for a period of fifty-two weeks.
We called this the "52-50 club." As indicated above, the $50-a-month benefit
continued during my time at Lehigh.

Billy Sheridan, the accomplished Lehigh wrestling coach and a friend of
my mother from her days in Scotland, wrote a letter endorsing my academic
capabilities and upstanding character.

I took the English placement test, which included writing a theme about
my experiences in WW II, and was accepted for enrollment in the spring
semester, beginning on February 27, 1946, with the requirement that I take
English zero, a no-credit course that reflected my lack of ability to put two or
more sentences together on paper. I graduated three years and four months
later, on June 20, 1949, with a bachelor of science degree in mechanical engineering cum laude.

Lehigh University was a challenge for me because all my classmates were also WW II veterans and motivated to achieve success in college. Students whom I knew in high school, who were lucky to make C grades back then, were now earning As at Lehigh.

But I was a new man, as well. My service in WW II benefitted me in three important ways. First, basic training had strengthened my body. I had gained thirty pounds of muscle and learned that I had the stamina to keep moving no matter what physical activity or stress I was enduring. These physical capabilities would help me to study late into the night doing homework and preparing for tests.

Second, during combat, I learned to live with the emotions of fear, anger, and hate while I lived outside through most of fall and winter; froze my toes during a thirteen-hour truck ride to the Battle of the Bulge in January with no canvas cover, no lights, and no stopping; wore the same uniform and had only one shower in eight months. I had been on the receiving end of German rifle fire, exposed to artillery barrages, including screaming Meemies and 88s, shot at numerous times by a sniper (who missed me by inches) and was still able to perform my duties as a soldier to the best of my ability, which in turn gave me great confidence in myself. This confidence motivated me to succeed at college and in all my endeavors in civilian life.

For my service during WW II, I received a Bronze Star, four Campaign Stars—Northern France, Ardennes, Rhineland, and Central Germany—and the Combat Infantry Badge, but the gift of the GI Bill of Rights in reward for my military service was clearly the most valuable. It was, in fact, a godsend, because my folks could never have afforded to pay my way. Consequently, I was determined to make the most of this wonderful opportunity for a college education. Indeed, going to Lehigh led to a lifelong career as an aeronautical engineer that furnished the means for me to marry and provide for my family. None of this would have happened if I had not survived the war. I have the Holy Spirit to thank for that.

My education led me to a successful forty-one-year career with three companies. First, I became an aeronautical research scientist at the National Advisory Committee for Aeronautics (NACA), which was the forerunner of NASA. There, I helped design Mach 7 and 10 nozzles for the eleven-inch hypersonic wind tunnel at the Langley Aeronautical Laboratory and later helped develop the prototype model and the final design for the X-15 Rocket Research Airplane. The culmination of my work at NACA was the presentation of a top-secret paper, "The Aerodynamic Characteristics of the X-15 from 100 miles per hour to Mach 7." All this was accomplished while I took night school courses to earn a masters' degree in aeronautical engineering from the University of Virginia.

Second, I worked thirty-one years at General Electric's ICBM Re-entry Vehicle Department in various capacities—i.e., aeronautical research scientist, supervisor of aerodynamic design techniques, manager of fluid mechanics, manager of penetration aids, project engineer for the Pen-aids on the Mk 500 program, chief engineer of the Electronic Decoy Program and as a consultant for the development of radar absorbing materials, all while pursuing PhD-level graduate courses in Engineering Mechanics at the University of Pennsylvania.

Finally, after retirement from GE in 1988, I returned to work for a few years at General Sciences Inc., as a program manager for Optical Penetration Aids Design and Tests.

It was October 27, 1946, a Friday evening and, taking a break from studying, I wandered into town to the YMCA hoping to meet someone I knew. My wish came true as Dean Garland, a onetime member of my Boy Scout Flaming Arrow Patrol, showed up. I had not seen Dean since enlisting in the army. He was attending Moravian College and I agreed to go to one of their football games to see him play in the band.

But on this night, he was going to a pep dance at Liberty High School and he asked me to go with him. Now I was twenty-one and did not think I would fit in with the teenagers; however, Dean begged me to go with him. He said he had a girlfriend at Liberty High he wanted to see, so I agreed to go.

We walked into the high school gym, which was packed with dancing couples and Dean introduced me to his girlfriend, Marie McCandless, who then introduced me to her friend Nancy Lou. Wow! I had never seen a girl as sweet and beautiful. For me, it was love at first sight.

We danced the night away. For a guy who did not know how to dance and hadn't tried to for eons, this was as close as it got to heaven. While dancing the second dance, I asked my partner once again what her name was, to which she replied above the noise of the band and the crowd, "Nancy Lou Ayre." I came close to ruining the whole evening by asking, "Are you Oriental? (thinking her middle name was Loo)" She hesitated briefly, then smiled sweetly and precisely said and spelled her name in a rather loud voice, "Nancy Lou Ayre, N-A-N-C-Y- L-O-U- A-Y-R-E!" Almost shot myself in the foot that time.

Nancy Lou and Herb at Lehigh Dance

Dean and I walked the girls along Linden Street toward their homes. When we arrived at Broad, we turned east on Broad where Dean and Marie continued one block to her home. There we separated and Nancy and I turned south on Maple to 401 East Market, her home.

At her front door I asked Nancy Lou if she would go to the movies with me the following night, Saturday. She did not answer my question but told me she was going to a dance at the Masonic Temple. I took that response as a "yes." After saying goodbye, I walked home with my feet never touching the ground. It was like walking on marshmallows. I know it is hard to explain but if you have ever been in love you will understand my feelings.

Thus began a wonderful four-year courtship. After graduating from Lehigh in the spring of 1949, I accepted a position with NACA in Hampton, Virginia. I asked for and received permission from Nancy Lou's father to marry her. I gave Nancy Lou a diamond ring and we became engaged at Walp's Pennsylvania Dutch Restaurant on Union Boulevard near Allentown. After building up enough funds in my savings account, we were married one year later, on June 24, 1950.

After seventy years of nuptial bliss, our family has been blessed with the addition of two daughters and two sons: Amy Lou, Herbert William, Jr., Leslie Ann, and Robert Thomas.

Amy Lou married Jeff Landers and gave birth to Chad and Kaitlin; Herb, Jr. married Kristine Poet, who gave birth to John Thomas and Douglas Graham; Leslie Ann married Mark Monahan and gave birth to Melissa and David; and Rob married Lori Forter, who gave birth to Robert Conner. We now had seven grandchildren.

In time, six of these grandchildren married and blessed us with eight great-grandchildren. Chad married Kayla Whipkey and gave us Kahlan and Alexa, Kaitlin married James Reder and gave us Wyatt and William, Melissa married Derek Schmitt and gave us Graham and Abby, David married Amber Peters and gave us Cali. Douglas married Sarah Bounty and gave us Eleanor, and John married Elizabeth Clain.

As of July 2020, the Herbert William and Nancy Lou Ridyard family including in-laws had grown by thirty wonderful people That's enough to make us sing and shout, "Halleluiah, Praise the Lord!"

APPENDIX 1

THE RIDYARD LINEAGE

Samuel[1] Ridyard—The oldest Ridyard ancestor for whom we have records is Samuel[1] Ridyard, a saddler of Pennington and West Leigh, Lancs., who was born around 1690.

Samuel[1] Ridyard married Sarah Rowbotham, daughter of Thomas Rowbotham, at Manchester Cathedral on 2/10/1711-12. Sarah was baptized on 5/20/1698 at St. James Didsbury near Manchester.

Their seven children listed here with their dates of baptism are as follows:

William,	9/21/1713
Samuel[2]	3/6/1714-15
John	9/6/1716
James	11/24/1717
Robert	5/29/1720
Thomas	1/23/1725-26 (buried 6/5/1732)
Richard	6/2/1731

Their father Samuel[1] Ridyard was buried 2/5/1748 at age fifty-eight and his wife Sarah was buried 3/12/1750 at fifty-nine.

Please note that the superscripts—for example, Samuel[1]—denote individuals who are in my direct line of descent with the numbers providing the sequence.

Samuel[2] Ridyard—Our line, beginning with Samuel,[1] was continued by their son, Samuel[2] Ridyard, baptized 3/6/1714-15, also of Pennington, who married Hannah Dunster, daughter of James Dunster at Leigh St. Mary's on 9/20/1737. Hannah was baptized 9/5/1716 at Leigh. Samuel[2] and Hannah had two children:

James, baptized 8/19/1739, died as an infant on 7/29/1740 at age eleven months

Ann, baptized 5/31/1741.

Unfortunately, Samuel[2]'s wife Hannah died and was buried about seven months later on 1/13/1742-3.

Samuel[2] then married Ann Wolstenholme on 6/30/1747 at Leigh St. Mary. Their three children are as follows:

William[3]	7/3/1748
Sarah	2/25/1749 buried 3/23/1766 (age seventeen)
Samuel	7/25/1753 buried 12/21/1753 (age seven months) at Leigh St. Mary

Samuel[2] was buried 6/8/1773 (age fifty-nine) and Ann was buried 3/5/1790 (age about sixty-three).

William[3] Ridyard—Samuel[2]'s son, William[3] Ridyard, a saddler of Pennington, married Mary Penkethman at Leigh St. Mary on 3/8/1774. Mary, daughter of Thomas Penkethman, was baptized 12/8/1751 at Leigh St. Mary.

Their children are as follows:

John	1/22/1775
James	4/1/1777
Samuel	1/23/1779 buried 4/3/1782
Mary	10/20/1781
Ann	9/20/1783
Robert	9/9/1787 buried 9/18/1787
Peggy	10/26/1788

Mary, wife of William[3], died and was buried 7/17/1789 at age thirty-seven.

William[3] Ridyard then married Betty Dean of Pennington, on 7/16/1793 at St. Oswald Winwich. Neither could write. Witnesses were Michael Ridyard and Robert Cross. Betty, the daughter of James Dean, was baptized 8/17/1750 at Leigh. William[3] and Betty's only child, Peter[4] Ridyard, was baptized on 2/2/1794.

William[3] Ridyard died and was buried 11/27/1812 at age sixty-three. Betty Ridyard died and was buried 6/20/1832 at age eighty. I have seen a record at the Mormon Church Library in Broomall, Pennsylvania, indicating that Betty Ridyard died in a workhouse, not a happy place.

Peter[4] Ridyard—Three generations of Ridyards as saddlers ended with Peter[4] Ridyard, an engineer of Golborne, who married Ann Davis on 2/1/1818 at All Saints Wigan. Neither Peter[4] nor Ann could write their name and there were no witnesses except for the church clerics. Ann, the daughter of Thomas Davis, was baptized 1/17/1794 in Wigan. Their seven children include:

Their firstborn, Mary, died as an infant and was buried 11/15/1818

John and Thomas[5], twins, were born 10/14/1821 and baptized 1/6/1822. John died and was buried 3/22/1824.

William was born 12/31/1822 and baptized 1/7/1823.

James was born 8/12/1823 and baptized 8/31/1823.

Henry was born 6/30/1825, baptized 7/31/1825 and buried 12/4/1828.

Henry was burned to death.

John was born 2/7/1827 and baptized 3/29/1827

Peter was born 5/14/1833 and baptized 6/16/1833

Peter[4] Ridyard of Edge Green, Golborne, was accidentally killed in a coal pit on 11/22/1833, at age thirty-nine. His wife Ann, also known as Nancy, died and was buried 4/8/1878, at Ashton at age eighty-four.

Thomas[5] Ridyard—My great-grandfather Thomas[5] Ridyard, a collier (coal miner), of Golborne married Martha Coates, a power loom weaver born in Cadishead, on 02/15/1846, at the Parish Church of England at Lowton, Lancs. Martha could not write her name. Witnesses were John Ridyard and Elizabeth Caldwell. John, the witness, was probably the brother of Thomas,[5] not his twin who passed away prior to Thomas's wedding. Witness Elizabeth Caldwell could not write her name.

A very interesting aspect of their marriage certificate is that both Peter[4] Ridyard, father of the groom, and Thomas Coates, a watchman and the father of the bride, were deceased at the time of the wedding.

Thomas[5] Ridyard and Martha's children include:

Sarah Anne, born 02/14/1847 at Edge Green Ashton in Makerfield

Thomas,[6] born 04/29/1859 at Golborne

Peter, born July 23, 1862 at Golborne

Miner Thomas[5] Ridyard worked in the mine as a doubler among the mine timber. He was accidentally killed on 08/17/1875 at age fifty-three by "a fall of the roof in the mine" in Golborne. He lived seven to eight hours after the accident. Tragedy seemed to abound in the Ridyard family at that time; both Peter[4] Ridyard and Thomas[5] Ridyard died in mine accidents

The 1881 census records show that Thomas[5]'s wife Martha, age fifty-eight, lived on as a widow and head of the household at 5 Heath St., Golborne, and worked as a grocer. Included in her household were her sister Mary Shaw, age sixty, a cotton weaver born in Cadishead, and Peter, a son age eighteen, who worked as a baker in Golborne. Ten years later, the 1891 census shows Martha at the same address living alone at age sixty-eight, still a grocer. Martha died at Heath St., Golborne, on 01/09/1892 at age sixty-eight after a two-year bout with chronic bronchitis. Her son Thomas[6] was present at her death.

Please allow me to digress for a moment from the record of direct descendants to include the following information on a certain Peter Ridyard. The 1881 census records show that a Peter Ridyard lived at 95 Walthew Lane, Hindley. Peter, a miner, was listed as forty-seven years old. This Peter is probably the one born 05/14/1833 to Peter[4] Ridyard and Ann Davis; therefore, he is a relative but not a direct descendant of our line. The census shows Peter's wife, Mary, age forty-five was a power loom weaver from Golborne. Four of their children, Sarah, age twenty, Jane, age nineteen, Ellen, age sixteen, and Mary A., age fourteen, were all power loom weavers born in Hindley. Son James P., age eleven, son John W., age nine, and daughter Amelia, age five, all born in Hindley, were listed as scholars.

The 1891 census lists this same Peter Ridyard, at age fifty-eight, as a collier (miner) underlooker, his wife, Mary, age fifty-eight, James P., age twenty-one, as a coalminer, John W., age eighteen, as a check weigh man, and Amelia, age fifteen, as a weaver, all at the same Hindley address, as in 1881. In case you are wondering, an underlooker is a supervisor whose "office" is down in the mine.

APPENDIX 2

TOM AND JOHN IN WW II

Thomas Ridyard

Staff Sgt. Thomas Ridyard, Battery C, 213th AA, US Army

In 1940, when Tom was twenty-one, he and some of his friends joined the Pennsylvania National Guard, Coast Artillery Unit stationed at the armory in Bethlehem, Pennsylvania. They were paid to train one weekend a month and to go on a bivouac each summer.

During the summer of 1941, just before the US entry into WW II, Tom's unit went on maneuvers in North Carolina. That was the time, according to Movietone News, when the US Army was simulating tanks by using trucks with a sign TANK on their side. Clearly, we were not prepared for war and everybody knew it.

When we heard from Tom that his unit was camped at Virginia Beach, Virginia, brother John, who owned a car, the first in our family, drove Mother and me to see Tom. The trip took a long time because in those days the roads had only two lanes and a speed limit of forty-five miles per hour.

Upon arrival we were amazed at the huge mass of tents in the camp on a very wide beach. After a nice but short visit with Tom, we said our goodbyes and returned home. John had to drive all night and well into the morning hours; that was a tiring, nervous ride for all of us.

Later that year, on December 7, 1941, Tom's birthday, the day the Japanese Empire attacked Pearl Harbor, Tom's unit was transferred to Coney Island, New York. Their anti-aircraft guns were positioned to protect New York City. That's when I learned that Tom, ASN 20329389, was a staff sergeant in Battery C, 213th Anti-Aircraft Artillery.

Once again, our family drove by car to visit him. I remember how very windy and cold it was, being so close to the ocean in December.

Both Tom and John served in the US Army during WW II. Because they were born in Scotland, they had to take a special oath of allegiance to the USA when they were inducted.

In November 1942, Tom took part in and received a medal for the invasion of Africa. He served as a gunfire control electrician specialist and saw combat with C Battery, 213th Anti-Aircraft Artillery in Algeria-French Morocco and Tunisia in Africa. After that campaign, he served in Italy in the Naples-Foggia and Rome-Arno campaigns, where he contracted yellow jaundice at the battle of Monte Cassino. He was evacuated and subsequently recovered in Sardinia.

Because the US Army Air Corps had achieved such superior command of the air in 1944, Tom's Anti-Aircraft Unit was disbanded and turned into the 360th Military Police. After the invasion of southern France, his unit protected US supply depots near Marseille because Black Marketeers were stealing us blind. Tom continued to serve honorably in the Rhineland campaign and in Occupation Duty. Upon his discharge he received the Good Conduct Medal, American Defense Medal, WW II Victory Medal, and the European-African-Middle Eastern Medal with five Campaign Stars and one Bronze Invasion Arrowhead.

John Ridyard

Pvt. John Ridyard, Co. A, 191st Tank Bn, US Army

Because John was married (to Alice Glassmeyer) and had a child (Regina), he had a deferment until 1943, when he was drafted. He trained as an infantryman at Camp Blanding, Florida, and was deployed to Italy, where he responded to a plea for tank drivers, figuring driving a tank was safer than being a foot soldier. He became a PFC, ASN 33835844, tank driver in A Company's 191st Tank Battalion, part of the 6th Army that invaded Southern France. From there the 6th Army drove the Germans back to their homeland.

After crossing the Rhine, John's tank battalion freed a concentration camp. The inmates did not know who the US soldiers were until they saw them playing pitch and catch with a baseball.

Upon his discharge, John received a Purple Heart medal, Good Conduct Medal, WW II Victory Medal, the European-African-Middle Eastern Campaign Medal with three Bronze Stars for the Rome-Arno, Rhineland, and Central Europe campaigns and a commendation as presented below.

HEADQUARTERS—45th INFANTRY DIVISION
COMMENDATION
PRIVATE JOHN RIDYARD
Company A, 191st Tank Battalion

On January 4, 1945, near Wingen, France, when a large force of SS troops entered the town of Wingen and threatened the supply lines of his battalion, Private Ridyard and his tank crew were ordered to accompany a small group of headquarters personnel to the road junction on the outskirts of Wingen to secure it. Proceeding to their destination, Private Ridyard and his comrades, realizing that it would not be enough to just secure the road junction, moved their tank 250 yards beyond the junction and engaged the enemy. Private Ridyard and his fellow soldiers were able to contain the enemy until a sufficient force could be moved into position to combat the SS troops, secure the supply line, and account for many enemy dead.

Germany—July 5,1945   Robert L. Frederick, major general, US Army Commanding

---

John Ridyard never talked about his exploits in WW II. His family learned of his Purple Heart medal and his commendation at his funeral service, on May 30, 2001.

WW II brought the three Ridyard boys together into a unity of purpose and action as they served their country.

APPENDIX 3

JOHN BARNETT

In addition to my brothers, Tom and John, having served in WW II, another immigrant, our cousin John Barnett, son of my mother's brother, Uncle James Barnett, served in WW II. Therefore, it seems appropriate to tell his story for the benefit of current and future family members and anyone else interested in the history of WW II.

A Time for Sorrow and A Time for Joy

Staff Sgt. John Barnett, Co. C, 417th Inf. Reg., 76th Inf. Div.

During WW II, my cousin John Barnett served in Europe, where he was killed in action. After the war, Uncle James elected to have John's body returned from overseas for burial in Bethlehem, Pennsylvania's Memorial Cemetery. My brother Tom and I were pallbearers. It was there I heard the saddest words I've ever heard and will never forget. Uncle James, in his time of grief, said, "Emmy (his name for my mom) had three boys and they all came home. I had one and he didn't come home."

Many years later, my wife Nancy Lou and I were invited to visit John Barnett's sister, Nancy, who was married to Ed Berger and living in Freemansburg, a small town near Bethlehem. We found Nancy and Ed to be a nice couple and had a lovely time with them. Over the years, we saw the Bergers again at several family affairs, including my brother Tom's ninetieth birthday party and a few years later at his funeral.

Interestingly, Nancy Berger showed us a Barnett family tree she had received from her daughter Jill, someone we had not met; however, I recognized that it was the same tree I had researched, prepared, and previously given to my brother Tom. Obviously, our families got together more than I realized.

In 2004, Ed called and asked for my help in acquiring John Barnett's army medals but my inquiries required discharge papers, which were not available. All I was able to do was enter John's name and army service records into the WW II Monument's Registry of Remembrance.

In the process of carrying out this task, I learned from Nancy and Ed Berger, who had obtained some of John Barnett's military records, that my cousin had been a staff sergeant in Company C, 417th Infantry Regiment, 76th Infantry Division, assigned to Patton's Third Army, the same army I served in at that time. And in the early hours of February 9, 1945, his company embarked in rubber boats at Echternach, Luxembourg, to cross the Sauer River to attack the Siegfried Line in Germany. Staff Sergeant John Barnett was killed in action when his boat was overturned during the crossing and John's body was found thirty miles downstream.

Shortly after helping Nancy and Ed, Nancy Lou and I visited both Belgium and Luxembourg in December of 2004 as part of a tour celebrating the sixtieth anniversary of the Battle of the Bulge. One evening near Christmas we found ourselves in Echternach, Luxembourg, where the tour guide showed us the very spot where the 417th Infantry Regiment of the 76th Infantry Division had crossed the Sauer River and attacked the German Siegfried Line on the other side. He told us the river had been swollen with rain and melted snow, such that the waters had covered the very plaza on which we stood.

Having a few minutes to walk the main street of Echternach, we found a gift shop and purchased a Christmas bulb in memory of John Barnett. Upon arriving home, we presented it to Nancy and Ed, who were most grateful and happy to include it with their Christmas decorations, ever since sealing our friendship.

A Time for Living and A Time for Dying

In 2018, I received from Ed Berger a copy of a book entitled *John Barnett*, written and published in August 2018, by Jill M. O'Connor, Nancy and Ed's daughter, documenting the letters written home by John Barnett during WW II. These letters described his training in the US and experiences overseas, as well as historical records of his division, and the circumstances of his death and burial—first in Hamm Military Cemetery and then Bethlehem Memorial Park.

After perusing this book, I realized that, by coincidence, the infantry divisions of my cousin and mine, the 76th and 94th respectively, were simultaneously attacking the Siegfried Line in Germany just eighteen miles apart from each other. The 94th's attack began on February 7, the same day the 76th began its attack.

Early that morning, I was instructed to lead my machine-gun platoon from our position in the woods across a farmer's field to a barn in the town of Sinz, Germany. This field was snow-covered the previous day, but rain during the night had melted it, uncovering the black boxes of a minefield in the path through which we had to hike. It was only because of the melting snow that the black objects were observable and my life and the lives of my platoon buddies were saved. For me, that was a frightening close call, one of many that I survived.

Very likely that same rain and resulting melted snow had swollen the Sauer River twelve feet above normal, widening it to 180 feet, making it more dangerous to cross on February 9, when my cousin, engaging in combat for the very first time, led his machine gun squad across the river at Echternach and lost his life.

Why one soldier survives and another does not during combat is beyond my understanding. Many GIs of the 76th Division made it across the Sauer during the attack. Why not John Barnett?

ENDNOTES

CHAPTER 1
Family History

I began my family history research by contacting the Wigan, England, town hall, where two volunteers helped me find my father's birth certificate and an appropriate census record. This process was too time consuming, so I contacted the Wigan Family History Society and they assigned genealogist Derek Horrocks to help me for an hourly fee. Over a year or so, he located six generations of Ridyards in our family line, as described in Chapter 1 and Appendix 1. These family history records are supported by birth, marriage, and death certificates, as well as census reports for each family member, and are kept in the author's possession.

1. Derek Horrocks, family history researcher, 32B College Road, Upholland Skermersdale, Lancashire, England, WN8OPY, 1999-2001.

CHAPTER 2
Grandparents

1. Derek Horrocks

2. Ibid.

3. Ibid.

4. Ibid.

Family History Records for my mother, Emily Paterson Barnett, were obtained by retaining genealogist Charlotte L. Cowe, who conveniently lived near the Scottish family history records in Edinburgh, Scotland.

Charlotte L. Cowe, genealogist, 151 Main Street, Davidson's Mains, Edinburgh, EH4 5AQ. 1998-99.

CHAPTER 3
Mom and Dad in the Old Country

The *Archive Photographs Series, Around Ashton-Makersfield and Golborne,* compiled by Tony Ashcroft and published by Chalford Publishing Co., St. Mary's Mill, Chalford, Stroud, Gloucestershire, GL6 8NX, 1997, pages 51 & 68.

Derek Horrocks
Charlotte L. Cowe
Ibid.
Google, Wikipedia, 2005
Google, Wikipedia, 2005

CHAPTER 4
My Birth Story and First Memories

1. Bethlehem Register, Bethlehem Area Public Library, 11 West Church Street, Bethlehem, PA, 18018-5888, July 29, 2017.
2. Ibid.
3. Bethlehem Steel Co., Bethlehem, PA, 1926
4. St. Luke's Hospital (Now St. Luke's University Hospital), 801 Ostrum Street, Fountain Hill, Bethlehem, PA, 18015, 1928

CHAPTER 7
My Family

SS White Dental Manufacturing Company, 1145 Towbin Avenue, Lakewood, NJ, 08701, circa 1930

CHAPTER 8
Pre-School Days

General Herbert Norman Schwarzkopf Jr., commander of Operation Desert Storm, Jan. 17 to Feb. 28, 1991.

CHAPTER 9
Neisser Elementary School

Neisser Elementary School was first built by the Moravians in 1853 and named after George Neisser, Moravian's first schoolteacher, back in 1740. Neisser School was torn down in 1897 and rebuilt. The author attended the second Neisser School from 1931 until 1937. It was finally demolished again in 1976.

CHAPTER 17
A Brief History Lesson
on WW II for My Children and Grandchildren

This history lesson is completely from my memory and, although brief, is as complete as I felt necessary. I lived through this time period and the major battles and events are imbedded in my brain and heart.

For those who are scholars and would like more detail, I refer you to the following six books (more like tomes) by Winston Churchill: *Winston S. Churchill, The Gathering Storm*, 1948. *Their Finest Hour*, 1949, *The Grand Alliance*, 1950, *The Hinge of Fate*, 1950, *Closing the Ring*, 1951, *Triumph and Tragedy*, 1953, Houghton Mifflin Co., Boston.

WW II has been recorded in numerous books. A few that I have studied and found educational and well written are noted for this history lesson are as follows:

Basil Collier, *The Battle of Britain*, Berkley Publishing Co., New
York, 1962.

Gordon W. Prange, *At Dawn We Slept, The Untold Story of Pearl Harbor*,
McGraw-Hill Book Co., New York, 1962.

John Costello, *The Pacific War 1941-1945*, William Morrow & Co.
Inc., 1981.

Gordon W. Prange, *Miracle At Midway*, McGraw-Hill Book Co., New
York, 1982.

William Touhy, *The Bravest Man, The Story of Richard Kane & U. S.
Submariners in the Pacific War*, Sutton Publishing Limited, Phoenix
Mill, Gloucestershire, 2001.

Thomas J. Cutler, *The Battle of Leyte Gulf, 23-26 October*, HarperCollins
Publishers, Inc., New York, 1944.
To learn more about the U.S role in WW II, I suggest the follow-
ing books:
Mark Bowden, *Our Finest Day, D-Day: June 6, 1944*, Chronicle Books
LLC, San Francisco, CA, 2002.
Stephen E. Ambrose, Band of Brothers, Simon & Schuster, New
York, 1992.
For the complete story of the US battles in the European-African
theater, read:
Rick Atkinson, *The Liberation Trilogy: An Army At Dawn, The Day Of
Battle*, 2007, *The Guns At Last Light*, 2013, Henry Holt & Co.,
New York.
For the history of the air war in Europe, read: Donald L Miller, *Masters
of The Air*, Simon & Schuster, New York, 2006.

CHAPTER 19
Enlistment in the Army Specialized Training Program (ASTP)

Chief of Staff, War Department, Fifty Questions and Answers on The
Army Specialized Training Program, 1943

CHAPTER 22
The University of Florida

Secretary of War, Subject: Reduction in ASTP, Memorandum to each
AST Trainee, Headquarters SCU 33418 ASTP, University of
Florida, Gainesville, Florida, February 23, 1944.

CHAPTER 24
The 94th Moves Overseas

The New Testament, American Bible Society, New York, instituted
in 1816

Lt. Laurence G. Byrnes, History of the 94th Infantry Division in WW II, Infantry Journal Press, Washington, DC, 1948, p. 24
Here After History of the 94th
History of the 94th, p. 23

CHAPTER 25
The 94th Deploys to Brittany, France

History of the 94th, p. 24
Ibid., p. 24
Ibid., p. 25
Ibid., p. 25

CHAPTER 27
The Rest of the Story in Brittany

History of the 94th, p. 53
US Armed Services in the European Theater of Operations,
The *Stars and Stripes*, Paris Edition, 1944, p. 1.

CHAPTER 28
Summary of the Battle of the Bulge

My favorite book on the history of the Battle of the Bulge was written by Charles B. MacDonald, titled *Time for Trumpets, The Untold Story of the Battle of the Bulge*, William Morrow & Co., Inc., New York, 1985.

Hollywood movies on the subject depicted the GIs involved retreating as in a rout. The retreat certainly occurred because of the surprise. Even General Eisenhower did not realize the magnitude of the German attack for two days. Our intelligence was caught napping as at Pearl Harbor. But the majority of our troops fought stubbornly holding up the German drive over and over again.

A good example is found in:

Alex Kerhaw, *The Longest Winter*, Da Capo Press, 2004

Another good example of the GI's tenacity is found in:

Robert F. Phillips, *To Save Bastogne*, Stein & Day Publishers. New York, 1983

CHAPTER 29
The 94th Is on the Move

History of the 94th, p. 70
Ibid., p. 73
Ibid., p. 79

CHAPTER 30
The 94th Attacks

History of the 94th, pp. 79-195
Ibid., pp. 84-94
Ibid., pp. 95-98
Ibid., pp. 99-116
Ibid., p. 109
Ibid., pp. 117-130
Ibid., pp. 132-138
Ibid., pp. 149-158
Ibid., pp. 159-176
Ibid., pp. 177-184
Ibid., pp. 185-195

CHAPTER 31
The Battle for Sinz

History of the 94th, pp. 196-199
Ibid., p. 199
Ibid., p. 154
Ibid., p. 176
Ibid., p. 199
Ibid., p. 184
Ibid., pp. 185-195

Ibid., pp. 200-201 & 205-208
Ibid., pp. 202-204
Ibid., pp. 214-219
Ibid., pp. 216
Ibid., p. 217

CHAPTER 33
Occupation Duty in Mettmann, Germany

History of the 94th, p. 467
Ibid., pp. 467-468
Ibid., p. 468

CHAPTER 34
Occupation Duty in Czechoslovakia

History of the 94th, pp. 448, 491, 492
Ibid., p, 494
Ibid., p. 495
Ibid., p. 495

ABOUT THE AUTHOR

A member of the "greatest generation," Herb Ridyard has lived a long, full life. At age ninety-five, he has a good memory, the fruits of which he shares in Do Your Best. When he was young, looking at airplanes in the sky and building model versions, Herb's dream was to find a career in aviation. It came true as he earned a master's degree in aeronautical engineering at night school. As an aeronautical research scientist, he worked in the Langley Aeronautical Laboratory's hypersonic wind tunnel for eight years and at GE's missile and re-entry vehicle department for thirty-two years.

Today, Herb lives in a cottage at Masonic Village, a retirement community, in Elizabethtown, Pennsylvania, with his wife of seventy years, Nancy Lou. They are often visited by their four children— Amy Lou and Leslie Ann, both schoolteachers; Herb Jr., a general surgeon; and Rob, a lead software developer—seven grandchildren, and eight great-grandchildren. In his spare time Herb sings tenor in the Sell Chapel Choir and Men's Chorus, participates in a weekly Bible study, is a member of the Veterans Committee and a Hospice volunteer.

CPSIA information can be obtained
at www.ICGtesting.com
Printed in the USA
BVHW050230100821
614004BV00004B/17/J